HOV
LEGENL
TRADERS
MADE
MILLIONS

HOW LEGENDARY TRADERS MADE MILLIONS

PROFITING FROM THE INVESTMENT STRATEGIES OF THE GREATEST STOCK TRADERS OF ALL TIME

JOHN BOIK

McGraw-Hill
New York Chicago San Francisco Lisbon London
Madrid Mexico City Milan New Delhi
San Juan Seoul Singapore
Sydney Toronto

The McGraw·Hill Companies

1 2 3 4 5 6 7 8 9 10 AGM/AGM 0 9 8 7 6

ISBN 0-07-146822-6

McGraw-Hill books are available at special quantity discounts to use as premiums and sales promotions, or for use in corporate training programs. For more information, please write to the Director of Special Sales, McGraw-Hill Professional, Two Penn Plaza, New York, NY 10121-2298. Or contact your local bookstore.

This book is printed on recycled, acid-free paper containing a minimum of 50% recycled, de-inked fiber.

Library of Congress Cataloging-in-Publication Data

Boik, John, 1961-

How legendary traders made millions : profiting from the investment strategies of the greatest stock traders of all time / by John Boik.

p. cm.

Includes bibliographical references.

ISBN 0-07-146822-6 (pbk. : alk. paper) 1. Stocks — Handbooks, manuals, etc. 2. Investments — Handbooks, manuals, etc. I. Title.

HG4527.B58 2006

332.63'22092273 — dc22

2005030051

CONTENTS

ACKNOWLEDGMENTS

To my wife Gina — the love of my life — I thank you again for your support and understanding.

To my daughter Daniella — you are truly God's most precious gift, and I already miss your nightly inquiry to me — "How many more pages, Daddy?"

To a great long-time friend Dave Chapdelaine — your gift (Barron's award plaque) really inspired me to continue on and write this book along with the encouragement from my parents.

To the authors of all the books listed in the Bibliography/Resources section — thank you for your quality works — all students of the market should read those excellent writings.

To Stephen Isaacs and the staff at McGraw-Hill — it was a pleasure again working with such a class organization.

To Mr. William J. O'Neil and the staff at IBD, especially Kathy Sherman — your assistance is greatly appreciated, and Mr. O'Neil's efforts and accomplishments once again speak for themselves.

A special thank you to Jim Roppel — for sharing your story as your passion and perseverance are to be admired by all — you are truly an inspiration.

AUTHOR'S NOTE

In trying to assist myself and others in better understanding how the stock market actually works, I increased my study of the market and its history. It resulted in this book, which includes what may be the first combination of history, market analysis and successful strategy to cover over a century of market activity. While trying to make money in the stock market is nowhere near the top of priorities for a successful, fulfilling and service-oriented life, I decided to study this topic more in-depth to help those who do try to increase their financial security and especially for those learning, as I was, how to avoid losing hard-earned money in the market. Since I believe that the stock market is one of the more complex and widely misunderstood topics, I decided to write this book so others can be better informed. And as this book will illustrate, few have ever sustained the highest levels of success in the market over extended periods of time. I believe this has to do with many people's misconceptions of how the market really works and their failure to realize that fact because they use information that is misleading and lacks solid historical analysis and factual data. William J. O'Neil, in his book "The Successful Investor," created the best definition of the stock market I believe there is, and one that more people need to be aware of and understand. It states:

> *The stock market doesn't care who we as individuals are, what we think, or how we feel. It's a beast like no other: indifferent to human desires, oblivious to common wisdom, maddeningly contrary, and seemingly bent on confounding the majority at every turn. The only law it obeys is the law of supply and demand. And until you, as an investor, come to grips with this reality and learn to move with the market rather than against it, you'll be plagued by results that are mediocre at best.*

As you'll come to see, personal opinions and others' opinions, which are what most people follow or mention when it comes to the stock market, don't mean a thing and usually end up getting most people in trouble in the market. Lack of discipline, patience and solid trading rules are reasons for failure as well. The successful traders profiled in this book lost money when they strayed from basic fundamental traits and skills, lost their discipline, and began to ignore trading rules that have stood the test of time in the stock market. I hope this historical real-world analysis can help others in discovering how these people battled the stock market and succeeded in a place where many others fail.

INTRODUCTION

How Legendary Traders Made Millions

"Most losses in the stock market can be traced to the average speculator's persistent disregard of the lessons of the past . . . "

— Jesse Livermore (1923)

". . . the market cycle of 1998–2002 was much like all those that preceded it. The losses suffered may have been extraordinary, but the mistakes that led to them were not. They were the same mistakes investors have made in every market cycle."

— William J. O'Neil (2003)

". . . recurring patterns occur over and over because stocks are driven by humans and human nature never changes."

— Jesse Livermore (1940)

"The first step in learning to pick stock market winners is for you to examine leading winners of the past to learn all the characteristics of the most successful stocks."

— William J. O'Neil (1988)

As two of history's most successful stock market operators of the past 100 plus years allude to, mistakes made by investors and patterns in the stock market just keep repeating themselves. Jesse Livermore in 1923 and then William J. O'Neil in 2003 — some 80 years later — remind us all that the same mistakes made cycle after cycle cause losses for generation after generation of stock market participants. Then, each through extensive experience, they remind us as Livermore did in 1940 and O'Neil did in 1988, that the most successful stocks follow certain patterns and that stock market cycles do repeat themselves throughout history as well.

The losses many experience don't have to recur time and time again. If you study and become familiar with how stock market cycles have worked in the past and understand how successful stock operators and investors have benefited from those past cycles, you will be better prepared for the future market cycles that will come. Great stock market participants over time have understood the power of knowledge gained from prior cycles and how stock market cycles work. They created rules to stay in sync with the market's current cycle and listened and paid attention to the cues the market presented to make sure they stayed on the profitable side of the market, whether that was on the way up (being long strong leaders during uptrending markets) or on the way down (shorting former leaders or just staying out of a bad market during downtrending markets). Though many may believe the market provides a smooth and steady return over its life (7.3% over the 105 years from 1900 through 2004 for the Dow and 12.5% for the Nasdaq from 1971 through 2004), it can be a bumpy ride along the way as can be seen in Tables I-1 and I-2. Many positive years over the past century that have produced solid returns are followed by some rough periods. In fact, what you will learn is that when the markets are in a clear uptrend, many leading stocks will outperform the index returns by a wide margin. And that is where the concentration of the legendary stock traders has been, which has led many of them to their outsized returns and accumulated wealth. But what you will also learn is that many of those same leading stocks that helped drive the market higher during its uptrend are the same ones that led the downside when heavy selling overtook the market. Those former leaders then can come down hard and fast, and in many cases they fall much more than the general market averages do as well. No wonder Gerald Loeb described the marketplace as a "battle." But learning how great traders navigated these turbulent waters by using knowledge from history, learning from mistakes, cutting losses short, and keeping in sync with the rhythm of the markets cycle can enhance one's results for the future.

DOW INDUSTRIAL AVERAGE–SIMPLE ANNUAL RETURNS

	Years +	Avg Rtn	Years –	Avg Rtn	Years =	Avg Rtn Tot
1900s	5	29.8%	4	-18.3%	1	7.6%
1910s	4	32.8%	5	-17.0%	1	4.6%
1920s	6	28.0%	3	-17.7%	1	11.5%
1930s	5	32.6%	5	-29.2%	0	1.7%
1940s	6	12.7%	4	-9.5%	0	3.8%
1950s	8	19.6%	2	-8.5%	0	14.0%
1960s	6	13.5%	4	-13.5%	0	2.7%
1970s	6	14.3%	4	-16.3%	0	2.1%
1980s	8	18.4%	2	-6.5%	0	13.4%
1990s	9	18.1%	1	-4.0%	0	15.9%
2000s*	2	14.0%	3	-10.0%	0	-0.4%
AVG	65	22.3%	37	-14.3%	3	7.3%

**2000s data is through 2004*

Table I-1 Simple Annual Returns — Dow average 1900–2004

NASDAQ AVERAGE–SIMPLE ANNUAL RETURNS

	Years +	Avg Rtn	Years –	Avg Rtn	Years =	Avg Rtn Tot
1970s*	7	21.2%	2	-33.1%	0	9.1%
1980s	7	20.9%	3	-6.6%	0	12.6%
1990s	8	37.1%	2	-10.5%	0	27.5%
2000s**	2	29.3%	3	-30.6%	0	-6.7%
AVG	24	31.9%	10	-23.8%	0	12.5%

**1970s data starts at 1971*
***2000s data is through 2004*

Table I-2 Simple Annual Returns — NASDAQ average 1971–2004

For just one example we can turn to O'Neil in 1962 — then still very early in his career — when he was studying the classic "Reminiscences of a Stock Operator" written by Edwin Lefevre, which was originally published in 1923. In "Reminiscences," which detailed the trading life of Jesse Livermore, O'Neil learned that Livermore discovered that a top in the market was occurring in late 1906 as many leading stocks that had led the previous strong uptrend in the market stopped advancing in price. Livermore then began shorting (borrowing stock from a broker in hopes of buying it back at a lower price and profiting from the difference) the market in early 1907, and he ended up making millions after he closed his positions out in the fall of 1907, due to the sharp downtrend that occurred throughout much of that year. O'Neil discovered a parallel to the market situation he was currently in at his time in early 1962. Many strong leaders that had led the prior strong uptrend in the market throughout 1961 began topping. O'Neil then began shorting Certain-teed and Korvette at that time as the market began to break. The market then broke hard, and O'Neil made substantial profits after he had closed out his short positions, just as Livermore did over a half century before. This was one of O'Neil's early successes — one of many that were to come during his career — that led to his becoming one of the youngest ever to buy a seat on the New York Stock Exchange. O'Neil used the knowledge of history's precedent from the market's cyclical behavior and one of the earliest successful stock operators and applied that knowledge to the current action of the market during his time to profit successfully. In the chapters that follow, we'll see many other real-life examples from the traders who actually had their own money on the line, rather than discuss investment and market theories based on academics or on what some others might think the market should do.

"How Legendary Traders Made Millions" will also illustrate how the stock market has performed for over 100 years dating back to 1897. Why analyze the market's activity? It's important that we start with an analysis of the market because most stocks follow the action and trend of the general market. And as you'll soon discover, following the actions of the market — not trying to predict its future behavior — is a key trading rule that led to the legends making millions of dollars. Now we have all heard of some of the more memorable moments and events in stock market history such as the Great Crash of 1929, the Black Monday crash in October 1987, the brutal bear market of 1973-74, the great bull market of the 1990s, the technology and Internet bubble that peaked and began to burst on the Nasdaq in March 2000 and probably some others as well. But what is usually missing from some of these more popular advertised moments in stock market history is how the market was acting just prior to each of these notable events, how the market presented vital cues before these events took place, and also how the best traders and investors acted upon those events to reap returns or avoid potential losses in their portfolios. It didn't matter if the event turned out to be a major correction or bear market or if it was the beginning of a major upturn that resulted in a strong bull market environment. The key to note is that when the markets begin to turn, in either direction, plenty of signals are usually present in the important market details for the astute investor, and this book will illustrate how the great traders applied their market knowledge and observation skills to reap profitable returns. The markets have been acting in a cyclical fashion for many decades, and as time moves on we have that many more examples to learn from.

The other vital information usually not presented in history's storied cyclical events is which stocks and industries led each of the upside cycles and how there were also profitable opportunities on the downside as well. The stock market is like one giant mirror that reflects economic conditions in a discounted matter, and it has also been one of the most reliable forecasting tools, as you will see when we travel in time and cover over 100 years of stock market history and how the best traders took advantage of the opportunities the market presented. There is simply no better historical guide to current and future economic prospects than the action within the stock market, which reflects millions of investors' perceptions for future profit potential. It also takes a keen sense of economic conditions and an understanding of what is in demand in the economic landscape of each era. The combination of economic understanding, stock market cycle knowledge, and how great traders succeeded in past market cycles is a powerful toolkit to help one profit in future stock market cycles.

The reason for understanding prior market cycles is that its daily display of emotional expectations showcased each week by millions of participants, and more importantly, by major money managers who control most of the real action in the stock market, doesn't change that much. It has been performing this way for well over 100 years, and it will continue to perform this way for many more years to come. The most recent example is the euphoric rise of the Nasdaq market in the 1990s and then its dramatic descent beginning in the spring of 2000, and how that environment looked eerily similar to the market environment of the 1920s and early 1930s, when another euphoric rise occurred in the stock market and then ended with another dramatic decline. Sure, the names and companies change because the time frames change, but the market has always experienced up and down periods and the actions during those periods are what create its cyclical rotation. Of the many historical moments in stock market history, we have seen extremes of great market crashes and then great periods of prolonged prosperity produced by great bull markets. The markets have continually acted this way, and the patterns usually repeat themselves, just like patterns in individual stocks repeat themselves. Let's not forget the famous observation by Jesse Livermore near the beginning of the 20th century, "Nothing on Wall Street ever changes, the names change, the pockets change, but the market never changes because human nature never changes."

To many (most who don't understand or take the time to study historical facts), the up and down cycles of the stock market represent random and haphazard action that simply cannot be explained. "Irrational behavior," they will say; "so either don't try to explain it and just invest for the long haul, or don't pay attention and just stay away from the market altogether." This book will illustrate just how "irrational" thoughts like that can be and will prove that with knowledge of history — especially in an environment like the stock market that keeps repeating itself — profitable opportunities *and* protection from possible future devastating losses will become much clearer.

This book will take us through each decade of the stock market starting from 1897 to the present time of this writing. It is not intended to chronicle the history of Wall Street and many of the influential people of each era, as there are already a number of good quality books that detail that type of Wall Street history (some are listed in the Bibliography and Resources section at the end of this book). Rather, this book will look more at the details of the market's action itself over the past 100 plus years. Don't worry — it will summarize much of the analysis so as not to bore the reader with dry "old" history. Again, it's critical to understand why it's so important to study the actions and history of the market to gain foresight. Because the action of the general market influences the majority of most all other stocks, one must first start in the most logical place for analysis, which is the market itself. From there you will see how parallels coexist between the market and the leading stocks that make up the general market. And as the four quotes from two of the most successful and influential stock market traders of all time during the past century at the beginning of this Introduction attest to, if you don't think knowledge of history in the stock market and past experiences and lessons can lead to future success, you will be at a huge disadvantage when it comes to battling the stock market for future profits. You'll also notice that no academic "experts" will be mentioned in this book for their take on the stock market. That's because this book only deals with facts and real-world results from a handful of traders who had their own money on the line, lost their own money, and then through their own hard work figured out how the stock market really works, so they could stay on the profitable side of the market and then make millions in profits.

What this book will also do is look at the leading stocks of all eras and the exciting leading industries that were created that represented strong bull markets and how those leading stocks of each era came to be the real leaders and how you can use past information to spot the new leaders in upcoming markets. It will illustrate how the market *always* looks ahead and how astute investors discovered when the markets began to turn upward after prolonged declines and offered up incredible profit opportunities. It will look at how the markets topped before they began some of their dramatic descents and how staying attuned to the market's action and acting on it preserved past profits and avoided future losses for the very best traders. Most importantly, this book will analyze how many of the greatest stock traders over history (all of those featured in my first book "Lessons from the Greatest Stock Traders of All Time," which included Jesse Livermore, Bernard Baruch, Gerald Loeb, Nicolas Darvas, and William J. O'Neil — and then adding in a few other notable traders and introducing a new one as well) acted upon the market environments of their time and how they recognized, profited, and avoided large losses on many of the leading and active stocks of their day. Make no mistake; they all suffered losses as well, but their discipline and trading rules limited their losses so as not to cause major damage to their portfolios. Their understanding of the actions of the market is proof enough that historical market knowledge can lead to very profitable future investment results. In addition, this book will illustrate how many times throughout history the market gave leading cues in advance of either topping or bottoming and gave those signals out in plenty of time for astute and observant investors to make profitable moves on either side of the market.

"How Legendary Traders Made Millions" will showcase the many lessons that you can learn as you analyze and understand history so as to be better prepared to profit from current and future time periods. And as the market has consistently proven, because human emotions are involved, repeatable patterns keep recurring over and over. If you have the blueprint of history, study and know it well, and understand how the very best performers managed to reap the best returns, that knowledge can only benefit you for future profitable successes. And though many may state that it is easy to look in the rearview mirror and then conduct reasonable analysis, "How Legendary Traders Made Millions" will show that experience and knowledge from the past does not hurt your probability for future success and can definitely assist in your quest for future stock market profits.

HOW LEGENDARY TRADERS MADE MILLIONS

1

Industrial Stocks Produce a Millionaire (1897–1909)

Bernard Baruch Considered the Action of the Market When Making His Plans

Charles Dow was actually a journalist. He was a financial writer who wrote articles for the *Express* and *New York Mail* concerning financial statistics. Eventually, he teamed up with a fellow worker, and they decided to strike out on their own. The two formed their own firm, and Charles Dow together with

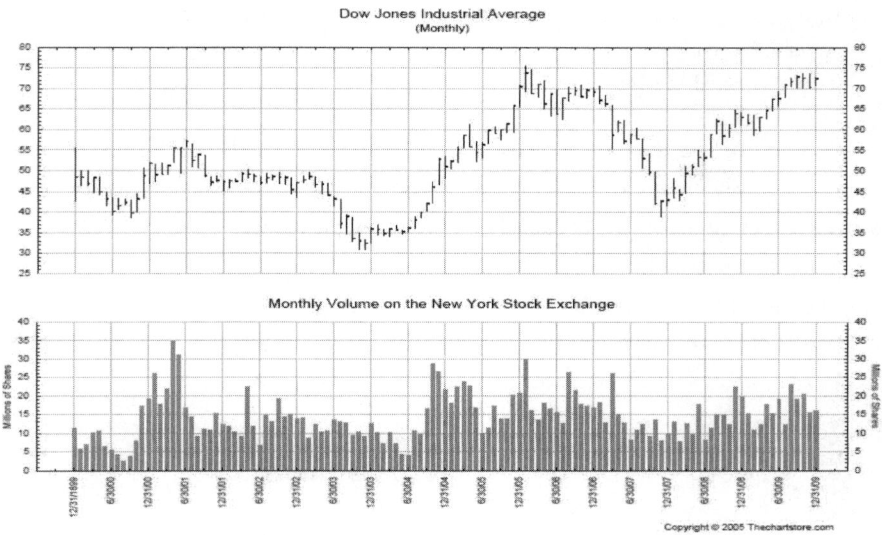

Figure 1-1 The Dow Jones Industrial Average 1900–1909.
Source: *www.thechartstore.com.*

fellow worker Edward Jones created a company called Dow, Jones and Company. On July 8, 1889, the company introduced a new product: the first edition of the *Wall Street Journal* was printed with Dow acting as editor and founder.

Charles Dow later created the Dow Average to help relieve the confusion that the numerous daily fluctuations in the market presented to many people as interest in the stock market began to grow. Dow wanted to create an index that would give an overall picture of what the market was actually doing in a summarized statistic. This average, or statistic, would provide a window, to the many that were following the market, into the activity of the overall market instead of just looking at the numerous changes in each stock and trying to interpret what the market in general was doing. Dow started this original average index in 1884 with 11 stocks, which were mostly made up of railroad stocks, the dominant industry of that time. In 1896, Dow introduced the Dow Industrial Average, and in October of 1896 the original and official average that he created in 1884 became known as the 20 stock railroad average.

The newly formed Dow Industrial Average, which consisted of 12 leading stocks, now provided the general public with a reliable statistic that would tend to mirror the general activities of the overall market. The original stocks chosen for the index were

American Cotton Oil	Chicago Gas	Distilling & Cattle Feeding
American Sugar Refining	Laclede Gas	National Lead
General Electric	U.S. Rubber	North American
Tennessee Coal & Iron	U.S. Leather pfd.	American Tobacco

These companies represented the industrial age of the coming 20th century. Throughout the decades to come the average would be expanded to 30 stocks and new leading stocks of new eras would replace older leaders over time. The only stock from the original average that is still present in the average today is General Electric. The first recorded average stood at 40.94. The current list of the Dow Jones Industrial Average stocks, as of this writing, now consists of stocks representing many different industries.

Baruch Makes His Mark

With the newly adopted Dow Industrial Average for measuring the overall performance of the market in place, stock operators could better gauge the actions of the market. One of those early stock operators was Bernard Baruch who was featured in my first book "Lessons from the Greatest Stock Traders of All Time." Baruch had spent the early part of his trading career making most of the same mistakes many investors make in the market. He wasn't doing his own research, he lacked experience and knowledge, and he kept listening to others' so-called opinions. He suffered many losses during his first six or so years being active in the market. But his refusal to give up and his constant study of his mistakes and how the market actually worked would eventually pay off for him.

The market was basically flat from January through May of 1897; the economy was still adjusting and improving as it was coming out of a recession period from the prior few years. In June 1897 the market began to rise sharply and did so for the next four straight months. As mentioned, business conditions became positive as the economy was coming off a depression-type period from early 1896. It was very common during those times to have sharp recession- or depression-like periods due to "panics" and then have strong reversals to the upside very soon afterward. By early 1897 banking, commerce, railroads and heavy industry were resuming activities at a rapid pace. The outlook for the country was improving steadily, and many business leaders were gaining confidence. It was a speculative period, and the markets were not regulated with many of the rules that exist today. Many who participated in the markets were wealthy and had access to information that the general public mostly lacked, but interest in the market was greatly improving. America was viewed as the next economic strength as it began to compete with Europe at a fast pace. The strength in railroads, agriculture and industrial sectors led to an exuberant and positive attitude. Two benchmark figures at the time, which were steel and gold, kept increasing in price. Bankers kept things in order in those days, and the most influential banker of the era was J. P. Morgan. Merger activity was very strong, as companies would combine operations to create "trusts." There were over 3,000 mergers from 1895–1904. In 1899 alone, there were 1,208 mergers. Some of the more notable corporations that were formed at that time due to industrial combinations consisted of Allis-Chambers, Amalgamated Copper, American Beet Sugar, American Car & Foundry, United Fruit and Republic Iron & Steel. The increase in merger activity created opportunities for many stock market participants. Times were good as America headed for the 20th century.

From Baruch's limited experience and as his observation of market activity began to improve, he noticed that many times during his era the market would experience many downtrending cycles only to bounce right back with strong upward reversals. He also noticed that the best profitable opportunities presented themselves when these reversals to the upside would begin. He thought that if he could time his purchases of new leaders that possessed very strong fundamentals when the market began to turn he could reap positive returns.

His constant observation and study of the market alerted him to the change in trend that was beginning to occur in the spring of 1897, and he purchased 100 shares of American Sugar Refining, which was a leading stock at the time and one of the representative stocks of the recently created Dow Industrial Average. He rode this stock up for a strong six months, as the market was strong at that time. He also used a pyramiding strategy to buy more of the stock as American Sugar kept increasing in price. His leveraging of a strong stock, as it kept moving up in price, only compounded his returns. Baruch ended up making a profit of $60,000 on that stock. The profit was substantial enough for him to purchase a seat on the Exchange. This was also the turning point for Baruch as it related to his stock trading. His ever-observant eye to the market, his study of the strong fundamentals of the stock he purchased, and his understanding of the strong economic and perceived perception of strength and profitable times ahead for businesses all combined to create what he thought was a solid speculative opportunity.

Baruch was one of the most successful stock market traders ever, and this transaction reiterated that his favorite time to purchase stocks was when the general market was beginning a strong upward trend after coming off a low market period. His observation skills and experience from watching and participating in the markets since 1891 gave him the confidence to take advantage of the strong opportunities when the market presented them. As mentioned earlier, he made most of the errors many market participants make in the market over the prior six years when he was starting out and learning exactly how the market operated. But he learned from his mistakes, decided he would never give up, and kept fast to his study. He was an avid reader, and he studied the fundamentals of companies extensively before he made any trade. He also learned how to wait for the market to confirm its new trend, and then he would trade with that trend. This he learned from the prior cycles in the market that had been occurring from 1891 to the then present time of 1897. His patience paid off in 1897, and with his pyramiding strategy to buy more shares as his winner kept rising in price, he kept a close eye on this big winner, making sure he would not give back his hard-earned profits. He also learned how to sell a good stock as it kept rising in price. Remember, he always would learn from his prior mistakes in order to better his timing for purchases and sales of his holdings.

The market flattened out and actually began to decline in the fall of 1897. Baruch made sure not to give back his hard-earned profits, and the actions of the market and his stock were huge warning signs to him that it was time to act. He therefore cashed in before the stock would break hard. His objective was to make a profitable return and not to declare himself a long-term or short-term trader. He just followed the actions of the stock and the market and made the right timing and profit decisions.

Baruch's Newly Established Rules Lead to More Profits

The market declined from September 1897 through early April 1898. It bottomed in April 1898 and did not touch this level again until October 1903, 5½ years later, due to the Rich Man's Panic (as it was called) of 1903. From April 1898 to April 1899 the market was in a strong upward trend with the only correction occurring in August and September of 1898. Coming off this brief correction the market rose from September 1898 to April 1899 from near 50 to near 75, or nearly 50%. One important item to understand is how the market seemed to anticipate the upcoming recession that would begin in June 1899, as the market topped and then began to decline. This helps confirm the forecasting ability that the market will continue to show as we go through the decades. It will continuously seem to decline and/or flatten out numerous times before an actual recession begins. And it will usually begin to turn upwards inside the recession before the recession ends and forecast better times ahead for American businesses.

Baruch discovered through his study that the market actually reflected the economic conditions of the day, rather than caused them. He noted that the market would act like a thermometer and the economy was more like a fever. It's important to understand this distinction. All the economic activity and factors that affect that activity (including interest rates, inflation, productivity, and profitability) taking place and being caused by supply and demand would be reflected in the stock market due to investors' expectations of current and future profitability. As the market constantly discounts the future to the present, it becomes a reliable resource as a forecasting tool. This could be seen all the way back to the late 1890s and early 1900s, and we will see this parallel as we move through each decade to come.

In early spring of 1899 while the market was still strong, Baruch purchased shares of B.R.T. (Brooklyn Rapid Transit Company) as a new executive manager had taken control months before and improvements were beginning to show in the company's results. B.R.T. was a leading stock at that time; its revenues were rising fast; and the stock price was reflecting the strong upward market environment, the leadership of the stock, and its strong fundamentals. By April the price of B.R.T. hit $137 and then began to pull back. Soon thereafter the new executive in charge died unexpectedly, a panic hit the stock, and it declined to near $100. But J. P. Morgan and others moved in to support the stock, and the price moved back up to hit $115. Although Baruch held on through this uncertain time, he did notice that as the months went on the market began to flatten and the price of B.R.T. began to stall as well. He decided to sell and retain his profit, due to his observation of the topping price and volume action within the stock. When he sold, he retained a profit of approximately $60,000. By the end of 1899 B.R.T. had declined to the $60s, as the market broke hard, and B.R.T. would never again reach the peak it had established earlier in the year. Here again we see Baruch latching on to one of the leaders of his day, as the market was moving upward. He also always would buy only fundamentally strong stocks that had good prospects for their products and future profits. He also liked to sell his winners on the way up, or in this case, when they began to top or stall in order to realize his profits. Again, his time frame for holding the stock didn't matter — it was the action within the market and his holding that alerted him of what action to take.

Richard D. Wyckoff — The Patient Trader

Another influential and successful stock operator of the early 20th century, who was not featured in my book "Lessons from the Greatest Stock Traders of All Time," was Richard D. Wyckoff. He was born on Nov. 2, 1873, and seemed to combine some of the early experiences of Jesse Livermore and Baruch. He also shared commonalities and early experiences that begot Gerald Loeb and also Nicolas Darvas, who came along decades later, as well.

Wyckoff, like Livermore, began his Wall Street career early at the age of 15. Like Livermore and Baruch, he became fascinated with the stock market and wanted to learn as much as he could about trading and speculating in the market. He began reading and researching on his own. He started reading the *Financial Chronicle*, just as Baruch had, and he began to study the financial statistics of many firms and different industries. Wyckoff also began studying the bucket shops that operated in those days. As mentioned in my first book, the bucket shops were more like gambling shops where one would bet on the next fluctuations in the price of a stock. Though Jesse Livermore became quite skilled at the quick action of the bucket shops and used those experiences later to aid his trading on the New York Stock Exchange, Wyckoff used the bucket shops as a study mechanism to observe how traders would act and participate in the markets. He wasn't active in the shops like Livermore, but he learned how trader's psychology would work both for and against a trader. For instance, Wyckoff discovered that most bucket shop operators would lose money due to the fact that they would take quick profits when they had them but would hang on to their losers in the hope they would soon recover. This observation of how traders would react to the actions of stocks within the market would become a key learning trait for Wyckoff. His discipline and patience and his observation skill would pay off for him during the remainder of his career.

As Wyckoff continued learning and educating himself on the market he began to move up in rank within the firm he had worked for, and his early career looked promising. But the aftershocks of the panic of 1893 caught up with this firm, and it was dissolved. For the next three years Wyckoff held odd jobs as he found it difficult to land another position with a Wall Street firm. At age 21, he was nearly broke, but he never lost his drive to return to and make a career out of the stock market. His break came when he finally landed a position with Price, McCormick & Co., which was a wire house. He began to study even harder than he had previously, and he also read books on banking, railroads, and accounting. We saw this drive to never give up and constantly learn more with all the great traders — Livermore, Baruch, Loeb, Darvas and O'Neil — no matter which time period they participated in the markets.

Wyckoff continued to work hard, and he kept advancing within the firm. With President McKinley's election in early 1897 the market began a move to the upside. It was here that Wyckoff made his first real stock purchase. Notice how he had been involved and interested in the market for many years up to this point. However, he knew he did not have much experience and that his learning and observing of others taught him how difficult and challenging the task at hand would be. This is in stark contrast to how many other traders began their careers. Wyckoff exhibited the skill and discipline of patience much more than many others in the market. It was one of the key reasons why he never experienced the many lows of losing all his money by trading in the markets. This patience and avoidance of a gambling nature was one of the more distinctive differences between himself and Jesse Livermore, though many of their observations and trading rules would coincide with each other. To show just how cautious Wyckoff was in this first trade, he purchased only one share of St. Louis & San Francisco common at the price of $4. He purchased this stock based on the pure fundamentals of the company, which he would learn later was not the only thing to consider if one wanted to buy and sell stocks in the market correctly for profitable gains.

During his early years of learning about the market, Wyckoff made the important observation that the market worked in a cyclical fashion that usually repeated itself. He would notice that the market would advance for about two years or so as it was coming off of a low point. This is exactly what Bernard Baruch discovered in his observation of the market at the very same time. The next wave of the market, as Wyckoff would discover, would consist of a decline over the next year or so right back to the original low point. Here he discovered that fear in the market was a normal cause for selling. The fear that investors and traders experienced in these early times was mostly caused by a badly organized banking system, overextended railroad construction, and unintegrated industrial organizations. Many of these led to instability, which in turn lead to uncertainty, which then lead to panic or fear selling. We'll see later how the overextended "construction" of other future industries led to some other major collapses in the market as well such as the auto industry in the late 1920s, when there were 166 automobile companies, and the Internet age of the late 1990s, when it seemed nearly everyone was starting a company with the words "dot-com" in their name.

As the market rose strongly throughout 1898 and early 1899 Wyckoff was still only trading in one-share lots and was by no means a big trader taking advantage of the positive market environment. He stayed cautious, in a learning mode, and concentrated on his career. In 1900 he decided to go into business for himself and deal in unlisted stocks and bonds. He brought in a partner, and in October of 1900 he created the firm of Harrison & Wyckoff. His firm cleared trades for other brokers and earned commissions off these trades. He also started to generate clients and acted as a broker, by giving advice to clients of what stocks to invest in.

In the fall of 1900 after declining for most of the year, the market began to turn upward. If you look at Figure 1-1 on p. 1, you will notice how the market begins to turn upward just prior to the official end of the recession that would end in December 1900. In February 1901, the largest buyout to date was announced as U.S. Steel was formed when J. P. Morgan purchased Carnegie Steel from Andrew Carnegie for a staggering $500 million at the time. Other new consolidations during this time that were created consisted of Borden's Milk, Corn Products, Eastman Kodak and National Distillers. In early 1901 with merger fever in full force many leading stocks were increasing in price on greater than normal volume. In fact in 1901 the total volume on the New York Stock Exchange was a record 265 million shares up to that point. As mentioned, many stocks were rising and taking the market higher, but the real leaders were U.S. Steel, Union Pacific and Northern Pacific. These were the true leaders of the day as the steel and metals industry and the railroad industry were reaping the economic benefits of their time.

Livermore Makes His First Big Trade

Jesse Livermore, also featured in my first book "Lessons from the Greatest Stock Traders of All Time," after making many of his earlier mistakes just like Baruch and many others, bought Northern Pacific stock in early 1901 and rode this leader out for a $50,000 profit. Livermore did exactly the same thing Baruch had done earlier — he traded with the trend of the market, which was up, and he purchased a strong fundamental leader from a leading group (railroads). This proved to be a milestone for Livermore, and it was one of his earliest successes. Though he was unaware of what was happening, he just followed the strong stock and sold out to retain his profit. It turned out that there was a raid on Northern Pacific stock as groups were trying to take control of the firm. On May 1, 1901, Northern Pacific was trading at $115. By May 7 it hit $143.50, as the stock became cornered by groups trying to take control of the company. On May 8 the price hit $160. May 9 was a truly remarkable day as Northern Pacific was whipsawed by both the groups trying to take control of the stock and the short sellers who viewed what they thought as a profitable opportunity on an overvalued basis. Northern Pacific hit a high that day of $1,000 but ended up closing at $325 for the day. Many short sellers couldn't buy the stock back to cover their losing positions due to the fact that there was no available supply. The next day, May 10, Northern Pacific fell back to $150.00. Because the many short sellers needed to raise money to cover their losing Northern positions, they sold other stock holdings that caused a major decline among many of those stocks. It was truly a wild day on the exchange, and it proved just how brutal the market could be in those days.

Wyckoff and Baruch See the Top

As mentioned previously, in the spring of 1901, railroad stocks were boiling over with Northern Pacific being the standout leader that Livermore had made a decent profit on. During the run-up Richard Wyckoff was gaining a successful reputation as a very good stockbroker who was picking winners for his clients. He made some decent returns for his clients during the current upward run. He also would still not trade much for his own account during this period, but his clients did benefit from his ability to spot leading stocks. As he was observing the action in many stocks, many of the leading railroads started to experience heavy distribution (selling action) on May 8 except for Northern Pacific, which was described earlier. Wyckoff started to get an uneasy feel for the market in general, as he would always look for changes in direction after a strong trend would occur in either direction. He then advised his clients to sell their holdings and go to a full cash position. This happened to occur right near the peak of the market. As many of his clients sold their positions and retained their profits, Wyckoff's reputation as a solid broker increased. His ever-observant study of the market and how cycles would occur and tend to repeat themselves, and how leading stocks would start to top and break, especially on heavy volume, were all clues that allowed him to come to conclusions about what action to take in the market.

Also in the spring of 1901 another leading stock, Amalgamated Copper, was selling for over $100. Bernard Baruch began studying the fundamentals of this company, and through his research he concluded that the current high price of copper was curtailing its use throughout the world. Copper exports also began to decline, and he thought his conclusions would hold true. By July and August, with the market starting to decline, Amalgamated Copper began to decline in price as well. On Sept. 6, 1901, President McKinley was shot in an assassination attempt. Baruch began shorting Amalgamated Copper because he thought the country's future looked uncertain, the stock had begun to fall, and the market was in a downward trend at that time. Unfortunately, President McKinley died a week after being shot. Baruch continued to add to his positions, and he aggressively kept pyramiding his short position as the stock fell further along with the market. Baruch held fast to his profitable position, and by December of that year, with the stock near $60, he closed out his short position and netted a profit of nearly $700,000. It was his largest transaction to date, and it established him as a major market operator.

For much of 1902 the market traded in a fairly tight and flat trading range and basically ended the year where it had begun, registering no gain or loss for the year. The prior merger boom began to slow down significantly. Business also began to slow down as some of the prior mergers that took place became shaky. Overleveraged consolidations began to feel some pain. A new recession began in September 1902 and would last through August 1904, or a total of two full years. Richard Wyckoff, in 1902, began writing market letters concerning market movements and conditions. Wyckoff, like Livermore and Baruch, would trade and advise his clients to trade both sides of the market. This market letter writing would turn out to be a prelude to what would help establish Wyckoff as a true market leading voice of his day. Also in 1902, because of the flatness of the market, Baruch sold most of his holdings as he discovered it was hard to make money in a sideways trending market. So when the ensuing panic was about to hit in 1903, he was mostly out of the market and sitting on cash. Here we see another strong trait and discipline of many great traders — the ability to stay away from the market when it is wise to do so.

A feeble rally during the first few months of 1903 didn't last long. By March the market started to head down. A panic then hit the market in early spring of 1903, termed the Rich Man's Panic (partly due to the wild speculation that followed the large merger period that created U.S. Steel and how many wealthy stock market participants were affected by the correction). Many former leading stocks declined significantly during 1903, and by October the Dow Industrial Average hit a level it had not seen since early 1898. It was the first real major decline (but not Wall Street's first by any means) reflected by the still newly developed index, and the Dow ended up with a 24% decline for the year. Meanwhile, the 20-railroad index, which hit a high of 192 in 1902, declined nearly 54% to hit 89 in 1903.

A few great stock traders however were basically unaffected by the Rich Man's Panic. Bernard Baruch, as noted earlier, sold most of his holdings during the flat market of 1902. By late summer 1903 after a prolonged vacation from the market, he decided he would leave the firm he was with for many years and venture out on his own. He was an established millionaire by this time, and he decided he wanted to trade alone and continue his career on Wall Street. Richard Wyckoff also decided to make a career change. He decided to fold his current firm and open another firm with a different partner. He opened Mallett & Wyckoff, which would cater to his current client base that stayed with him. He also continued his writings on the market. Here we see two successful and experienced market operators mostly staying away from a bad market environment and actually planning ahead and making positive changes to their lives to further their future successes. While others were wiped out by the panic, here are two illustrations of how successful, disciplined and patient market operators stay ahead of the market by following its trend and observing its supply and demand action.

Just when many would give up on the market and most thought it would never improve, the market began to turn around. We'll see this many more times in the chapters that follow. It's the great traders who keep their personal opinions at bay and always stay attuned to the market and look for turning points that seem to reap the best returns because they never give up on the markets ability to change course. After bottoming in the fall of 1903, the market rose slightly in the last two months of that year. As if forecasting better times ahead while still mired in a recession, the market then flattened out a full seven to eight months before the recession officially ended. Here again is the forecasting ability of the market. For those who would give up on the market during the latest decline, they would surely miss out on the upcoming rise that would turn out to be the greatest ever up to that point.

Wyckoff Sees the Trend Change

Keeping his ever-observant eye to the actions of the market, Wyckoff noticed that the selling had dried up. He also knew from his past study of market cycles that an inevitable rise was maybe just around the corner. He also began to become more involved personally in the market by trading in his own account on a more active basis. Early in 1904 he began purchasing shares of U.S. Steel as the selling had subsided. He bought shares at $8⅝, which happened to be just a quarter of a point off its historic low. What Wyckoff discovered during this observation period was that when the market began to flatten out after a long decline this would usually lead to an upward trend for the market. The decline had worked itself out because the selling had exhausted. His bearishness over the prior few years began to change mostly due to the action of a recent bond issue that hit the market from the City of New York. This issue experienced a heavy oversubscription response, which was something the market had not experienced during the decline. He also noticed the bottoming of many stocks, especially many that he still considered leaders of the day. What also added to his newfound optimism was that the economy was picking up. Industrial production and agriculture, with wheat crops rising, were the leading industries, and markets began rising in other countries as well.

While the market continued trending mostly sideways (though it was more of a slightly choppy and whipsawing market) during the first half of 1904, Wyckoff sent out a market letter to his clients in June 1904. The last statement of the market letter read, "GET BULLISH." It was impeccable timing, as the market as measured by the Dow registered its strongest gain since its inception, up 42% for the year. In the letter he also made recommendations to his clients of stocks that he thought were beginning to be accumulated by big traders. The stocks recommended in the market letter were Reading, Union Pacific common, Atchinson, Missouri, Kansas & Texas preferred and U.S. Steel.

Wyckoff was 30 years old at the time, his firm and reputation were growing (though he still had relatively few clients and most were not large traders), and he was right there at the start of the most dramatic rise in the market up to that point, which would witness the Dow more than doubling in a little less than two years. Near the end of 1904 Wyckoff dissolved his firm and joined a firm called Ashwell & Co. He did this in order to lessen his responsibilities of running his own firm, though he did bring along his current client base, so he could spend more time studying the stock market. Intense study of the market was his real passion, and he was determined to find a way to become consistently profitable in dealing with the operations of the market.

In early 1904 while the market was beginning its upward move, Baruch was continuing his studies of the market as well. He became interested in the Soo Line, which he heard was planning to expand its rail line westward due to an expected rise in wheat traffic. When the economy started picking up again as the current recession was winding down, Baruch noticed that agricultural was a leading industry and was providing new leadership to the market. He studied the prospects of the Soo Line and wheat economics very intensely. He then began to purchase shares in the Soo Line at between $60 and $65 per share. As expected, a bumper crop of wheat came along, the Soo Line benefited from this crop, and their revenues rose 50%. The stock kept rising and hit $110 per share. Baruch liked to sell his profitable holdings on the way up, and his further studies of the company and wheat economics told him the demand would not last. He therefore took his substantial profit just before the peak price of the Soo Line and just before the stock broke. This transaction proves how he stayed in tune with the market action of the stock and the underlying conditions, which supported the rise in the stock. It also shows how he quickly adapted to any changes he was aware of and how he would lock in profits when it was wise to do so. The market finished 1904 at near 70, as mentioned earlier, for a solid 42% increase for the year after coming off the panic of 1903.

The market started off 1905 by continuing its upward trend through March. A sharp pullback in April and early May didn't last long, and the market continued to move higher to finish the year at right near 100, good for another solid gain for the Dow that year, up 38%. During 1905, Wyckoff was making good money for his clients, though they would still be considered small accounts. It was during this time that Wyckoff really began to pique his curiosity of how big traders operated in the market and how one could acquire the skills and knowledge needed to succeed consistently in the market. He had been involved in the market for nearly 17 years by then, but he realized that understanding the ways of the market was a continuous learning process. Along the way he experienced gains and losses just like everyone else. His own trading was still considered fairly small at the time as he usually traded in 500- or 1,000-share lots. This was a far cry from the status that Baruch and Livermore were establishing for themselves at that time. Wyckoff also moved from the firm of Ashwell to another firm called Wasserman Bros. Though his own results were improving, he still had an insatiable desire to learn all he could about successful trading. As he began to study great traders he discovered the best lesson he had learned was to keep his losses small. Wyckoff would come to learn, as all the other great traders featured in my first book did, that this was clearly the Golden Rule. He also discovered just like the other great traders that the greatest challenge was in eliminating any emotion. He wanted to learn how to trade with a poised mind, without fear and without hope. He wanted to acquire a trained judgment, combined with experience that comes from practice.

In 1906, Wyckoff made another change and he left Wasserman Bros. He felt as though he had learned much and was now ready to start his own firm alone. He opened Wyckoff & Co. Here he wanted to trade in bonds and unlisted securities, and he did not want to expand on attempting to gather an investing clientele. He also detailed the traits of a successful trader as he learned and observed from others through his experience. The following is a summary of that profile, which comes from his book "Wall Street Ventures & Adventures through Forty Years":

> To be clever, alert, and not only quick to act, but able to reverse a position at a moment's notice. One should exhibit no hopes or fears. One must participate without a sign of nerves or mental strain; must look upon profits or losses with equal equanimity. One must develop the kind of intuition that becomes a sixth sense. These traits must evolve over a series of failures over many months and years. The education could be completed only through a long series of transactions, spread over long periods, which would perfect the operating personality to carry one through adverse times without discouragement, until ones expertness and self-confidence match that of the surgeon who performs many operations, losing some patients but never losing his nerve. Such a man, with such character and experience should be a success in the market.

Livermore Gains His Prominence

As 1906 began, following two of the strongest years recorded by the Dow Average up to that point, the market began consolidating its recent gains. From January through June of 1906 the market retreated from just above 100 down to near the mid-80s. A sharp spike back to the upside occurred in July, but then the market seemed to flatten out and closed the year down 2%. Jesse Livermore, in his ever-observant study of the tape and market action, began to notice how the market could not advance further and its leaders began topping by having trouble keeping their advances going. Livermore then began to send out probing trades (small positions to test the direction of the market) on the short side of the market near the fall of 1906.

Industrial production had just hit an all-time high in early 1907, and it seemed as if the good times were here to stay. The stock market was however forecasting a slowdown of the times. As mentioned previously, the market actually peaked in January of 1907 and began backsliding and flattening out for much of that year. Here again we see the market discounting back to the present and looking ahead. In April 1907 another recession began, and the market was by then in a clear downward trend and by March 1907 the Dow was near 75. Livermore's probes began working, and he began pyramiding his more profitable short positions. A tightening of credit began growing, and mining stocks were especially hit hard. Livermore continued to short the market as the trend had clearly turned down and he was taking advantage of fallen leaders. He pyramided his positions in Reading, Union Pacific and Copper & Smelters. By the summer of 1907 the market began stabilizing briefly, but railroads, which of course were a leading group, began reporting down earnings. With capital shrinking and drying up, conditions weakening, and railroads reporting slow earnings and finding it difficult to obtain financing, the market was set up for a fall.

From July through mid-November the market fell almost straight down from near 60 to just below 40. And to show, as we will again see, how the market crumbles when its leaders fall, we can look at Union Pacific's action. Union Pacific was a leader throughout the strong uptrend of 1904 and 1905. In September 1906, Union was trading at $195. By October, it fell back slightly to the $170s. In early February 1907, well before the major break to the market occurred, Union Pacific was already flashing warning signs as it declined to near $120. This was one of Livermore's short positions. By late October a run on the banks had begun as the panic had spread. Jesse Livermore, sensing the bottom, closed out his short positions on Oct. 24, 1907, and realized profits of nearly $3 million. He did this by holding his winning short positions as they worked out well and kept adding to them as the stocks kept declining. This biggest payday yet had now established him as a true market operator.

J. P. Morgan who eventually had to save Wall Street by injecting needed capital even sent a letter personally to Livermore in late October asking him to stop shorting the market. The 1907 decline turned out to be the worst crash up to that point, as the Dow fell 38%, since it had just followed one of the best periods during the prior few years. Meanwhile, Bernard Baruch was also a contributor during the crash injecting nearly $2 million of his own money. We can see from this that Baruch was basically unaffected by the crash, most likely due to his disciplined trading approach and paying attention to the actions of the market. Wyckoff also noticed during this time that the bond market had also dried up, which offered a clue as to what might be coming. He also had an idea of publishing a magazine on trading and investing so he could educate the general public on the ups and downs of Wall Street so that they would be better prepared for future cycles. He would call his publication the *Ticker.* For his first copy (dated Oct. 1, 1907) he received $300 worth of advertising, and he printed 15,000 copies and sent them out to prospective interested parties.

The market bottomed in November 1907 (and ended the year down 38%) after assurance from Morgan and receiving needed capital. This panic was severe and needed the help of J. P. Morgan to bail out the exchange and keep it running as a viable institution. Livermore and Baruch both profited from this decline, again by staying in touch with the market, not getting biased opinions in one way or another, and just moving with the trend of the market's action.

The market made a strong comeback in 1908 right after it started the year by declining slightly in January and February. Again, as if anticipating better times ahead, the market began its climb in March, three months before the recession would end in June 1908. From there it trended upward, overcame a choppy period in late fall, and then ended the year near 85, recouping all the losses it experienced during the Panic of 1907 and then some, as the market rose 47% for the year.

The market took a short dip at the beginning of 1909 but then climbed higher until August. The remainder of the year it traded in a choppy fashion but ended the decade near 100 (up 15% for the year), or right near its peak for the decade, which it also reached back in early 1906. During 1909 Wyckoff kept up his study of the market and his writings. He kept experimenting with market tactics that would work, and he kept eliminating those that did not. He also began a series of articles entitled *Studies in Tape Reading* (which later became, and is still available today, published material). He originally ran these articles in his magazine from November 1908 to October 1909. The articles were meant to educate the public on his findings of positive market rules and skills. This was the first time anything like this had been presented to the general public. He discussed such market tactics as

- Determining the trend of the market.
- Supply and demand means everything in the market.
- Volume action within the market and stocks is vitally important.
- Keeping losses small is the number one rule.

Wyckoff was determined to assist the public in the ways of the market for the upcoming decade. As the passing decade showed, the market moves through many swings and cycles. To summarize the results of the prior period: From 1897 to 1909 the Dow Average went from the 40s to near 100. It peaked at a little over 100 in January 1906 and bottomed at the beginning of 1897 near 40. The period analyzed experienced three recessions, but they were long recessions. The first one lasted 19 months, the second lasted 24 months, and the third lasted 14 months. All told, the 156 months of this period would witness recession periods for a total of 57 of those months, or 36.5%. What was interesting to discover was that the market declined and/or flattened out prior to each recession period and rose sharply before each one officially ended.

2

A Few Sidestep Landmines to Profit (1910–19)

Jesse Livermore Followed the General Trend of the Market to Do Well

As if sensing another coming recession, the market began to trade in a choppy and flat range for the last five months of 1909. The market then started off the new decade by declining from January through July 1910 to just under 75, or nearly 25%, as a new recession began in January to usher in

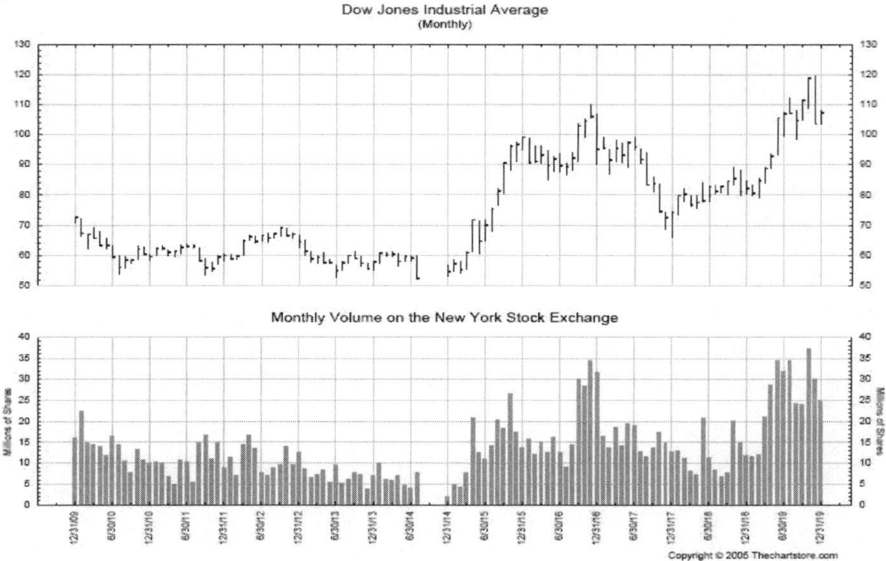

Figure 2-1 The Dow Jones Industrial Average 1910–1919.
Source: *www.thechartstore.com.*

the new decade. This long recession would last through January 1912 for a two-year total of 25 months. After a strong comeback from the Panic of 1907, the markets two-year uptrend began to weaken. There was still much apprehension concerning the market following the Panic, as investors still hadn't forgotten how fast a market could decline and the aftereffects of a severe downtrend. Participation slowed as well even during the uptrending years of 1908 and 1909. In fact share turnover declined each year on the New York Stock Exchange from 1909 to 1914, as did the average daily volume. This was a result of the lingering effects from the Panic of 1907.

During this slow time for the market, Wyckoff's magazine the *Ticker* wasn't making much money. But his strong interest in studying the market and trying to educate the public on how it really worked kept his drive moving forward. He also wasn't making much progress in his own trading, but perseverance can usually overcome short-term defeats. He then decided to take a job with a firm called Thompson, Towle & Co, mostly so he could have a steady income flowing in to help offset losses on his magazine. His responsibilities with Thompson were to generate new clients for the firm mostly through his publication. He then began to write another series within the *Ticker* called "Studies in Stock Speculation." He also now had more time during the trading day to observe and study the market. Through this study, his ability to forecast market movements began to improve. This analytical study was what he'd been looking for, and his judgments of the market started to show that his continuous curiosity and hard efforts of study were beginning to pay off.

At about this same time the government also began to get more involved in the markets. After the Panic of 1907, many wanted more scrutiny from the government to help protect investors. Then in 1911 the Taft administration began to level a heavy hand to many of the trusts that formed in the prior decade during the merger mania that occurred. DuPont and U.S. Steel were hit with antitrust actions, but the two major firms that were hit hardest were Standard Oil and American Tobacco. Both of those firms were dissolved due to their monopolistic structures. It was a striking blow and a loud sounding to American businesses concerning competitive practices. Meanwhile, Wyckoff began new additions to his magazine. In October of 1911, he created the *Trend Letter*, which was a separate weekly advice. This weekly would advise on what stocks to buy and sell and when to buy and sell them. The initial response was greater than he expected, mostly due to the fact that many of his forecasts were turning out to be correct. His popularity began to increase, and he then resigned from the firm of Thompson, Towle & Co, as his revenue stream began to increase from subscription sales of the *Trend Letter*. As for the market, it was still a mostly unexciting and dull market environment, as after the market rose to near 85 in October 1910, it then traded mostly sideways through July 1911. It then declined and bottomed four months before the end of the recession and then began to rise slightly and finally ended the year just slightly under where it began 1911.

The year 1912 witnessed the end of the long recession in February that began two years before. It should be noted that these flat years were very frustrating to many active traders at the time. One, of course, was Jesse Livermore. As mentioned in my first book, Livermore lost all his millions in profits that he had made from his successful short positions during the Panic of 1907 when he became involved in the commodities market and took a tip from Percy Thomas, who at the time was considered the Cotton King. Even though Thomas had been hit by a losing streak and lost many of his profits, Livermore still listened to him and ended up losing his entire stake trading in cotton. Taking tips from others is a dangerous way to try and make money in any market. Desperate to get back his capital, he traded constantly during a flat and dangerous market environment. This proves one of the major lessons from the great traders: it's not always wise to be active in market environments that don't offer profitable opportunities. We saw Baruch heed this advice back in the flat market of 1902 when he decided to stay out. One must trade with the trend of the market instead of constantly trying to force profits in a dull market.

Livermore became more indebted and began to become depressed as well. Livermore, of course, did not do well during this time, and he would later mention how he stayed out of future market cycles that were flat and directionless because they offered no good profit opportunities. We also don't hear much during this time from Bernard Baruch, as mentioned, due to his knowledge and experience. Baruch would also try to stay out of markets that offered no solid profit opportunities either to the upside or to the downside. Baruch was a much more disciplined trader than Livermore, so it would not be surprising to not hear of much activity from him during dull and listless trading patterns within the market. Baruch also retained his profits that he earned in Wall Street and when the war broke out, through his many business contacts from Wall Street, he became directly involved in servicing the country and he would leave trading for the time being. It's worth repeating that it is very important to remember that one of the key traits that all the greatest traders would employ was that it was wise to stay away from the market from time to time when opportunities to capitalize were minimized. This discipline protects one from one of the worst enemy's of a stock trader — overtrading. This time away would also allow them to do more analysis, review past trades for mistakes made, and just escape the challenges of day-to-day activity in the markets to clear their minds.

Meanwhile, Wyckoff's patience and hard work were paying off for him. His reputation continued to increase, and many firms were now approaching him. Wyckoff was discovering that the more time and thought he put into the market the better his judgment of the market's action became. He also at this time decided to change the name of his magazine from the *Ticker* to the *Magazine of Wall Street*. As for the market, it rose coming out of the recession from February to March 1912. It was however a short-lived rally as the market basically flattened out again through April and then rose slightly until it peaked in October. Then, just as many times before, it seemed to sense another impending slowdown and declined throughout the rest of the year as another recession period was just around the corner, though the Dow did manage to gain 8% for the year.

Another recession did begin in January 1913, and this one would also linger for two years until just after the beginning of World War I. The market would again offer up a slightly downward trend for much of the year, which was another mostly dull one for stocks and saw the Dow lose 10% for the year. Also in 1913 Wyckoff then joined a stock exchange house called Alfred Mestre & Co. as a special partner who put in a capital stake. Here he would look for the fastest growth opportunities, and he continued his intense analysis of the market. He began to analyze leading industries and the leading stocks within those industries and make recommendations to his firm's clients. A few of the leading industries he discovered during these tight market times were chain stores, especially S.S. Kresge, and mail-order companies, especially Sears, Roebuck and Co.

The year 1914 would turn out to be a historic time for the stock market following the mostly dull and listless prior years of the decade up to that point. With the country again mired in the middle of a recession, stocks continued their flat to slight downtrend from January through early July. In late

July, as uncertainty began to grow stronger over Europe and an impending war, the market sank on July 30, its worst day since the Panic of 1907. On that day some of the current leaders broke hard as General Motors fell $19⅞ and International Harvester fell $13. The following day, Friday July 31, 1914, the London Stock Exchange closed for the first time in its history. Fearing a rush to sell stocks, the New York Stock Exchange also decided to close for an undisclosed period of time. It was only the second time in U.S. history that the NYSE was closed. When trading did resume though on December 11 (for only issues that had no international nature), prices rose. This relief caused the exchange to resume all trading three days later on December 14. As the year came to a close stocks rose slightly, removing some uncertainty and fear, though the average volume on the NYSE would be recorded as the lowest average trading volume for the entire century and the Dow would lose 31% for the year. The year 1914 was also when Jesse Livermore filed personal bankruptcy after losing all his 1907 market profits. In addition, Wyckoff was not making much money as the slow dragging downward market with light activity caused him to reduce his publishing expenses and cut back on any expansion plans due to the slowed interest in the market. When the exchange did reopen for business in December, and as mentioned, it rose higher, there was a renewed demand for Wyckoff's products as well, which included stronger subscriptions for both the *Magazine of Wall Street* and the *Trend Letter.*

As the two-year recession ended in January 1915, the war in Europe had begun. Some uncertainties were lifted, and the market started to rise. After a slow beginning in January and February, the market sprang forward in March, which can be seen clearly in Figure 2-1 on p. 19, and continued rising strong throughout the year except for one major correction, which occurred in May. The war brought many to view the U.S. as a safe haven since many infamous predictions of disaster had not come to fruition. Also demand for American exports began to escalate. With the economy coming out of recession and allied countries looking to the U.S. for goods to expand their war-time efforts, many companies' profit prospects began to increase. The expected positive profitable picture started to send stocks upward. As America started to become the supplier of arms and food for the war, many leading stocks look poised for solid returns. Some of the leading stocks that stepped forward included American Smelting, Bethlehem Steel, General

Electric, General Motors, U.S. Steel, Baldwin Locomotive, Union Pacific and Reading. Volume also rose again since the prior year's volume was the lowest in history, so it was with renewed conviction that the market was finally coming back around.

Livermore Begins His Comeback

Though Livermore was still broke, because of his bankruptcy filing he now at least had a clear head to concentrate on the market and begin to regain his stake. One of the brokerage houses that he would trade with offered him a line of 500 shares. Livermore then, noticing the general trend of the market had turned upward, began observing market action and who the leaders of this renewed uptrend would be. He did nothing for six weeks but just watch and observe market action and leading stocks. He noticed how stocks would act when they would approach certain par levels. A par level, he observed in his bucket shop trading days, was when a stock's price came near a round figure such as $100 or $200 per share. He noticed that as they came close to this level and then crossed it a certain psychological threshold was reached and the stock would be free to resume its advance past that level. This was by no means a 100% certainty, but his market observations of how stocks traded, especially during a strong uptrending market would convince him that the chances of the stock rising were greater than normal. He began watching one of the strong leaders benefiting from the war-time economy, which was Bethlehem Steel. Livermore purchased Bethlehem Steel as it rose strongly and hit $98 per share. It actually finished the prior year of 1914 at $46⅛, so you can see how much momentum the stock had going for it. He bought another 500 shares as it kept racing upward to hit $114. The very next day it hit $145, and Livermore sold out for a quick $50,000 profit. It turned out he actually broke one of the vital rules of trading: don't be quick to sell a winning leader. Bethlehem Steel was one of the strongest stocks to have because it had benefited from the war-time economy as allied countries that used its product kept orders high. Bethlehem Steel's profits increased from $5.5 million in 1914 to $17 million in 1915 and then would soar to $43 million in 1916. Bethlehem Steel finished the year of 1915 at $459½, or up nearly 900%, and actually hit a high of $700 in 1916. But Livermore at this time was more interested in keeping a solid gain and regaining his stake and his confidence. With now some trading capital and his confidence back intact he was ready to get back into the game. Livermore would actually end the year with $150,000 in his account as he clearly stayed attuned to a rising market and made trading and investment decisions within the context of a healthy and profitable market environment.

As foreign trade continued to grow, exports increased and gold imports soared. Railroad earnings also began to jump and would end the year up 203% over 1914 levels. With this there were many renewed leaders from this group, among them Reading, Union Pacific and Baldwin Locomotive. Baldwin would end 1915 at $117⅞, or 192% higher than what it closed at the end of 1914. The market would finish the year strong, up 82%. This was clearly a golden opportunity in the stock market. Some of the best leading stocks, as is the case in most bull markets, rose quite further. As mentioned previously, Bethlehem Steel was up 900%, American Smelting rose 93% and General Motors shot up a whopping 517%.

Wyckoff Trades with the Trend

After a strong run-up like the one of 1915, the market pulled back and consolidated its gains over the next seven months. Then in August the market shot back up and rose until November. The war activity in Europe was still demanding American products, and companies continued to show strong results. Industrial businesses and agriculture were especially strong. What was also benefiting the market at the time was a renewed interest in stocks from the general public. Throughout the rising market after the start of World War I, the only real corrections to the upward trend were caused by rumors of the war ending. This adverse effect from a positive news item reflected the market's outlook on company profits and how they would recede back to more normal levels without the strong demand from overseas to help the cause for war requirements. Meanwhile, Wyckoff's *Trend Letter* kept gaining in popularity, since more and more people became subscribers and his keen eye to the trend of the market had resulted in many more correct recommendations. It should be noted that he always advised in the *Trend Letter* to have a stop-loss of three points in place to reduce losses as quickly as possible. Remember that the greatest traders' number one rule was to limit losses. Wyckoff was no different in his day, and it was a major reason why he never suffered large losses in his trading career. He was a strict disciplinarian when it came to this rule.

In early September 1916 after the market had staged a strong two-month advance, Wyckoff advised taking profits in his leaders. (It should be noted that when Wyckoff made recommendations he also personally followed them.) He, as Baruch did, liked to sell on the way up to take profits. Wyckoff had positions in all the strongest leaders that represented the strongest groups at the time, and he realized quick profits from the following: U.S. Steel (+17⅞), Baldwin Locomotive (+12½), Smelters (+9⅞), Union Pacific (+7⅛), and Pressed Car (+6⅝). Wyckoff stayed out of the market in October (being disciplined as mentioned before) when the market seemed to stall, and then in November he advised to short the prior leaders as the market began to quickly turn down. Here we see the flexibility of an experienced market operator not becoming biased in one direction or the other but rather moving with the actions of the market itself.

As always, even back nearly 100 years and as it also will in the future, the market looks ahead. The main reason for the sharp decline was that there was more uncertainty surrounding the war. Stocks started to peak in mid-November and then began to decline. Many leaders after rising strongly for quite some time began to pull back and stop their incredible uptrends. General Motors hit a peak of near $850 in 1916, or over 950% higher than when it closed out the 1914 year. Stocks simply don't keep going up forever, as we will see many times in the chapters to come. Bethlehem Steel peaked near $700 after climbing over 1,400% since its close in 1914. As the leading stocks of the prior bull market began to peak and break down, the greatest traders knew from past market cycles what that meant. Baruch and Livermore were right there watching the action of the market and its current leadership as they both started to fade. Baruch then began shorting the market leaders as they weakened.

Livermore also began sending his probes out to test the market to see if indeed it had topped. He noticed that when the current leaders corrected several points, which is normal market action, many of them didn't come back, as they had done during the prior few years when a normal reaction in the market took effect. This was also the first time in many months that leading stocks, which were correcting did not bounce back, which when they do is a sign of strength during a strong market. This weakness was the first signal to him that a top might be near. He had learned this lesson and profited handsomely during the 1907 market, as he noticed the exact same type of behavior — leading stocks topping and then starting to break down without a bounce back in price. This topping action in market leading stocks will repeat itself over and over in the coming decades when other market peaks have been reached. As his probes proved him right, Livermore pounded the market hard on the short side. He would begin by sending probes consisting of 5,000 shares in total, spread among a few of the prior leaders. When the probes began to work, he would pyramid his positions. He was now adding former leaders to his short positions and adding shares to these positions to compound his returns. He would pyramid these short positions when he was ahead by four points on each position. He would end up being short 12 different market leaders (General Motors, Baldwin Locomotive, etc.) with 5,000 share positions in each. With 60,000 shares short in the hard-falling leaders and a sharp break in the market during November and December, Livermore ended up with another incredibly profitable year in the market. He netted profits of nearly $3 million in 1916 as he rode the rising uptrend during the latter part of the summer until the fall, and then he shorted the market leaders during the latter few months of the year. When his earlier leading holdings began to top and break down, he quickly turned his operations around to follow the lead of the market. His short positions became profitable, and he showed again how staying attuned to the actions of the market can lead a great trader to huge gains. All this action occurred seven weeks before the famous "leak" that is mentioned next. In fact, when the leak came out, the market broke even further, but that was when Livermore covered his short positions and cashed in his profits.

Many leaders in late 1916 began to falter as a news leak that President Wilson was about to offer a peace plan to the Germans scared many traders into fear selling since it meant that the war-time economy would soon come to an end. Baruch was said to have taken advantage of this famous news leak and that he made $3 million from the advanced word. A congressional committee was actually formed to investigate the news leak and those who could have possibly profited from it. Baruch and Livermore were both called on to address the committee. Baruch denied he made $3 million stating that he had not heard of the news leak. He did however disclose that his short profits during the market break amounted to approximately $470,000, but stated this was due to his ability to trade with the market and not to some news leak that he acted upon.

Wyckoff was also right there watching the market, and in late November, as mentioned previously, his advice was to short the prior leaders as well. Though not as notable and large a trader as Baruch and Livermore, he made profits on the following stocks as he shorted them in November and then covered his positions in mid-December, just as Livermore did: U.S. Steel (+13), Smelters (+12¼), Baldwin (+14), Pressed Car (+7) and Central Leather (+6⅝). Notice how many of the same stocks he rode up during the uptrending market and made profits on were the same ones he shorted as the market topped and began to break. Again, we see the flexibility and change skill benefiting the best traders.

As 1917 began there was more uncertainty as rumors that the U.S. would enter the war began circulating more heavily. The markets whipsawed up and down for much of the beginning of that year. Also the earlier war effects that were positive for many businesses were beginning to level off. The markets always anticipate, and here it was again forecasting what the future would hold. On April 6 it was announced that the U.S. would enter the war. By late May and early June the market continued its downtrend mostly due to the uncertainty of the involvement of the U.S. in such a major war. Stocks dove almost straight down until the end of the year with the Dow losing 25% in 1917. As is always the case, the former leaders that rose the most also dove the most. The bigger they are, the harder they fall. Bethlehem Steel reached a low of $66¼ in 1917, a far cry from the $700 peak it had reached the year before, or 90% off its peak price. General Motors fell from its $850 peak to $74½, or 91% from top to bottom. Baldwin Locomotive fell to a low of $43 from its prior year peak of $118⅝, or 63%. The best traders throughout history sell their stocks when they begin to crumble, and they make sure to take their profits and not ride a stock all the way back down again.

Wyckoff would look at the market in 1917 with a shorter view, and he at times traded within the market to take advantage of quick turns. For example, in May the market made a quick upturn during a choppy period. He took four long positions on May 14 and then closed them out quickly on

May 31, as the rally was short-lived. His results were U.S. Steel +14⅛, Bethlehem Steel +12, Lackawanna Steel +10 and Studebaker –3¼. Notice how he kept his losses small — the 3¼ point loss on Studebaker — as he kept to his strict loss-cutting rule of three points. By early August the market was heading down again and Wyckoff took short positions in the following and then closed them out in September, mostly due to the still choppy nature of the market. His profits on these transactions were as follows: U.S. Steel +15⅛, Baldwin Locomotive +14¼, Crucible Steel +15, Republic Steel +11⅝, Bethlehem Steel +11, Lackawanna Steel +13¼, Beet Sugar +13¼ and Central Leather +13⅛.

Notice how he kept his focus on only a handful of stocks at any one time, another key trait of all the best traders. This focused concentration on leaders relates to active issues on both sides of the market. His *Trend Letter* was now making decent profits for his subscribers, and news began to spread concerning his recommendations. Soon he became the talk of many of the brokerage houses, and they would get copies of the *Trend Letter.* In late October he noticed the market began showing major weakness. He advised and shorted again the leaders that were breaking down. He shorted U.S. Steel, Baldwin, Bethlehem Steel and seven others. He was following the actions of big traders as volume surged higher as the market weakened. He also utilized a pyramiding strategy on every stock as it dropped by one point. That pyramiding strategy, as you'll see, is a key strategy that all the very best traders utilized to create their best gains. For every one-point drop in his positions, Wyckoff added to his position but he also kept his three-point loss protection with each stock as well. On the first day he held a position in U.S. Steel, it fell 7½ points on huge volume. He held these winners out and realized more profits when he covered his short positions. His popularity kept increasing, and he was now getting subscriptions from very high-level business people. He continued to focus the *Magazine of Wall Street* as a publication endeavored to show the trading and investing techniques as not get-rich-quick schemes but rather as a specialized business that was just as intricate as other professions such as law or medicine. This was exactly the same conclusion that Livermore, Baruch and Gerald Loeb (see Chapter 3) came to as well.

Right at the end of 1917 the market bottomed and began moving higher the first two months of 1918. The market then began to trade in a choppy range again and would continue that way until the summer. Wyckoff stayed mostly out of the market during this choppy environment. He had scored big profits in 1917 and he wanted to retain his positive returns. He also, through his recent success, began to refine his strategies. The keys to his success were much of the same that relate to each of the five traders featured in "Lessons from the Greatest Stock Traders of All Time." They were as follows:

- Trade only with the identified trend of the market.
- Stay out of flat or directionless markets.
- Pyramid your winning positions to compound your returns.
- Adhere to a strict loss-cutting policy. His was three points from his buy point.
- Stay focused on only a handful of stocks at a time — usually 10 or less.
- Trade only the real leaders from the leading industries.

During the prior 7½ years Wyckoff had now made enough money so that he would be financially independent. It took many years of trial and effort, just as the other great traders discovered. He would hop from job to job (as mentioned) in order to try and gain his footing. His perseverance is similar to what we will see in Nicolas Darvas when we get to the 1950s and Jim Roppel when we get to the late 1980s and beyond. Though Wyckoff never attained the big trader status as others of his day, he was a moderately profitable trader and would at times trade in 8,000- to 10,000-share lots, which qualifies as a rather large-scale trader. For Wyckoff, his now-profitable business publications of the *Trend Letter* and the *Magazine of Wall Street*, along with other business ventures, and his trading profits would now allow him to concentrate solely on his mission rather than worry about personal financial issues. That mission was to continue educating the public on how the stock market actually worked. He also discovered that his judgments improved as he stayed focused and disciplined. His strength, he thought, was in advising others, and as he discovered (as many others agree), he was more cautious in his advice to them than he was to himself regarding his own account. The one thing that he never would change was his view that being successful in the market over the long term was one of the most challenging and uncertain endeavors.

By 1919 the *Magazine of Wall Street* would become the number one financial publication of its time and would have a circulation larger than all other financial publications combined. In May of 1919, he would actually cease publication of the *Trend Letter*, due to the fact that so many brokers were gaining access to it without paying for it and using it to move to stocks that Wyckoff thought his paid subscribers were now at a disadvantage. He wanted fair information for all, and he even canceled writing it at the peak of its popularity and while there existed a waiting list to get a subscription.

In the summer of 1918 the market moved up, as the Germans were being pushed back in the war. But it would be a short-lived rally, as another recession would begin in August. This recession would be a much shorter one as compared to the many others that occurred in the prior 20 years. This shorter-lived recession was mainly due to the end of World War I, which finally occurred in November. The market then rose slightly to finish 1918 up 11% for the year, but a brighter future seemed to be just ahead as peace replaced uncertainty.

The market started 1919 off by dipping in January, but then it turned upward and began to climb. From 1917 to 1919 the national debt rose from $1.3 billion to $27 billion as a result of the war and due to the granting of credit to our Allies. The recently formed Federal Reserve, however, did a good job in handling this. It also started to look like postwar prospects were good even though many industries would be hit by the reduced demand for war goods. The war transformed the U.S. into the world's largest economy, and New York replaced London as the central market of the world. Based on this the stock market continued to climb in early 1919. The economy was also coming out of its recession, and the Federal Reserve was still in the expansive monetary policy that was in place during the war — it kept interest rates low to finance the war while pumping money into the banking system. There was a sector rotation that began that was directly tied to the end of the war. The huge exports that occurred during 1914–18 began to shrink in early 1919. Those industries that led that cycle (which consisted of steel, chemical and other industrial manufacturers) would begin to be replaced by other peacetime and rebuilding industries. Another skill of the great stock traders was their ability to always understand what was happening in the economy and the world as new industries took shape and older ones matured. In 1919 new industries that stepped up to the leadership role included agricultural products and railroad equipment (used to help rebuild Europe's damaged systems). Other leading industries included clothing, food processor and machinery companies. Activity was also increasing on the NYSE, as share volume in 1919 hit a new high of 318 million shares.

Just as things were looking bright, the Federal Reserve began raising interest rates in November for the first time in its brief history. The Fed wanted to put the brakes on the easy money environment that was still currently in place following the war. Also, many sector rotations, as mentioned earlier, take time to complete. Many also thought that there was an overexpansion that took place during the war and winding that down would not go unnoticed in economic terms. And once again we see the stock market looking forward; in early November prices peaked and then sharply broke until the end of the year, again foreseeing the next slowdown that was right around the corner as the new decade would begin.

It was a challenging decade for the market as war and recessions (totaling 47.5% of the entire decade) would dominate, but a few great stock traders were successful. Richard Wyckoff really got on the profitable side of the market after his many years of study and learning from his mistakes. He observed and studied the market in intricate detail, and he moved with its actions, even through some very challenging periods. He proved how one could take advantage of cycles and then profit successfully. We also saw Livermore make a profitable comeback from some of his prior mistakes. His legendary skills again proved that the best can profit, even in challenging market environments as well.

3

Shrewd Traders Made *and* Kept Millions (1920–29)

Richard Wyckoff Learned by Judging the Action of the Market

The markets began the 1920s where they left off in 1919 — sliding downward. A recession began in January 1920 — one that would last 19 months. The year 1920 saw the Dow drop from just over 100 to around 75, as some early choppy action gave way to a steadier decline as the year went on. It would be,

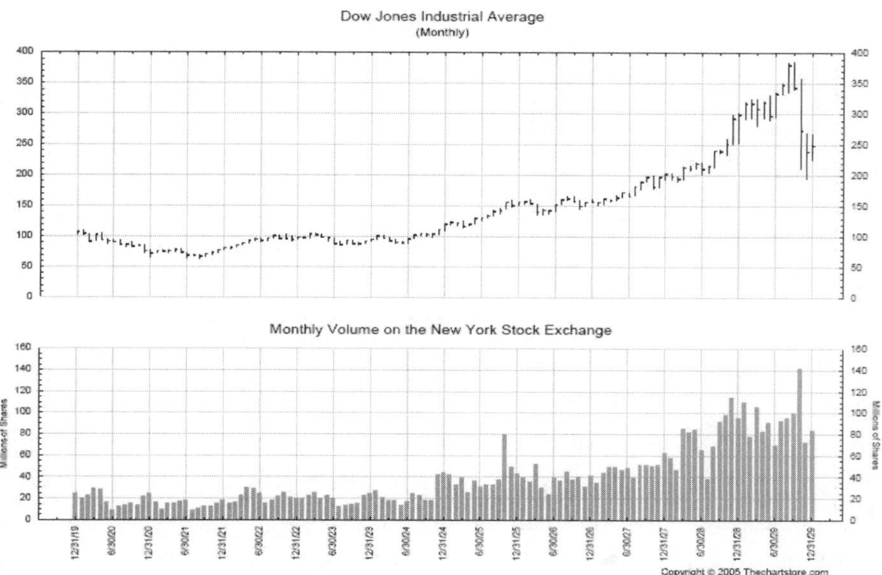

Figure 3-1 The Dow Jones Industrial Average 1920–29.
Source: *www.thechartstore.com.*

however, a start to some new exciting technological developments: the radio would be introduced as the new communication medium. The year 1920 also experienced an economy that was slowing down, as a recession began to set in while construction and crop prices were falling, which back then were vital industries to the American economic landscape. Because the market reflected an outlook of slowing conditions, many leading stocks, as they do when the market experiences heavier selling rather than buying power, pulled back and fell with the market. A few of these were American Woolen closing the year at \$60½, which was off from a high of \$165; Baldwin Locomotive, which closed 1920 at \$86, which was off from a high of \$118½; and Crucible Steel, which fell from a high of \$278 in April to \$75 by year-end, or a fall of 73%. This latter decline shows how the prior steel leader was caught in an industry rotation that was just beginning. Early 1920 also witnessed a time when many racial riots were beginning to unfold in many major cities throughout the country. It would be a tumultuous beginning to a decade that was about to witness both historical highs and lows for the stock market.

Wyckoff Expands His Analysis

Richard Wyckoff, during his continued study of the markets, remarked in 1920 that the market was changing. He noticed how, after the war had ended, that there were many more industries vying for the lead in the market. This was in contrast to the preceding decade when really only a handful of industries seemed to lead most market upward cycles. There also were more stocks to follow currently as diversity began to increase. As we will see he was correct in his thinking as more consumer-related industries began to crop up in addition to the existing industrial industries. Through his observation he concluded that he needed more than just pure market action to discover the real standout leaders for the future. Since the economy seemed to be in an early stage of expansion from a widening-out position and with recently enacted organized structures in place that had exertive powers such as the Federal Reserve, Wyckoff thought he needed to correlate many economic factors into this study as well. He thought that money and credit issues should be considered for their impact on the overall economy and how they directly affected profitable operation environments for organizations. With this new expanded study in mind he set out and formed Richard D. Wyckoff Analytical Staff, Inc., in which he was the sole owner. This firm was an advisory firm — it did not handle individual clients and their investments.

Wyckoff divided his firm, for research, initially into two different segments. The first segment was a Trend Trading Service (a takeoff from his earlier publication the *Trend Letter*), which focused on speculation. A second segment was called Analytical Staff Services, which focused more on swings within the market. He later added a third segment, called Investor's Advisory Board, which catered more to income investors. With these three segments he now covered most traders' and investors' needs from an advisory perspective. As Wyckoff refined his study he discovered what he called "10 vital traits" that he began to use as his new selection criteria. The 10 traits were split among three groups or categories: corporate related (based on trends of the fundamentals), industry related (based on trends of business in general) and technical related (based on technical swings in the market). Under each of these groups were specific vital factors that would comprise his 10 vital trends that related to each, as just mentioned.

Here we see early on a major experienced market operator adjusting his strategy to the changes in the marketplace and the economy to include many interactive issues that affect stock prices. We see a focus on combining fundamental analysis (corporate trends) with some technical features (technical trends) of the market and individual stock price action. We also see an expanded interest in general economic conditions and how they affect the market and stock prices as well. Wyckoff made a constant study of the market and its actions, of what was happening in the world and with the economy, and of how industries were constantly trying to innovate and adopt to ever-changing needs of people and events. He wanted to understand how the market discounted events and reacted the way it did as its many participants made predictive investment decisions.

From the beginning of 1921 to the end of April, the market nearly moved in a straight sideways fashion. Then a sharp drop from May through June occurred. The first part of the year was met by more negative news from an economic standpoint, as many businesses continued to fail. Because of the slowing economy and the many failed businesses, unemployment rose to over 5 million people (that was a large number back in the early 1920s). Steel prices also fell by more than half in early 1921, and it's interesting to note that one of the stocks listed earlier that broke in 1920 was Crucible Steel. Crucible was a leading stock in the steel group as that industry enjoyed strong returns from WWI activity in the preceding decade. As the steel industry began to slow down, this former strong leader broke hard (1920) before news (1921) of weakness in the industry. Here again we see how stocks peak months in advance — within certain leading groups — of actual weakness occurring as the market's ability to look forward repeats again and that those breaks usually occur with the leaders first. We'll see this play out time and again. This is exactly what happened with Union Pacific in 1907, before the panic mentioned in Chapter 1 really set in.

As the market kept falling further in early 1921 and the recession continued to drag on, there were a few bright points. For one, President Harding began his administration and his Republican status was viewed as more business-friendly than that of his predecessor, President Wilson. Also the Federal Reserve began to lower interest rates. Here we see again the market falling for somewhat of a prolonged period of time and many possibly giving up on the market when in fact what was happening was the market was just beginning to shake off the decline and begin one of its greatest moves in market history. By June the market had begun to flatten out, and by July the recession would officially end. We have seen instances of this in the prior decades — a flattening out of the market after a prolonged decline and the end of a recession period. By the end of the summer a true recovery was taking shape. Combined with an easing of interest rates, an economy that was beginning to broaden in terms of industries, and consumption starting to improve, the market was looking ahead to better times. The year 1921 would serve as a pivotal point in the economy as it started to strengthen with accommodative policies. In fact, the Federal Reserve would lower interest rates to 4.5% by year-end. This was quite a reduction since they stood at 7% earlier in that year.

The year 1921 also witnessed the birth of a market career for Gerald M. Loeb, one of the traders featured in "Lessons from the Greatest Stock Traders of All Time." He would begin his career by working in the bond department for a brokerage house in San Francisco, and he also wrote some briefs concerning financial statistics and bonds that were published later that year. Richard Wyckoff would also begin more detailed discussions with Jesse Livermore, for the two had first met back in 1917. As they got to know each other better, Livermore would grant interviews to Wyckoff regarding his strategies in the market. During those years Livermore would comment that his experience is what developed his judgment to lead him into the right stocks and it was his intuition that would lead him out. Livermore would also comment on how the stock market also discounts information and events and that in order to be successful in the market one had to anticipate business conditions six months to a year forward in order to understand how the market truly values stocks. Wyckoff would use the information from the Livermore interviews to gain more perspective from a successful market operator, and his findings later became available to the general public in a short pamphlet-style booklet that today is published by Windsor Books entitled "Jesse Livermore's Methods of Trading in Stocks." As for the market, it rose steadily from the fall until the end of the year and finished just above 75, a good 13% gain for the year.

The year 1922 began with the market continuing a slight but steady climb. This would also be a year in which many economic trends were moving up and business conditions were continuing to slowly improve. Wyckoff also continued his interviews with Livermore. The *Magazine of Wall Street* actually began reporting on some of the comments made by Livermore. In the summer of 1922, it stated that Livermore was mentioning that investors needed to adjust to the now improving postwar era and that conditions were strengthening. He also stated he had a bullish bias and some attractive leaders consisted of Delaware & Hudson, Northwest and Great Northern pfd, among others. He also stated how critical it was to adjust to new and stronger industries that were appearing. He mentioned that railroads, which were the leaders for many years earlier on, were now weak and would continue to weaken. His experienced market observation was steering him to new industries that were shaping the economic landscape of the future. Here we see one of the most respected and legendary market operators staying in tune with everything that affected the market, and adjusting to the changes in it and other relevant factors, right near the start of one of the greatest runs in market history. After a steady climb, the market began to flatten out in September and then traded mostly sideways until year-end when it finished right near the 100 mark, up 22% for the year.

The year 1923 started off positive as the market moved up in January and February, but it peaked at just over 100 in March. A steady decline began in April and lasted through May, again as if signaling an impending recession or slowdown. Sure enough, beginning in June a new recession set in that would last for 14 months (note that some of these later recessions were shorter in length than the preceding ones from the prior two decades). The market meandered for most of the middle months of that year and then sprinted higher in November and December to finish the year slightly below where it began, or down 3%. It's also interesting to note that during the 1923–24 recession period, the market barely gave up any ground, as can be seen in Figure 3-1 on p. 33. This is in stark contrast to the many other prior recessions, where the market showed much more weakness, especially inside a recession. With a more stable financial system in place and a rotating industrial sector away from just a few major industries, astute observers of the market during this time would have noticed this. There just were not as many major breakdowns in leading stocks during this slowdown period. Also, and more importantly, during 1923 the average daily volume on the exchanges was increasing (an average of 860 million shares a day), and throughout the year there were consistent instances of where the market would move higher on increased-volume days and would decline on lower-volume days. This price-volume interaction is one of the main determinates of market activity and individual stock activity. It was one of the main trading strategies of all the great traders featured in my first book regardless of the time period. No doubt, the great traders during this era noticed and acted upon this vital trait.

Loeb Learns a Lesson

It was also during this time that Gerald Loeb was really beginning his personal operations in the market. He actually began his trading account with an inheritance from his father of $13,000. Though he fairly quickly brought his account up to around $25,000 with a successful bond issue during the prior year, he would soon discover how challenging the market really is. No doubt, inexperience and a dull sideways market can serve to be valuable lessons to an aggressive aspiring young trader. Sure enough, in early 1923 Loeb bought on a tip from someone and put everything he had into Maxwell-Chalmers, an auto stock that was being run by Walter Chrysler at the time. Loeb bought 5,000 shares on margin at $40 per share. He, in effect, had $200,000 worth of stock in which he only had to put $20,000 of his own money (10% margin requirement at the time). Shortly after this purchase the stock began to decline as the market topped and began a slight correction. As the stock continued to fall Loeb refused to sell. Once the stock hit $20, with Loeb's gut-wrenching emotions out of control, he finally sold out. This major loss for him, as he was just about completely wiped out, taught him that it was important to pull money out of the market when trends in the marketplace have turned against you. He also discovered that his timing was completely wrong, as the market was not presenting solid buying opportunities. But even though he was discovering some valuable market lessons from this loss, a determined but inexperienced and impatient trader needs more time to learn. Hoping for a quick comeback, his mother sold some jewelry for $10,000 to give young Loeb a new stake. Here we'll see a few more rookie mistakes. One was that he traded on comeback determination instead of waiting for the market to present opportunities to him. He also fought against the market's new trend, which was correcting, as he bought on another tip concerning an oil stock. The stock was priced near $20 when he made his purchase. He ended up taking another major loss as the stock eventually fell to $2 per share, though he was out before that drastic plunge. This second loss taught him one of the most valuable lessons for success in the market — do your own research. And with time, research and experience will lead one to better judgment. Loeb would later say that those first two major early losses for him were keys to why he did not lose money in the Great Crash of 1929. And as we know, it takes losses in the stock market to make future great traders. When it comes to the stock market, perseverance is one of the best traits to have, and learning from mistakes is one of the best teachers.

The year 1924 started off with a gain in January, but then the market dipped down from February through May. In early 1924 Livermore began getting more bullish on the longer-term prospects of the market. This was probably due to what was mentioned earlier as the downside selling was drying up and wouldn't produce as severe a correction as previous periods did. After a few months of a drifting market, things began to turn up in June and July as the market lifted higher two months before the recession would end. Remember, that when markets were coming up off of corrections, especially with the economy coming out of a recession, that's when Baruch began to see the best opportunities. He began actively buying leading stocks right near the ground floor of a market that would begin an impressive upward trend. Some of the positions he established were 3,000 shares of

Consolidated Gas (he would later add another 3,000 shares as it moved higher); 8,100 shares of Baltimore & Ohio Railroad; 7,500 shares of American Smelting; 8,000 shares of U.S. Steel (he would later add another 7,000 shares); 5,000 shares of International Nickel; 4,900 shares of Sloss Sheffield and 12,000 shares of Northern Ore.

Here we see an experienced market operator making commitments in an environment that he was familiar with since he had witnessed this type of market movement many times in the past. He also took major positions in a handful of stocks as the market began turning upward. Experience and judgment play key roles in participating in the market, and Baruch's intelligent insight into market activity would pay positive returns to him. As in the prior year, 1924 witnessed an increase in trading volume, and for the first time in history the average daily trading volume on the New York Stock Exchange would exceed one million shares. Also that year the market continued its action of rising on increased-volume days and declining on lower-total-volume days. As for Wyckoff, he also saw the market begin turning its trend to the upside, and he went long in June as well. But as we've seen many times with him, he took his profits quickly, when in August the market flattened out. Wyckoff was more of a shorter-term participant, and he always made sure to retain his profits when he had them instead of giving them back.

A flattening out from August through October then led to a strong push upward in November and December, and the market ended the year near 125, or at an all-time high, for a good 26% gain for the year. Also in 1924 Gerald Loeb, after bouncing around for the prior few years with several firms, accepted a position as a stockbroker with E.F. Hutton in New York. He would end up staying with Hutton for the remainder of his career. The skittishness from his earlier losses still showed up in his market operations as he made 30 trades during the month of August. But his strict loss-cutting policy earned him a net profit of $2,500 for the month as his 19 winning positions exceeded his 11 losing transactions. He did confine his trades to active leading stocks, and he conducted his own research. He would commonly trade what he called the "four horsemen" of speculative stocks, which were American Can, Studebaker, U.S. Steel and Baldwin Locomotive. He traded American Can frequently due to its quick activity and the fact that he knew and studied the company extensively. Also at this time he was writing daily market letters for E.F. Hutton and sending them out to other brokerage firms and the company's client list. He was young (24 years old), learned quickly, and worked extremely hard. He was also gaining a reputation for his market insight. He was quickly given a promotion within the firm and was named head of E.F. Hutton's statistical department. He was also given more brokerage clients, in fact six large accounts that had net worth's of over $1 million each. Success was coming his way, and he decided to begin studying even harder by paying more attention to fundamentals and the backgrounds of companies. He was also much more conservative with his clients' money than he was with his own account (just as we saw with Wyckoff). Loeb was still very young and in a learning mode, but his desire and determination became key skills and strengths that aided his later success, much as we saw and will see with the other great traders as well.

After starting 1925 off flat and then dipping slightly near the end of March, the market turned up and steadily increased until the end of the year, closing at above 150. It was a nice solid gain for the average (up 30%), and the period became known as the beginning of the "new era" bull market. The economy was also picking up as the prior recession was now over and worker productivity and the use of power and credit were rising, and America was becoming more upbeat about the future. During the uptrend of the market all the great stock traders mentioned so far in this book were right there staying in sync with it and riding stocks up as the market kept climbing. Along with the rising market we see volume playing a strong role again. The average daily volume that year rose solidly to 1.7 million shares per day. Clearly this price and volume action was signaling that buying power for stocks was strong. Baruch's trading records show that he made a profit in 1925 of just over $1 million. His winning positions totaled $1.4 million, and his losing positions totaled $416,000. Here again we see a large individual operator experiencing losses as everyone does but keeping his market losses minimized compared to his winning positions by a rate of nearly 3½ to 1 (ratio of his winning positions to his losing positions in dollars). Livermore was also in the market with long positions as was Wyckoff, as will be discussed subsequently. Gerald Loeb was also beginning to learn from his exhaustive study of the markets and his experience.

In 1926 the market edged higher still through February when it began to lose steam. After a nearly uninterrupted run of close to a year, the market was due for a pullback. You'll notice if you view the charts at the beginning of each chapter that nearly continuous run-ups rarely lasted greater than a year at a time. Consolidations in market activity are a normal occurrence due to human reactions as people tend to take profits at certain times and stocks begin to build new bases. March and April did offer a noticeable correction, as profits were cashed in from the prior advances. Wyckoff was one of those that cashed in his profits. He made good profits on the ride up in the 1925 market. In February of 1926 he started to sense a top to the market as his earlier experiences had always taught him to be on the lookout for when the market begins to change directions. By late February, after the market stalled, he sent out an advice through his analytical staff that stated, "Sell at the market." By March 1, he was totally out of his positions and 100% in cash, as one never knows how strong the selling could get. As his subscriber base kept increasing and the buying power of his services grew to a large number, Wyckoff mentioned that his continuing challenge was to improve and ascertain when certain turning points would take place in the market.

Near this time Wyckoff began to plan his retirement (mostly due to health reasons). As he did so, he wanted to stress those challenges to his analytical staff as being the basis of further training and focus. Remember Wyckoff's goal was not to make the most money, but rather to perfect his skill and efficiency in the market that he operated in and then to communicate his findings to the general public. He issued a circular called a *Record of Results* for the 10-month period ending March 4, 1926. The circular showed the results that would have been achieved if one would have taken his advice through his research, if trading in 100 share lots. A person following his advice would have realized net profits of $31,650. These profits would have been achieved by winning positions totaling $36,450 and losing positions totaling $4,800. Notice again how all the great traders experienced losses in the market but that their strict loss-cutting policies enabled them to easily overcome the losses with strong profits (here by better than 7 to 1) in their winning stocks during a strong upward-trending market environment.

Loeb Gets Burned and Then Rights Himself

Although Wyckoff was gaining advantages from his valuable experiences, Gerald Loeb was still continuing his learning ways. As he started managing more money for others, he started to do less in-and-out trading. He was also more cautious and tended to stay with slower-moving stocks. In early 1926 when the market corrected hard, Loeb got caught and didn't act. He ended up losing a whole year's worth of profits in a very short time. He was discovering just how brutal the market could be if one doesn't pay attention and act swiftly. What he discovered was that his conservative approach on the way up was wiped out in a speculative manner on the way down, which was just the opposite approach to how he thought it should be. He discovered that staying with only conservative stocks, for example, might net a 15% rise in appreciation over a longer period of time and then could be totally wiped out by a correction in a much shorter period of time. On the other hand, faster-rising and more speculative stocks may advance, for example, 200% over a longer period of time and then correct 30% when a sharp market break occurs. Though the correction of 30% is twice the correction of the 15% in more conservative stocks, the much stronger advance would still leave one with positive returns over the length of the holding period. This experience was a huge wake-up call to him. He then decided he would lean more toward active speculative issues, and he also discovered that the real importance was how the general market was responding and he needed to follow its action closely. He also increased his observation and study of the market in general and decided to only follow a handful of strong active leaders in the market. His persistence paid off as the market began a turnaround trend in May, and in six weeks he was active and rode with the market on the way up to recoup all his prior losses. Here again he learned from his experience and mistakes. He took two very important lessons to heart from this time frame. First, he would increase his study and research to focus on only a few strong leaders. Second, and most important, he discovered that flexibility in the market is the most important trait one could possess. He would use flexibility to change with the market and to also become an expert in many industries that would be leading the market. For example, throughout his success he did not concentrate on one particular type of industry. He became knowledgeable in many industries such as automobiles, photography, oils and energy, entertainment and others, since many stocks from each of these groups would become leaders of the market as those industries continued to evolve and create new products for consumers and businesses.

As mentioned, after a basically flat period through May, the market turned back up and rose strongly from June through August. In May, however, Wyckoff closed his association with the *Magazine of Wall Street*, the publication he had started 19 years earlier. The magazine was now self-sufficient from a financial perspective, as liquid assets for the magazine were well over half a million dollars. In June, Wyckoff was confined to bed rest for an extended period due to health issues.

The short-lived rally stalled, two months before another impending recession was ready to set in. This recession would last another 14 months until November 1927. The market sold off in September and October of 1926, and then bounced up to finish the year basically where it began. It ended up being a choppy year for the market, though again the major declines after prior run-ups and another recession setting in didn't seem to contain intense selling pressure. This would now be the second time in the prior few years we have seen the market hold up well despite some variables that earlier would have resulted in much larger corrections. For 1926, Baruch actually ended up making a profit of $457,000 during a fairly choppy market environment, mostly due to his experience, judgment and ability to be flexible with the market's action as well.

In 1927, while in the midst of a recession, the market sprinted higher after a brief dip in January. From there though the market moved steadily higher. By then market participation was increasing even further. More people continued to use margin (borrowed money) to buy securities. This was in contrast to times before the war, when margin was utilized mostly by professional speculators. By the middle to late 1920s the public became heavier users of margin as the use of credit was gaining popularity in the purchase of other goods, mainly the automobile. This surge of buying in automobiles sent the shares of many of those firms to new heights, as auto stocks were a clear leader during that time. Also, advertisers were more prevalent and touted the ability of the general public to borrow money to purchase stocks, and buying on margin was viewed as the "in" thing to do if one desired to get rich in the stock market. It's interesting to note that while the economy was in recession, the market again barely declined and actually rose throughout much of its current slowdown period. The industrial production index was falling, and America was feeling the pain of a depression-type environment from the English and from Canada. But an easy monetary policy from the

Federal Reserve flooded the banking system with cash, which the banks in turn lent out for collateral loans that were starting to be used for stock purchases. From 1925 to 1927 the amount on loans for securities increased by 40% versus the amount of loans for commercial purposes, which increased only 12%. The signs that an imbalance was beginning were clear in 1927. It was becoming a highly speculative era as another event that took place proved as well. Charles Lindberg's flight to Paris buoyed airline stocks to new heights. Wright Aeronautical, which built the *Spirit of St. Louis* plane, rocketed from near $25 to $245 in only 19 months after the successful flight took place. Seaboard Airlines, which was another airline stock at the time, also soared rapidly higher in price following the historical flight.

It was also in 1927 that Loeb began to really notice how psychology and crowd behavior played a major role in the market and how certain Wall Street valuation methods didn't matter as much. For example, every stock he purchased in 1927 was based purely on fundamentals and a model he would use to value stocks. As his stocks rose to higher levels he sold them because his models informed him that the prices had reached an overvalued basis. What he noticed however was that once he sold them they continued to rise in price due to the strong trend of the market during that time. He then came right back into the market and bought them again. This understanding of how crowd psychology worked was the exact same discovery that Livermore and Baruch had learned in their early years.

Baruch Makes a Mistake

In order to fully understand how best to succeed in the market, it pays to study your mistakes, as that is how all the best traders over time perfected their market skill — they kept learning from what they did wrong so they would not repeat those mistakes in the future. Even the best still made major mistakes as they went along. One was Baruch in 1927 when he thought that General Motors (GM) had risen too high in price. Remember, the market doesn't care what you may think, not even if you're Bernard Baruch, someone who had achieved many positive returns in prior years and was viewed as one of the best market operators ever. His "thought" was what got him in trouble with GM. Instead of listening to the actions of the market and its participants, which were clearly in a continued buying phase, he thought GM's valuation was too high. It is important here to distinguish between thought and judgment. Judgment gained from experienced market observations and knowledge of past events leads one to make sound decisions. Thoughts like Baruch had can creep into the mind of a stock operator and overtake sound judgment. When you begin to think that you are right no matter what the situation or circumstance, you can get yourself into quite a bit of trouble in the market, and it will end up costing you money. You may find yourself arguing with many participants and their decisions, and no matter how big your positions may be, you will find yourself on the end of a losing transaction if you fight the trend of a certain stock just because you have a thought on where its value should be.

Baruch actually began shorting GM in late 1926 when he took a position of 3,000 shares at $150 per share. By January 1927, he increased his short position by 12,000 more shares at $155. Notice how he already made a mistake of averaging down (in this case shorting more of a stock that was going in the wrong direction for him). It should be pointed out that none of the great traders featured in this book averaged down. They all did the exact opposite — they pyramided their best positions as they moved up in price, if they were long the stock. Livermore and Wyckoff would add more to short positions while those holdings kept falling. As GM kept increasing in price, since the market was moving higher, Baruch covered 8,000 shares of his position at $160¼. By late March, with GM continuing to climb, and Baruch staying fast to his thought of overvaluation, he shorted another 26,000 shares at $176. Remember that the market was still in a clear upward trend and GM was one of the strongest leaders of the upward move. With automobiles enticing everyone, not only were automotive stocks rising, but many other industries that were created to support the automobile were all rising as well. After a short consolidation in June, the market surged higher from July through September. It was in July that Baruch finally threw in the towel as GM had appreciated to $213½ and he bought the stock to cover his short positions. He ended up losing $405,000 on this venture. Notice how he also did not limit his loss, as was usually one of his strongest disciplines and trading rules. This proves how dangerous and costly personal opinions and fighting the market can be even if you have many years of success and experience.

After a sharp consolidation in October, the market bounced right back in November and then finished the year near the 200 mark (which it hit on December 19) for the first time. Also, the recession officially ended in November that year. It was a solid 29% gain for the Dow in 1927, as the momentum and excitement about America's prospects continued to grow.

The bull market was gaining momentum, and 1928 would turn out to be a high-flying year for stock market gains. The market started the year off flat during January and February. A nice upturn lasted from March through May. Then a modest consolidation pullback occurred in June and part of July. From mid-July onward it was a surging market. General participation kept increasing, and many more people kept buying on low margin requirements. Excitement was widespread, and new industries were gaining momentum. The radio, automobile, air flight, television and color movies were all fairly new and exciting industries. The public, driven by credit, had a consuming appetite with many new products being introduced. Investment overseas by American businesses was also increasing. To try and better measure the changing face of America in the late 1920s, the Dow Industrial Average was expanded to 30 stocks in 1928. Joining the list were new leaders in the automotive industry. Nash, Chrysler and Mack Trucks joined the list to represent new strength. To show just how much the public began taking to some of the new products being introduced, Radio Corporation of America (RCA) reported earnings of $15.98 a share in 1928. This was a 1,100% increase from the $1.32 a share it reported just three years earlier in 1925. The stock of RCA was one of the high-fliers of the late 1920s. From $32 a share in 1926, it hit $101 in 1927, and would eventually rise to $574 in 1929. Here is a classic example of a leading stock in a new leading industry reaping the benefits of demand for its products by reporting record earnings and the stock leading in price appreciation during a strong uptrending market.

Some Experts Get Cautious

From near the end of July at just above 200, the market surged through November to near 300 with only one month of rest (September). Some of the best market operators however, tried to keep their heads during this tremendous rise that many on Wall Street had not seen before. Livermore was said to have been looking for a top to the market by late 1928. He'd seen how markets top from some of his earlier days, for example back in 1903 and 1907. His remembrance of those experiences and how people's behavior really doesn't change kept him alert. It was a major reason why he would profit so handsomely in the coming year. He also kept his head and didn't get too excited. This is part of the critical emotional control that the best traders employ. Bernard Baruch, however, seemed to get more caught up in the excitement. He actually moved his offices closer to Wall Street — a mistake of getting too wrapped up in the action. We will see this happen to Nicolas Darvas as well in the late 1950s. Though Baruch was extremely bullish on America's prospects for the future, he would start to feel uneasy about the rapid increase in share prices, and he mentioned a few times that prices seemed exceedingly high. He was also an astute observer of crowd psychology, and he studied it well. He knew that a "mob"-type of behavior was somewhat responsible for the rise of the market, but he also believed very strongly in the economic prospects of the country. He did sell out of his positions a few times during the rapid run-up in prices, as he liked to sell his winners on the way up. His often quoted saying is, "Repeatedly, in my market operations I have sold a stock while it was still rising — and that is one reason why I have held on to my fortune." But each time he sold in 1928 the market kept moving higher. Being the astute operator he was though, he would come right back into the strong market and buy more and benefit from the current rapidly rising market.

A sharp pullback then occurred in November, but it didn't last long as the market shot right back up again in December and finished the year near 300. The 1928 gain was a solid 48%. Also, the Federal Reserve began to get concerned about the rapidly rising market and began to raise interest rates to help curb some of the more speculative buying. They raised rates from 3.5% to 4%, then to 4.5%, and then by December rates were raised again to finish the year at 5%.

The year 1929 started off with another buying frenzy as the markets bolted higher in January. From there it would be mostly whipsaw action (up and down) until May as the bulls found a fight with some cashing in their profits. But the continued frenzy for stocks was not over yet. A continued strong demand for margin money raised those rates to 12%. Even at those high rates, people thought that since the market was rising so fast, their returns on the increase in stock prices would dwarf the higher margin rates they were being charged. Consumption by consumers stayed strong, as the gross national product (GNP) had risen by 50% since early 1921 to the current time of 1929. It was clearly a remarkable increase in many respects from an economic standpoint. Worker productivity had increased by some 40% during the same time frame, from 1921 to 1929. Taxes had also been cut to spur investment. Buying on credit, advertising and consumption were all rising. It was clearly continuing to be the roaring 20s, and most everyone was caught up in it and excited about continued prosperity.

By the summer of 1929 many of the more active and astute traders of the day would again be questioning the euphoric rise in stock prices. Livermore was beginning his probing on the short side looking for a top. As mentioned previously, he remembered his successful experience in 1907 to know that all markets don't go straight up forever. Baruch, by August, when the market was rising so fast, would buy stocks one day and then turn around and sell for profits the next day. As the market kept shooting up he would continue this fast-paced trading, though he had sold out most of his positions on the way up prior to this. Baruch and Joseph Kennedy (father of former President John F. Kennedy and a successful stock market operator in his own right) near this time really started becoming more suspicious when beggars and shoeshine boys began offering stock tips. The action of "mob psychology" was in full force, as more people where racing to get in the markets. Many would leave their jobs during the day and just watch the tape in brokerage houses or at the Exchange (a little bit similar to how others in the late 1990s would quit their jobs to day-trade full time as the Nasdaq was sprinting higher).

By mid-1929, because of demand, the broker rates for margin loans was near 20%, quite an increase from where they were just two years earlier at 3.5%. Because of this high demand for money and the attractive rates in the market, corporations even started lending money to consumers for securities purchases. Chrysler, Anaconda Copper, Bethlehem Steel and others saw good returns from lending money that actually exceeded their corporate investment strategies. Therefore, money was being funneled into speculative stock purchases and being directed away from productive capital investments that could eventually create new jobs and opportunities.

A sharp spike upward in the market in June was followed by only a pause in July, and then the final climax run began in August. By this time many leading stocks were rising in dramatic fashion in what is called "classic climax runs" (we'll see this occur again later in many other market cycles as well). American Tobacco, RCA, Standard Oil of California, Union Carbide, National Cash Register and many others were racing up in price. Montgomery Ward was also a huge winner. In fact, this would turn out to be one of Loeb's earliest and biggest winners. He ended up making a multimillion-dollar profit on this stock alone. How did he do it? He stayed in rhythm with a very strong market and one of its leading stocks. Montgomery Ward was a major leading stock at the time as consumer demand was in full swing and the company was reaping the benefits of increased revenues and earnings. Loeb kept pyramiding this stock on the way up, and he held fast to this rising leader. He kept watching it closely and heeded one of the key rules for big gains — let your winners ride. He also sold correctly and made sure he didn't become too emotionally attached to a winning stock, even one that produced over millions of dollars for his account. He always liked to sell on the way up, and he was absolutely one of those smart money traders who sold right into the very strength of the stock before it would then weaken and break with the rest of the market.

Volume on the exchange was also rising. From the fall of 1926, the market would not witness a single day with a volume under one million shares traded until the summer of 1931. One curious divergence that was occurring for the astute observer was that economic conditions were slowing down even though optimism was running at an all-time high. Auto and construction figures that were coming out were all down. Also, European stocks had already begun to fall. In August an official recession set in, and this would be the first time that the market would actually rise and keep rising just before and right into the beginning of a new recession. Clearly, all caution was pushed aside.

The peak close of the market was September 3, as the market stood at 381.17. Gerald Loeb observed this and began to question the almost uninterrupted rise of the market. From near 200 in June of 1928, the market surged to over 380 in a little over 14 months, or up 90%. The market had nearly quadrupled from the point of when it started its historic run in late 1924. Here now are some of the interesting details of how that market topped and gave out plenty of cues before it really started to sink. Some smart money began to sell in September, and some of the best traders in history were either liquidating their stock holdings and retaining their profits or beginning to sell short. Remember that a key trait of the very best traders is their ability to control their emotions. The difficulty in not getting too caught up in the hysteria but following sound judgment and using experience from either prior mistakes or successes is a main reason why so few are able to conduct sustained profitable operations in the market.

After the market peaked in early September, heavy selling began to set in and actually became quite common. This is a very strong signal that gradually smart money was leaving the market. The Dow Average suffered five declines on heavy volume throughout September. Those days were September 5, 12, 17, 20, and 24. Within three weeks the Average experienced noticeable selling pressure. Also, on September 19, the market reversed from an earlier gain to close with a loss on another heavy-volume day. We will see as we go along that if for numerous days after the market hits a high, heavy selling begins to build and continue, the markets will start major correction phases. This action and pattern has repeated itself time and time again throughout market history. All this selling during September was occurring a full month before the bottom fell out. It was clear that the price action of stocks, especially the leaders, and the volume activity that was taking place were causing a change in the general trend of the market. In fact, the Dow was 45% off from its peak by October 29, which is when most say the Crash began. A 45% correction is a definitive change in trend and a pretty significant and loud signal that things were already crumbling by the time late October came around.

After the fall in September, a sharp rise on October 6 calmed some nerves on the street as RCA, Westinghouse, U.S. Steel and American Can posted sharp increases that day. Was this to be just a temporary decline and a new buying opportunity? Optimism rebounded after the quick comeback. However, the big and astute selling traders were not quite finished yet. As trading began to slow down a bit, more economic reports came out showing continued weakness. Steel production was poor, and construction figures continued to weaken. Also, the momentum of the October 6 rebound was short-lived. After a sharp fall like the one in September, one good day is not enough to turn around what was becoming a new direction in the overall trend of the market. On Friday, October 18, stocks sank again, and leading stocks were taking more hits. U.S. Steel, General Electric and

Westinghouse were all down over five points each. People then started getting more concerned, and many started talking about the Panic of 1907. But many thought that, due to the fact there was a more organized banking structure because of the Federal Reserve, more established leadership in the market, and previous experience from 1907, an event like that could not occur again. Of course, Livermore remembered 1907, and his thoughts were that since human emotions are involved, an event like that could happen again no matter what was in place. His memory of his actions and the market during that time helped him tremendously during this current time. On Saturday (the markets were open for short sessions on Saturdays back then), October 20, the markets fell again on heavy volume. This also was the first day that heavy margin calls were being placed by brokerage houses. Also, rumors started to circulate that Jesse Livermore might be responsible for the selling and that he was trying to pound the market lower. By that time though, he had already established plenty of short positions in the market since he had seen the change in trend to the downside weeks before. From there it was the beginning of panic selling. The next few weeks looked like this:

- Monday 10/21/29: Prices were down and volume surged to over 6 million shares (a record).
- Tuesday 10/22/29: Prices were up in the morning and then reversed to close for a loss.
- Wednesday 10/23/29: The market was down sharply again (American Telephone, GE, Westinghouse, Hershey — all down over 15 points each).
- Thursday 10/24/29: Known as Black Thursday. The market opened lower, and then around 10:00 a.m. volume picked up and the market sank. Volume was almost 13 million shares, and the tape was four hours behind in quoting prices.
- Friday 10/25/29: The market staged a minor increase for the day.
- Saturday 10/26/29: Volume rose again, and the market fell slightly.
- Monday 10/28/29: The market sank 12.8% on huge volume. GE, Westinghouse and American Telephone fell 48, 34 and 34 points, respectively, all on huge volume. Margin calls increased as the losses piled up for those who didn't sell.

- Tuesday 10/29/29: The Dow fell another 11.7% (down 24.5% in two days), and volume crossed 16 million shares. All leaders were slammed hard, and U.S. Steel and American Can declared extra dividends to try and relieve the panic.
- Wednesday 10/30/29: The market soared 12.3% recouping the prior day's loss on relief from positive comments from many in order to stop the heavy selling.
- Thursday 10/31/29: The market's open was delayed, and it was announced that the market would be closed until the next Monday so clerks could catch up from all the delays due to heavy volume. The market posted a rise for Thursday's short session.
- Monday 11/04/29: The market opened lower and then fell throughout the day.
- Tuesday 11/05/29: The market was closed for Election Day.
- Wednesday 11/06/29: This was another heavy down day on large volume.

From that point on in early November to the end of the year there averaged only one up day for every three down days in the market. In a few short months over 1½ years' worth of gains were wiped out, if one hadn't sold correctly. By the end of November a mild rally brought stocks up off their low point for the year and breathed some life back into the market. U.S. Steel rose from $150 to $171, and General Electric rose from $168 to $243. It goes to show that markets usually don't go straight up or straight down, but clearly the longer-term trend had changed.

Livermore, Kennedy and Loeb were mostly out of their long holdings by the time the end of October came around. Their astuteness and observation skills, while keeping their emotions in check, are just a few of the key successful traits of the great traders that were featured in my first book. Baruch's records are a bit more uncertain, but he did unload many of his holdings. For example, he sold 121,000 shares that he held in the sulphur industry right before they broke because he began to get a bit uncomfortable with the high prices and also because he liked to sell on the way up. Livermore, through his short positions, netted another multimillion-dollar profit when he finally closed those positions out, just as he had done in prior market tops.

Gerald Loeb believed strongly that stocks had risen to unrecorded and overvaluation statuses. A few instances alerted him to come to this conclusion. One was that leading stocks had topped and then began to fall from their peak prices. Another was that tips were flying everywhere, which is what Baruch also discovered and alerted him to be more cautious as well. Loeb knew his own rules were being compromised when a certain stock he had known about for quite a while, but vowed he would never own due to its bad price action and fundamentals, was being talked about by tipsters. He then purchased the stock as he got caught up in the talk and excitement. Quickly after his purchase he realized what he had done and soon thereafter sold out the entire position. He knew that he had lost his "sense of proportion." Another clue to him was that there was a new issue coming out from an investment trust. New issues in those days were hot items, and most would take off like they were made of gold on their initial trading days (sounds similar to the late 1990s). Though E.F. Hutton had a hard time getting any of the issue, Loeb discovered that the backers of the stock kept putting up support orders for the issue to prop up its price. This was a clear indication to Loeb that the market was saturated. In the meantime, in September, he was offered a partnership with E.F. Hutton. At 30 years old, he was the youngest ever to make partner at the prestigious brokerage house, and it occurred just before the bottom fell out from the market. Because of Loeb's observations, he sold out all his positions in early October and all the positions of the nearly 200 clients he was managing money for at the time. He was therefore 100% in cash over three weeks before the major damage was to occur. What did he do after he sold out? He went to Europe for a six-week vacation and was not even in the U.S. when the worst selling was about to hit the market.

As the year and the decade ended, the economy was still in recession. Volume zoomed to new heights during 1929 and hit a record 1.1 billion for the year. The last few months of record trading days increased the average to 4.2 million per day. It was quite an incredible decade for the market, which began at near 100, peaked at 386, and finally finished near the 250 mark after a mostly steady climb during the first three quarters of the decade. And though there are many theories and books written about the Crash and why it occurred, how many were affected, how suicides were rampant, and so forth, studies did show that still only less than 5% of the public was active in the market at that time. And it's debatable as to whether the stock market collapse caused the Great Depression that would shortly follow, though it certainly did not help it. As for the cause of the Crash, many cite installment buying, capital stagnation, questionable financing and an overabundance of greed. Whatever it was, it most certainly was caused by a change in the trend of the market (which could have occurred because of all those reasons cited and others as well) as witnessed by its price and volume action. And as we progress further down the road, we will see repeatedly how these changes can be foreseen by observing price and volume activity.

4

Patience and Flexibility Lead to Profits (1930–39)

Gerald Loeb's Flexibility Allows Him to Profit in Difficult Times

Loeb Quick-Trades an Upturn

The 1930s started off with the market sprinting higher from January through mid-April as it rose back up to near the 300 level. This shows just how tricky and challenging the market can be. Gerald Loeb was back from

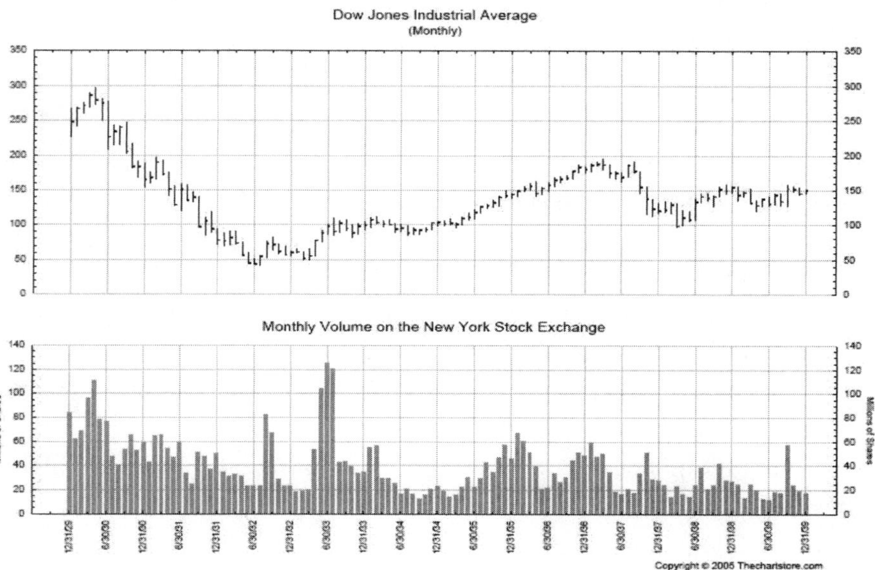

Figure 4-1 The Dow Jones Industrial Average 1930–39.
Source: *www.thechartstore.com.*

his vacation, and he still remained active and attuned to the market. With his profits intact from the strong run-up in the market in the late 1920s and plenty of cash on hand for his inventory, he stayed involved in the market but on a more limited basis. He also found out that short selling was not well suited for him. This is another vital trait we will see from some of the greatest traders — they find a place in the market that is suited to their own personality and strengths. Loeb would discover through his experience that short selling never was very profitable for him, and he felt it was too difficult to master, even in bear-market environments. What he would rather do in bad market times was either stay out of the markets altogether or trade in very quick turns from the long side on a much smaller scale than if the markets were in a confirmed uptrend. In 1930, when the market snapped back, he of course noticed this and did get back into the market. He was much more cautious though, as his skittishness had increased after he had witnessed how much damage a severe break in the market could cause. As he went along in his career, Loeb would many times mention how valuable experience, knowledge and judgment are in the quest for stock market profits. Here in 1930 he stated, "... knowledge born from actual experience is the answer to why one profits; lack of it is the reason one loses."

Because Loeb would come into the market on a smaller scale and dart in and out of certain stocks, always cutting his losses short, he had a profitable month in February as the market bounced back. During the month he netted himself a profit of approximately $8,000 while trading in 12 different stocks. He realized profits ranging from $43 to $2,500 in nine different stocks (Chrysler, Fox Film, General Allegheny and Indian Refining, among others). He experienced losses in only three stocks (Gold Dust, Warner Brothers and Montgomery Ward) and kept those limited. Notice that he kept active during this short rising trend in the market and he kept his mistakes small. He would actually end up trading similar to this as the market was falling all the way down in the early 1930s. The fact that he made profits each year during the worst decline in the history of the stock market — and from the long side — is an amazing accomplishment. He was still, at that time, a very young man whose hard work and attention to the market were paying off. His achievement of remaining profitable during those difficult times also raised his confidence. And as I mentioned in my first book, lack of confidence is a mighty strike against any market operator. With Loeb's confidence high he was sure that if he could make it profitably through the tough bear market he could surely prosper greatly when things turned around again, as they always had in the past.

After April, the market would begin its dramatic decline, as that would be the highest point it would reach until the early 1950s, or more than 20 years from then (so much for long-term holding). As we'll see, the rallies up over the declines were short lived (many times called "sucker rallies") and lasted just a few months or so and just led the way to steeper declines. We'll see something similar to this nearly 70 years later with the Nasdaq as that average began its decline (which hurt many traders who were told to "buy on the dips" during a dangerously falling market). The end of April experienced a sharp drop, while May was stable. June brought another sharp decline. July and August experienced another short-lived whipsawed rally. The end of 1930 was another sharp sell-off, as the market from September through December fell from near 240 to finish the year at near 170 (a 29% drop in three months).

It was a rough year for the market in 1930 as the Dow declined from near 250 to near 165, or 34%. It was the second worst yearly decline in the Dow's history, only exceeded in 1907, due to the Panic of that year, when the Dow fell 38%. Those types of market environments can be very difficult and frustrating for novice investors and professionals alike. If the longer trend is not convincing, it can suck one in for quick fake-outs and then quickly turn around and cause more damage. Remember the market is designed to fool most of the people most of the time, and that includes the so-called experts. But this is why Loeb was so successful during these times — he stayed with the flow of the market and its actions from the past and didn't let himself get caught up in a particular bias one way or another during a difficult market environment. Though what he did is not recommended unless one is extremely disciplined (as he was with his strict loss-cutting rules in place), has an experienced eye kept to the market, and most importantly adopts a flexible approach. This type of market environment is what made him use the word "battle" in his upcoming book to describe the market's environment. And because the market doesn't change that much, he continued to use the same word when he wrote many years later as well.

As mentioned in Chapter 3, Baruch's records seem to be a little unclear as to how he was affected by the Crash in late 1929 and then in the early 1930s. He did sell many holdings prior to the crash, and he was largely unaffected by the decline as far as his lifestyle was concerned. He continued to hold millions in cash, took his annual extensive vacations, and continued giving generously to many charities. His records do show a sharp reduction in trading activity — another trait of experienced stock operators—that of staying away from dangerous market environments. It does seem evident that Baruch did not cash out totally like Loeb had done and he then went on to generate positive results during the downtrend. It was discovered that Baruch wrote a memo to himself in 1930 with reminders of the many rules that led to his most successful years and defining his take on speculation and investing in the stock market. The memo mentioned key traits and rules to be a constant reminder of the proper way to participate in the markets. One of the main messages contained in the memo was the advice that one should never try to find the exact bottom and purchase there — it is much too difficult. He also mentioned that trying to time or wait for the exact top in order to sell is just as difficult. There was also a section relating to psychology, as Baruch was well aware of the important role emotions could play in a stock trader's day-to-day operations. Here we see one of the most respected and experienced operators — by that time Baruch was in his early 60s, had been in the markets for nearly 40 years, and had made a fortune many times over — still reminding himself and reviewing key skills, disciplines and trading rules to stay focused and alert in one of the most challenging environments of the stock market. The section on psychology mentioned to always cut short losses and let profits run, be quick to act when the market moves, stay in sync with the current market's actions, think of adverse possibilities and always become familiar with and *understand history to learn from the lessons of the past.*

The year 1931 began in similar fashion to the prior year — a sharp rally upward during January and February. This would be the third attempt for the market to come up off of its severe decline. Again, it was short-lived. After a flat March, the market headed downward again with a sharp decline in April and May. Another attempted rally in June was even shorter-lived, as the market slipped back in July and August. Similar again to the prior year, September began another steep sell-off. A slight bounce in October just set up another sell-off for November and December, though one of the days in October would witness the largest percentage increase on the Dow for a single day. On October 6 the index rose 12.86 points to 99.34, or 14.87%. But once again there was no confirming buying power following this strong gain, and the trend in the market (which always takes more than just a couple of days) was not confirmed. This market was clearly in a downtrend and was a dangerous market to be in. Unless one had the skillful eye and nimbleness of a Gerald Loeb or was highly skilled in shorting stocks, there was no reason to be active in a market like this.

The Dow ended up closing 1931 at near 75, or down 53% for the year, which to this day stands as the worst-performing year on the Dow. It also marked the first time in history, up to that point, that the market fell for three consecutive years. The economy was now deeply mired in a severe recession that would eventually become a depression, which by the end of 1931 was 29 months old and the longest of the 20th century up to that point. With economic conditions worsening due to the overhang of negative psychology from the crash and slow growth leading to more unemployment, the overall pessimistic mood began to increase. Bank closings were becoming more common — many of them due to the fact that high balances lent for margin trading in securities could not be paid back. Also, as the economy kept weakening, businesses kept failing, which meant more defaults on bank loans. Credit problems began to mount, and the banks felt the brunt of it. It seemed a spiraling negative effect was consuming just about everything in sight.

The year 1932 started with the markets meandering up and down in a fairly narrow range for January and February. March began the final descent for the brutal bear market as the market declined uninterrupted to July when it finally hit a low of 41.22 on July 8. At this point the Dow had declined 89.5% in 34 months from its peak of 381 in September 1929. After hitting its July 8 bottom the market surged upward on its fourth day of an attempted new rally (we'll detail more of this type of market analysis as we get to the 1960s and beyond, when we discuss William J. O'Neil's meticulous study of how market tops and bottoms have occurred throughout many of history's market cycles) as it surged 5.2% in heavy volume. That confirmation of a turning trend in the market, after it finally bottoms, will occur over and over again as we move forward, and it is a clear indication that serious selling in the market had been exhausted. From early July, at its low and through August, the market put together a strong spurt upward that would see the Dow double in a short two-month time period. After a run like that (too fast in too short a time frame), nervous investors who had been burned by many short rallies over more than two years probably were quick to take profits when they had them. From September to the end of the year the market backslid and actually finished the year at 65, or down 23%. It was now the fourth straight losing year for the Dow — the first time it had ever achieved that dubious feat, and as of this writing it has not equaled that losing streak. While the 1920s would be the era of promise, optimism, and living high, the early 1930s became the era of lost faith, little hope, and frugality. Many former leading stocks would succumb to the severe declining market (since most stocks follow the general market), but the reversing trend in July and August would be something that caught the eye of the most astute traders. While it did seem that a new trend was just beginning, former high-fliers can come back down to earth during severe breaks in the market (prices are adjusted for stock splits and dividends) such as Anaconda (1929 high of $175 to 1932 low of $3), New York Central (1929 high of $257 to 1932 low of $9), RCA (1929 high of $574 to 1932 low of $12) and General Electric (1929 high of $1,612 to 1932 low of $136).

Gerald Loeb, as mentioned before, actually made money each year from 1929 to 1932 using a smaller and quicker style of profit taking. Baruch mostly stayed away from this bad market as he drastically cut back his activities. We'll see in many of the following chapters that due to the cycle rotation of the market, it is wise to stay away from the market during challenging times. The best traders, through their many years and decades of experience, all mention that being in the market all the time is not a prudent and profitable strategy. Only a select few can ever make the distinction of sustained success over many market cycles.

As the market kept sliding to historic lows in 1932, economic conditions continued to worsen. By mid-1932, the GNP had fallen by one-third from its levels in 1929. Banks weren't the only ones feeling pressure from unpaid margin loans. Remember that many corporations began lending money for securities purchases back in 1929, as rates hit 20% and companies saw an opportunity for decent returns. As many margin calls went uncollected due to the fall in stocks, many corporations had to take write-offs and withhold issuing new debt, which led to slower expansion. Also, mergers slowed down significantly due to weakening credit conditions. But as we've seen in the past, and we'll see many more times to come, the market always looks forward and senses changes in economic conditions caused by inflation, interest rates, productivity, profitability and so forth. Here is another look into the market's forecasting ability, as decreases in corporate profitability during those trying times had already begun to appear. From $9.6 billion in 1929 to –$0.8 billion in 1931 and then –$3 billion in 1932, things finally began to improve in 1933, as corporate profits rose to $0.2 billion.

These details show that when things are rosy and look as though the good times will never end, the market may look out and foresee something different. As the market sank in late 1929, corporate profits were booming. But what was to come would be a drastic slowdown. As business began to decline, more jobs were lost as companies cut back on hiring and producing. This is a typical economic event especially if it follows an exuberant period where all caution is cast aside (we'll see this again later in the 20th century). Back then as more businesses saw their revenues decline, even more jobs were lost as all hiring basically went flat. In fact, unemployment worsened significantly from 1.5 million people in 1929 to 12.8 million by 1933 (the unemployment rate reached 25% in 1932). With more people unemployed and their credit balances high, due to the increased consumerism that took effect for much of the mid- to late-1920s, goods purchased on credit were being repossessed. Repossessed goods then led to more pessimism, which in turn led to less consumption and to still lower corporate profits. The cycle then kept repeating itself until many economic variables spiraled downward. In fact, industrial production fell by 50% from 1929 to 1932, and in 1932 was running at only 12% of capacity. U.S. Steel, a leading stock that has been mentioned many times, saw its earnings sink 62% from 1929 to 1932. Stocks usually exaggerate the rate of increase and decrease in most economic statistics because human traits can sometimes get out of control. On the way up stocks can get way overpriced as caution is ignored, and on the way down fear inspires quick reactionary responses. In the case of 1929–32, stocks fell by over 89% from their peak in early September 1929 to their low in mid-1932, when on July 8 the market hit bottom. Because psychological factors are involved, this will continuously happen as we move forward and that is what creates the cyclical nature of the stock market.

Baruch in 1932 would begin to invest heavily in gold. He continued to do so into 1933 as well. He would also start to become more involved in politics again. It was in the fall of 1932, that Baruch wrote a brief forward for a new edition of the popular 19th-century book, titled "Extraordinary Popular Delusions and the Madness of Crowds" and written by Charles Mackay nearly

100 years before. Baruch praised this popular book and pointed out how it would always be relevant due to its take on how psychology, especially during economic movements, would constantly repeat itself. Baruch wrote, "... many begin to wonder if declines will never halt; the appropriate abracadabra may be: 'They always did.'" His remarks couldn't have been more timely.

The year 1933 continued the light selling as January and February pushed the Dow back down to near 50. But hope finally began to appear in a few areas. A new leader was coming into power to provide hope and plans in reviving an America that just a few years before seemed destined for long prosperity. The vision and innovative ideas and products of the roaring 20s seemed long since forgotten after three long years of a depression-type economy. Franklin Roosevelt came into power in early 1933, and the recession period officially ended in March of that year. The markets responded favorably, and in April 1933 a sharp rise, on a noticeable increase in volume that can be seen in Figure 4-1 on p. 57, lasted until July in which the Dow doubled again. It was the longest rally since the crash and became the most rapid rise in the markets history up to that point. By July the Dow had passed the 100 level for the first time since November 1931. This strong run-up equated to a 100% gain in just 5 months, now the second time in a year that the Dow had staged two short runs in which it doubled in value. From July through the rest of 1933 the markets consolidated their powerful gains off the bottom and traded in a fairly tight trading range.

There were many regulatory changes getting ready to take place as Roosevelt vowed to fix the county's problems. His New Deal took the U.S. off the gold standard in order to protect the economy. He also wanted the government engaged more in Wall Street. One area of concern was to reproach short sellers and refine that practice as many abuses were still taking place. He wanted stronger ethical conduct standards between brokers and customers. By 1936, all commercial banks were completely out of securities and stock market activities. Also, the Securities Act of 1933 was passed, which required all new companies that came to market to register their securities. All these measures were being put in place to restore confidence in the economy, the banking system, the stock market and the future of America.

The Dow would end the year at near 100 as it moved mostly sideways in a choppy fashion from July through December, as Wall Street was somewhat skeptical and needed some time to digest all the new regulations that were taking place. The skepticism showed up in the trading volume, as the average daily volume came in at only 2.5 million, quite a drop-off from the 4.2 million averages of 1929. The one major positive here, as opposed to the prior few years, was that the rally early in the year did not give way to another major sell-off. Rather, the gains from the longer rally held intact, and the market only experienced minor and normal consolidations. The market also finally broke its streak of four losing years in a row and produced a very strong 67% gain for the year.

It was also in 1933 that Gerald Loeb received a letter from an E.F. Hutton customer stating that the customer purchased stocks in 1929 from the advice of a Hutton broker in a California office. He lost most of his money, as he was still holding those shares. He wrote to Loeb asking for advice and what his next step should be. This letter made an impression on Loeb, and he wrote the man back and asked him if he just wanted advice or if Loeb could help him get his money back with an aggressive strategy. The man agreed to have Loeb try and earn his money back, as he mentioned he had not much else to lose. Loeb researched thoroughly, saw the market rising quickly during the early part of the year and bought a stock called Standard Cap and Seal. He paid $10 a share after he researched the company and liked its prospects. It quickly zoomed higher and when it hit $45, he sold out the man's position as he had made all the man's money back for him that he had lost during the prior several years. As for Loeb himself, he bought General Motors and Chrysler in early 1933 as the market began shooting higher. He purchased 10,000 shares of each and then sold them both out within six months and made a solid profit, as the market then flattened out.

The year 1934 continued to bring regulation change to the market as Roosevelt's administration created the Securities and Exchange Commission (SEC) in order to regulate the securities industry and attempt to prevent securities manipulations. The Securities Exchange Act of 1934, which created the SEC, was designed to outlaw certain practices such as insider trading and the creation of pools to manipulate stock prices. One of its key rules was the establishment of the "uptick" requirement for short sales. This meant that before one could sell short a stock, the preceding price before the transaction could take place had to be at a higher price. This would help maintain a more orderly market for declining stocks. Wall Street's reaction to additional newly enacted regulations was pretty much ho-hum, and the choppy and overall flat movements from the second half of the prior year continued.

The market started 1934 off by moving higher and peaking in February at 111.90. From there the market slumped lower and declined on lower volume until late summer. It seemed to be a typical slow summer trading season, and there was still much apprehension on the street concerning all the new regulations that had recently passed. The decline from February through July brought the market down 24% — a decent-sized correction. On August 1 though, the Dow surged 2.9% higher on stronger volume than it had traded at during most of the summer months. This key price and volume surge occurred on the fourth day of a new rally attempt, just like we saw in July 1932 when the market hit its absolute bottom, and it would also signal the bottom had occurred in the market at this time as well, indicating that selling had dried up and a new trend was beginning to the upside. From there the market traded in a fairly tight range for the next four months until November when it sprang forward. The Dow then reclaimed the 100 mark and ended the year at 105, a basically flat performance for the year, but good for a 4% gain. The highs and lows of the year barely made the headlines, but that crucial bottom in late July and then the strong follow-through in early August would propel the market upward by 131% into the spring of 1937.

The action in 1934 was actually a calming welcomed change resulting from the aftereffects of the crash that included many bad periods from 1930–32. This mostly consolidating action after a strong downtrend is what Richard Wyckoff observed during his early days as a good basis for an upcoming rising market as it showed that the intense selling had exhausted. The year 1934 was still a very slow period for the market as only 324 million shares traded that year, less than half that of the prior year, which averaged only 2.5 million shares a day, and well below the 1929 average of over 4 million, as caution concerning the regulatory changes still weighed on investors' minds. New issues also hit rock bottom in 1934. Just as we've seen in the past though, when things look their worst, and it seems the market may never rise again, the market often starts a new trend.

After starting 1935 off with a continuation of the flat trading from the prior year in January and early February, the market dipped slightly in March. From mid-March to November it seemed the old 1920s were back. The market zoomed from 100 to near 150, or 50% in just 8 months (and would eventually double again when it hit 200 in March of 1937). Many things started turning up in 1935. New issues (which are always a positive for the stock market) began climbing back. They would reach $2.2 billion that year, an increase of 340% over the prior year. The following year, in 1936, they would more than double again to hit $4.6 billion. Confidence was beginning to return, and many of the regulatory changes were taking effect in a positive way. For example, more people were prosecuted for abusive activities, as more discoveries were made due to the efforts involved. Fraud, embezzlement and deceit were discovered as more inquiries were made into those whose names came up (a bit similar to another time when things got out of control many decades later). The SEC pressed Wall Street harder for reforms that resulted in the formation of a trade group called the National Association of Securities Dealers (NASD). This name would later be given to the unlisted over-the-counter securities market.

As the economy continued to strengthen, the market rally was becoming the strongest since the late 1920s. While the market stalled in late 1933 and 1934, Gerald Loeb became active in some foreign markets, mostly in Canada and London. He researched Canadian mining stocks, which were strong at the time, and he also invested in three strong London stocks. It shows his never-ending search for the best possible returns — wherever they may be. He did well with these stocks, and when the American market picked up in 1935, he sold those positions to concentrate again on the U.S. market. He also used the down period of the prior few years to continue his research and writing. He came out with his first book in 1935, the classic "The Battle for Investment Survival." The book became a bestseller, was updated several times over the coming decades, and to this day is considered one of the best investment classics ever written. It also became a major resource for education on the market and trading for some of the best traders in the decades to follow. For Loeb, at the time, we see an experienced (though still very young at only 36 years old) market operator staying on top of his profession during one of the worst periods ever. His determination, never-give-up attitude, and refusal to get discouraged complemented his hard work efforts that paid off handsomely for him throughout his career. Riding the market up in 1935, Loeb did very well in his trading.

The market experienced a slight dip in December and then finished the year near the 145 level, for a strong 39% gain. Some of the best leaders of this newly revised uptrend were American Express, Air Reduction, AT&T and General Motors. The year 1936 started off basically flat, but then the market quickly rose from February through the first part of April. A sharp but quick retreat to where it had opened the year occurred throughout the rest of April. After a flat May, the market renewed its strength and rose from June through November. Many strong economic figures were coming out in 1936. The GNP rose solidly as it hit $82 billion, an increase of 46% from the 1933 figure of $56 billion. Corporate profits (before taxes) zoomed to $5.7 billion in 1936, a very strong increase over the $200 million it had been just three years earlier. Loeb was still there riding this new bull market up, but he started to get more cautious near the end of the year as his experience was telling him not to get too caught up in the excitement when long periods of almost uninterrupted rising markets occur. By late fall the market had doubled in just two years. Again a slight pullback in the market occurred in December, but the market ended the year at near 180. It was another solid gain for the market (up 25%), and the gain padded that of the prior strong year.

Loeb Sees the Top Again

The year 1937 started off strong and continued the upward momentum. By early March the market approached the 200 level. As mentioned before — at this point the market had doubled in just two years — and from its bottom in July 1932 the market was up 385% in little over 4½ years. Also at this point the market began to turn down, two months before another recession was to hit the economy in May. This recession would be considered short-lived compared to the Great Depression, as it would last only 14 months. But it was still severe in its own right as the unemployment rate rose again to near 20%, invoking still more fears of the very bad times just years before. From mid-March until July the market experienced its first pullback that exceeded more than a few months since late 1932, over 4 years ago. Beginning the second week of March, the market experienced some heavy selling action. From March 8 through March 22, the market sold off four times on heavy volume in a little over two weeks. On April 2 and 7, it did the same thing — sold off hard on heavy volume. It was here that Gerald Loeb began to see a parallel to the 1929 market — the market began experiencing sell-offs in heavy volume after a strong run-up. He noticed that many leading stocks were topping and the market was having trouble advancing. It was also a time when the market had just staged an incredible run-up and the country was in the beginning stages of a newly formed recession. He knew from his experiences that the market needs time to digest strong gains made after years of almost uninterrupted advances. He also listened to his intuition, and he decided to trust his judgment. He therefore cashed out completely and once again was 100% in cash when the market then broke wide open. A sharp bounce back in August back to near its high for the year didn't last long though and actually turned out to be a "suckers rally." These are the important lessons to learn from one of the greatest legendary traders. Loeb controlled his emotions due to his experience and now well-trained judgment. He also used his profitable past to benefit in his current time. Watching and then acting on details of the market and leading stocks simply forced him to manage his positions in the most prudent manner.

There were many other problems occurring at that time in the economy as well. Large budget deficits began to attract more attention from the government. In order to make an attempt at balancing the budget, government spending would need to decline sharply. During those times government spending was a stimulus to the economy, so a slowdown there was viewed as a negative overall. Also, labor unrest and strikes were becoming more plentiful, which distracted and disrupted business. Capital spending was also down. From mid-August through November the market sold off hard, dropping from near 185 to 130, or nearly 30%. It regained its footing a bit in December and finished the year at 135. It was still a 25% negative return following two strong years. Some leading stocks, including AT&T, Bethlehem Steel, Chrysler, General Electric and General Motors, fell hard during the latter half of the year.

In 1938, with the recession still lingering, the market meandered back and forth for the first two months of the year and then in March it sold off and hit the 100 level, which it had not touched since March 1935 — three years earlier. More reforms and regulations continued to come to Wall Street. The market responded and quickly bounced off its low level and traded sideways until it flattened out in June. A month before the 14-month recession ended in June the market flattened out and then shot up to end June near 140. This rise was accompanied by only average volume levels, which did not display the strong conviction that is needed to keep a sustained rally moving forward. Hence, the market followed up with three more flat to slightly down months and then jumped back over the 150 level by early October and then traded sideways until year-end where it closed right at 150. It still turned out to be a fairly decent year with the Dow up 11% and the country coming out of recession.

The market continued its flat trading at the start of 1939 through mid-March. It was a rather uncertain time again as talk of war began spreading and bringing up memories of the past. A sharp pullback to near 130 occurred in late March. Trading activity was extremely light as the month of April experienced only 20 million shared being traded. This was a sharp reduction from prior periods as April 1930 saw 111 million shares traded. But from April through August the market moved higher to near 140. September saw the beginning of World War II, and the market jumped back to 150, as war orders began to lift the economy just as it had during the early years of World War I. In fact once war was announced, the Dow jumped 20 points during the next three days. But this time there seemed to be far more fear and uncertainty, as it looked as if Hitler might be unstoppable, and also since many still had vivid thoughts of the depression on their minds. From the fall until year-end the market traded flat and finished the year and the decade right near 150, down 3% for the year. With so much caution and uncertainty lingering, the market registered little activity for the year, as trading volume came in at less than 1 million shares on average per day, the lowest since 1923.

The 1930s was a trying decade that experienced the Great Depression, drought, a brutal bear market, regulation change, and then the beginning of World War II. Overall, the market lost 40% from the beginning of the decade to its end, but there were some opportunities for observant investors when the markets rose strongly from early 1933 through the beginning of 1937, as Loeb demonstrated. Also, his feat of being profitable through some of the worst years ever in the market, especially from the long side, really proved his abilities to profit from the market using his key strength of flexibility while also sticking to his strict discipline of cutting his losses short.

5

Victory Creates More Opportunity for a Legendary Trader (1940–49)

Gerald Loeb Entered the Market When the Trend Seemed Clearly Enough Established

The new decade began with the uncertainty of World War II hanging over the market. Reflecting this uncertainty the market continued in an almost perfect sideways fashion through April. Then, when the Germans

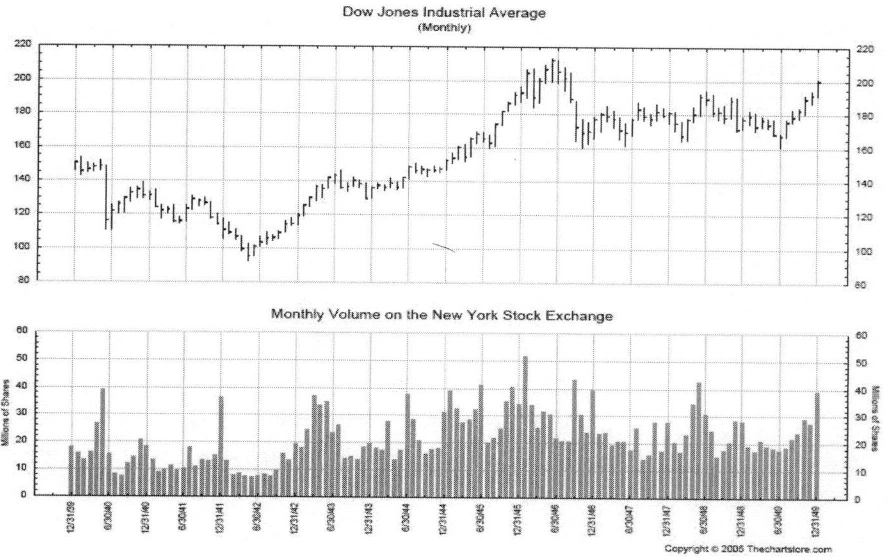

Figure 5-1 The Dow Jones Industrial Average 1940–49.
Source: *www.thechartstore.com.*

took Paris, the market dived from 150 straight to 120 in May, or nearly 20%. It also seemed certain that the U.S. would eventually enter the war as well. It would be a huge task to finance another war, especially one as large as World War II was turning out to be. In order to finance the war, bond drives were set up throughout the country. After the plunge in May, the market slowly moved higher until November, though volume trailed off and came in over 200,000 shares lighter, on average, each trading day than it had in 1939. Then the market flattened out again and finished 1940 at 135, for a loss of 13% for the year.

Loeb Gets Cautious and Offers Words of Wisdom

The year 1941 began with a downward market in January and February. From there through May, it traded basically sideways as war uncertainty continued to hang over the market. Trading volume was again light as more eyes continued their focus on looming world events. There was though, just as always, some action going on in the market. Many companies from railroad and steel industries began gaining popularity. Loeb also made some important statements that all stock operators need to heed. Through his experience and attention to the market he was constantly refining his take on how the market actually worked and reacted to certain situations. In previous chapters, we saw Richard Wyckoff having this same incredible interest in trying to understand the market thoroughly during his time. One of the statements Loeb made was, "There's always the discounting factor in any stock. The price of a stock doesn't reflect its value at the moment, ever. It reflects the expectation of the value and there's no precise measurement of the amount of time involved in that expectation. It's not a mathematical thing; it's a human thing." He then went on to say, "That's why investing can't be an exact science." From those comments he concluded that this is the reason why no one, ever, can be right all the time in the stock market. And because of that fact, he stated, "And I think the big secret of those who have made more money than others is to realize their mistakes and get out quickly." Here we see another testament, from someone who has made millions in the market, to the number one Golden Rule (which is usually never taught in academic courses on the stock market) — cut your losses short.

In June and July of 1941 the markets rose slightly and then flattened out and traded in a slightly choppy fashion through September. By October the market started heading down (almost forecasting what was to come) and continued its downward trend until early December. On December 7, Japan attacked Pearl Harbor. The next day the market only fell slightly, as if it had already expected something of this sort. December 9 though experienced a steeper loss. The next day the market rose slightly easing a few fears, but then it fell back again on December 11. The market then ended the year near 110, or down 15% and registering its third straight losing year. There was a lot of uncertainty during the year, and many fears were realized on that tragic day in early December. Activity in the market during the year was tepid, as average daily volume on the exchange registered only 619,000 shares, 18% lower than the weak figures of the prior year.

The year 1942 continued the steady downtrend through April as the U.S. was now deeply engaged in the war. In February of that year trading slowed to its lowest level since 1915, as war dominated everyone's attention. By the end of April the Dow sank just below the 100 mark for the first time in nearly 7 years. From that point on, however, the market would never revisit the 100 level again. And just as we've now seen more than a few times, when things look their worst and most people give up hope, that is when the smartest traders keep up their study and observation skills. In April, a reporter from California who wanted to get a take on the market at the current time interviewed Gerald Loeb, who stated, "… the market today offers opportunities of 1932, even though, as yet, it is clear that the trend has not changed from down." Here we see an experienced and knowledgeable operator relying on his past market cycle knowledge and understanding of how the market works to try and identify what the current situation looked like. He stated this when the trend had not yet changed, but he offered up at least the point that one should not take their eyes off the market when there could be the possibility of a change based on historical market action. He made those statements just before the market turned and would advance over 130% during the next two years. Also in the interview he stated, "When the news gets good, and the situation clarifies, it will be too late." He of course saw the trend change shortly after his comments, and he bought heavily into U.S. Rubber, as the prospects for the rubber industry were strong and he latched onto an early leader. He also bought at the right time, which is usually when most are scared and afraid to take a position. But, again, his experience gave him the confidence to know that the timing was right.

A steady climb began in May and lasted throughout the rest of the year, though one major ingredient was lacking, and that was strong volume. As the market moved higher there was still much apprehension, and it showed in the lack of strong buying power in the market. Trading volume for the year would average only 455,000 shares per day, a sharp pullback of 26% from even the slow period of 1941. Nonetheless, the market seemed to have exhausted its selling pressure, and the Dow ended 1942 at near 120, or 8% higher and halting the three-year skid for the Dow. It was actually quite an accomplishment and statement for the overall market that things might be changing even right in the middle of a major war. But as we heard from Loeb, being observant to the market's action and moving with it usually pays rewards. Remember, the market always looks ahead, so its rising action was a clear sounding that something better might be just around the corner.

The year 1943 began where 1942 left off — the market kept climbing and volume surged as well, as can be seen from Figure 5-1 on p. 71. From January right through July the market steadily rose to near the 150 level with only a few small minor corrections along the way. This would be a nearly 50% rise in 15 months since the Dow slightly undercut the 100 level in early 1942. In April 1943, the same reporter who interviewed Loeb exactly one year earlier interviewed him again to get his current take on the market. The Dow at this time was near 135 and had risen nearly uninterrupted for almost one year. Loeb stated, "... those who expect us to win in Europe next year and in Japan the year after had better look at the 155 stock average of 1939 when World War II began, or at 1937." He was nearly right on these remarks as well, as the market would then begin to consolidate its gains during the summer months. Again, we see an expert using his past market cycle knowledge and experience to relate to his then-current time.

In August the market experienced a pullback, and then it traded sideways in choppy action through October. The market then dipped in November and managed a slight bounce back in December to finish the year near 140, or up 14% for the year. Though the year started off slow as far as trading volume was concerned and as had been the trend the prior four years, activity did pick up as the year went on, and the daily average trading volume came in right at 1 million shares and was the highest showing since 1936. This was quite a pickup from the other years since the decade started and showed that some uneasiness was beginning to fade. Lingering effects from the depression and World War II issues had been heavy burdens on the market. Also, during the early part of the 1940s, more money was filtered into savings and war bonds than was directed toward the market. The many lessons learned from the depression had their effect in the lower-volume activity and as people continued to be frugal and pay down personal debt loads. But in 1943 some optimism began to shine through as unemployment fell, mostly because of the war efforts. Also, the economy was picking up, and by the end of 1943, the economy was celebrating its sixth straight year in which it had not experienced a recession period. This was the longest stretch by far since the beginning of the 20th century.

The year 1944 saw choppy action in the market from the beginning of the year through April as the market made no overall progress during that time. Progress on the war front though was turning more positive, and Loeb again was asked, in April, for his assessment of the market — for the third straight year. At this point he declared that he had become more bullish on the prospects for the market. He thought that postwar earnings estimates and prospects would be strong, and since the market always looks ahead, the current time was a prime time to be positive for future market action. Here again his timing could not have been better as the market would advance some 65% from that point on over the next 22 months. He thought that corporate profits were poised to double (after taxes) from even during the best levels of 1935 to 1939. And he believed they could grow by five or six times, if measured before taxes. This research reiterated his strong belief that it was a ripe opportunity to buy stocks. As for which groups he thought would lead the continued uptrend of the market, he mentioned they would probably not be the war stocks. Because of the forecasting ability of the market, most war stocks rise before war and then usually decline while the war is being fought. At that time during 1944, he started looking at peacetime stocks since he knew that peacetime stocks rose strongly right before the end of World War I. Using history as a guide, he thought the same action would happen again. One of the groups he favored at that time was aircraft manufacturing. He also bought heavily into Warner Brothers, as its profits were soaring, and he had researched and knew the company well. American Can was another of the stocks in which he continued to actively trade. Its profits were strong, and he would buy this stock when heavy interest would propel it upward and then sell out and cash in his profits when the market or the stock would flatten out or level off. One thing he also mentioned in this interview was that he thought the market might have a hard time sustaining strong gains some time soon after the war. We'll see a bit later that his assumption here was also correct. In May and June of 1944 the market rose and hit the 150 mark. Volume in the market rose following D-day (which occurred in the summer of 1944), but the market didn't make much progress as it basically flat-lined in a relatively minor choppy fashion until the end of the year. It would be another positive year for the market — its third straight year — as the Dow finished up 12% for the year.

The year 1945 started with a slight dip downward for the Dow in January. A new recession began in February, the first time the economy had been in recession since 1938, quite a stretch for those early decade periods of the 20th century. It's also interesting to note that the flat market action of late 1944 correlates to the many other times preceding a recession in which the market either fell or traded in a flat range. While the market spiked up in February and then spiked back down in March, news on the war front was becoming more positive. In April the market moved back up, and from there it traded sideways again. After a basically flat trading summer, Japan's surrender in late summer 1945 inspired a rally in the stock market. It was now finally peacetime, and many celebrated the good news, including the stock market. From August to the end of the year the Dow rose to finish the year over the 200 mark. This would mark the fourth straight yearly rise for the Dow as it advanced a solid 27% for the year. Volume also rose on the exchange, especially once the war ended, as more interest began to be directed to the market and many of the uncertainties that were created by the war were lifted. The recession also ended in October, as it turned out to be a short-lived downturn of only nine months. Some of the leaders, which still happened to be many older-line companies, helped lead the market higher, which included IBM, General Motors, AT&T, Bethlehem Steel and U.S. Steel.

Following the jubilant celebration of peace in the preceding year, the market continued moving up in January 1946. But many other concerns would begin cropping up at that time. Inflation began to rise following the war mostly due to a still aggressive Federal Reserve policy of increasing the money supply. Also, the economy began to weaken mostly because the government reduced its spending sharply due to the end of the war. It should be noted that, because the government was such a large part of the economy in those years, a sharp reduction in spending then would be felt with greater impact than it would today. There were also some pre-Cold War tensions with Russia and issues that began to surface along with many labor upheavals here in the U.S.

After a sharp pullback in February and then a quick rebound in March, the market traded in a very choppy fashion through April, May and June. The market actually peaked in May of that year and then began to show some classic topping action. In June and July there were three days within a four-week time frame that the market sold off in heavy volume. All three days saw the market fall by at least 2.5%. That classic distribution action was similar to the same action we saw in prior markets when they seemed to peak and would then begin to turn down (we'll see many more instances of this as we move forward as well). As the market headed toward the end of the summer months, a few more heavy-selling days accompanied by large volume occurred. As the market really began to wobble more and leading stocks started stalling and turning downward, many analysts started coming out with their expert predictions. On September 3, some Dow theorists started to say that according to their analysis the market would not breach a resistance level of 186.02. That very same day, the market fell hard and broke that line as over $3 billion in value was wiped out.

Loeb Makes a Mistake

While the market was weakening and showing classic topping action, Loeb started to sell his holdings, but he sold too slowly. He later admitted that he had made a major mistake as he was thinking that a rebound would occur in the market. Even though he saw the same type of action that had alerted him to quickly sell out of his holdings and go to a 100% cash position in 1929 and again in 1937, he hesitated. He ended up losing money during this downtrend, but he did sell out in time to not get hurt in a major way. It still shows just how challenging the market is and how your own thoughts can at times become your worst enemy, as we also saw with Baruch and his mistake in shorting General Motors that was mentioned earlier. But here was Loeb, one of the best stock traders of all, knowing from past experiences what he should have been doing, but instead hesitating because he thought his contradictory idea might be right. Remember O'Neil's definition at the beginning of this book, "The stock market doesn't care who we as individuals are, what we think, or how we feel … it only obeys the law of supply and demand." Even if you're Gerald Loeb, now entrenched in a successful career after having obtained many successes in the market, what you think should happen might prove to be wrong. If you are proven wrong, you must correct your judgment by reversing your positions. Another example is the one given earlier of Bernard Baruch, who in his early sixties in the 1930s wrote a memo reminding himself of the dangers of psychology and how one's own thoughts can be damaging if one becomes too biased to them and ignores the action in the market. These are the constant challenges one faces in the market each day.

Even Loeb, in the late 1940s, commented that it was easy to write a book and say "cut your losses" and "never let emotion out-rule investment principles," but much harder to do in practice because we are all human and as humans we all make mistakes. He made other mistakes too. Once, after he had bought heavily into New York Central, as it was being accumulated by many investors and the price was rising fast, he hesitated again. Because the company declared a high dividend, many investors began selling, as they thought the dividend was too expensive for the company to maintain. The action in the stock, which was now being sold off in heavy volume, was a clear indication that the trend in the stock had changed. Loeb knew he should have sold, but he hesitated and hoped the stock would bounce back. It didn't, and he eventually gradually sold out of the position and ended up taking a large loss. As for the market, it fell hard in September and then whipsawed up and down until the end of the year. The Dow would lose 8% that year, snapping its four-year winning streak.

The year 1947 started off with a decline in early January but was quickly followed by a sharp spike up in February. It wasn't a very convincing rally, and it soon faded as the market fell back in a whipsawed fashion during March, April and most of May. There didn't seem to be much strength or even interest in the market, as volume began to dry up again, and there was a clear lack of leading stocks, which are always required to lead a strong market upward. The new-issue market also dried up significantly. Rumblings of the beginnings of the Cold War had people on edge. There were also more actions from the government coming out. The Marshall Plan was enacted to help divert funds in order to rebuild a tattered Europe after the war. The Taft-

Hartley Act soon followed, which was created to help soothe many of the conflicting labor disputes at the time. On May 28 the market zoomed higher on what looked to be a confirming change to the upside. Volume, however, was not very convincing, and even though the market did rise to hit the 200 level again by July, it was only a short-term rally. Volume, which indicates strong demand for stocks, just wasn't there in the heavy levels that had been seen in other uptrends that extended well beyond just a minor upturn in the market. This was a clear signal that strong buying power was absent. From there the market mostly zigged and zagged in a fairly narrow range until it ended the year near 180. It turned out to be a 2% gain for the year, though the choppiness would have made any participant a bit uncomfortable.

By late 1947 many economic figures were starting to turn up and strengthen. GNP numbers were improving over prior years, as the total of $234 billion in 1947 was up strongly from the $211 billion in 1944. Corporate earnings were gaining strength, but the market continued to languish, dropping the PE ratio of the S&P 500 under 10 and near historic lows. The main culprit to the market at the time was inflation. Inflation is a danger to the longer-term outlook in any market, and with very high inflation still present, the market in late 1947 would be challenged to move higher. There were some positive things going on under the surface, though. The savings levels by consumers in the economy were increasing, since the depression memories were still vivid for many. The forced and disciplined savings would actually be a building block that would contribute to future market demand. There were also some new technologies being introduced, most notably the invention of the transistor. Also, mass production of the television was in full swing.

The year 1948 started off on a down note as the market slid lower in January. After a basically flat February, the market rallied 19% until June, as it once again crossed the 200 mark. Then, once again, just as in early 1947, the rally soon faded and the market pulled back again. There was very little convincing buying power in the market as noted by lagging volume numbers when the market would put together these suspect rallies. From there the market traded mostly down until October when the market spiked up again only to pull back down sharply in November. A new recession set in during November that would last 11 months. The GNP slowed way down and ended up rising less than $900 million from the prior year. Here again we see the market almost correctly anticipating this with its downward trend that began that summer. A flat December ended the year with a 2% decline, as the market made no headway for two straight years but along the way was constantly being whipped up and down. Times like those in the market can be very frustrating, and many great traders decide to just stay away from it altogether and wait for better opportunities that will always come around again. We'll see another whipsawing period for the market that featured high inflation when we get to the 1970s.

With the country entrenched in a new recession and Truman back in the White House, the market yawned again in early 1949. A flat period through April led to a sharp spike downward in May. As had been the pattern though, the market spiked back up in June, and on June 20, the Dow gained a solid 1.1%. Volume here again was not overwhelmingly convincing. After a listless August and September, the market seemed to finally find a spark in October. During 1949, corporate profits before tax fell to $26.4 billion from $33 billion in 1948 and the GNP fell 0.9% for the year. The PE ratio of the S&P 500 stood at 6.6, near a historical low. But business was starting to pick up in late 1949. The recession officially ended in October. The stock market again sprinted higher months before the recession ended and then ended the year up 13%, and consumers were beginning to spend their money. Consumer-type industries were beginning to expand, and it seemed as if the many long periods of rationing, shortages, and saving were beginning to pave a way toward more spending. Industries that started to exhibit strength were gold (which often is a bearish sign), soft drinks and radio and television stocks. These consumer-driven stocks were signaling a change in direction; for example, television companies were growing at a fast clip as only 3% of households had a TV in 1948, but that grew quickly to 10% by the end of 1949. A few technology stocks also began springing to life as well. With business conditions improving, consumer spending growing, and the market moving higher on increased volume — its first real stretch of higher prices followed up by heavier and growing demand — it seemed good times were right around the corner as the 1950s were about to begin.

6

Innovative Stocks Produce Fabulous Profits (1950–59)

Nicolas Darvas Saw the Trend and Took Full Advantage of It

As the new decade began and many areas of the economy were improving, there was a new sense of optimism in the air, though it was still measured. The market would begin what would turn out to be a slow but steady rising trend in the early 1950s. From January through the beginning of June the market marched steadily higher. While the market rose, new leadership

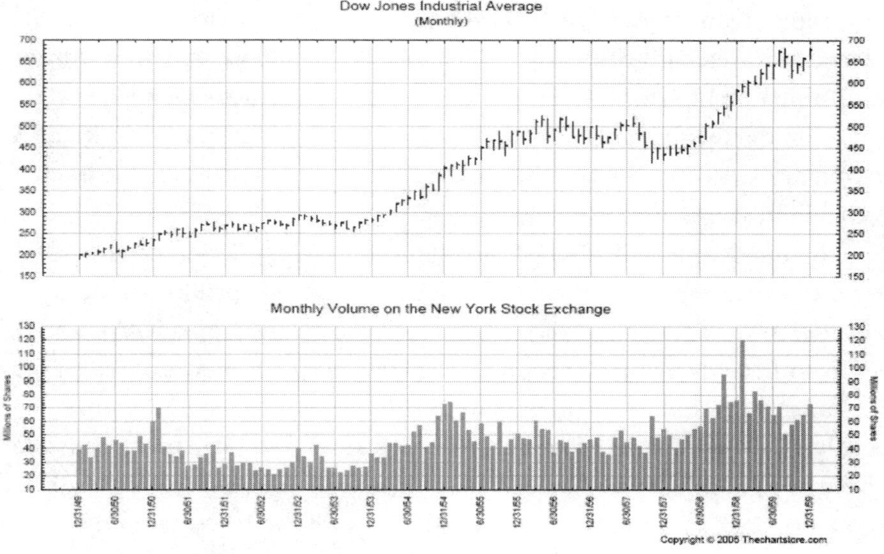

Figure 6-1 The Dow Jones Industrial Average 1950–59.
Source: *www.thechartstore.com.*

began taking shape, as is usually the case when new uptrends begin. Zenith, mostly due to the new TV craze, stepped up to help lead the market. It rose from $31½ to the high $70s just during the first part of 1950. Motorola was another strong leader. It doubled in just a few months in early 1950. It was benefiting from strong orders as its revenues jumped 134% in 1950 to $35.5 million from $15.2 million the preceding year. Net income soared 207% to $3.50 per share from $1.14 per share. This was clearly a new emerging leader displaying strong fundamentals during a rising market. In fact, new offerings that year would hit $7.8 billion, which would be a new high. Of the new offerings (including bonds and others) coming to market, 30% of them were in common stocks, which was a large percentage at that time.

A sharp drop near the end of June coincided with the beginning of the Korean War, when on June 24, North Korea attacked South Korea and it looked again as if America would get involved and engaged in war issues. The setback in the market was slight, and from August to the end of the year the market continued its steady climb. Strong corporate earnings and new war orders that were coming in seemed to blunt the negative impact of the start of the Korean War. It also became clear as the months went on that the war would not be as large (possibly World War III) as many had originally feared. The economy was also picking up as GNP rose to $285 billion in 1950, or 10% higher than it was from its $254 billion level in 1949. Corporate profits before taxes were also rising; they came in at $40.6 billion, up strongly from the 1949 figure of $26.4 billion. The Dow ended up 18% for the year, following up on the revised uptrend that began in 1949. Activity in the market also started to rise as average daily volume in 1950 came in right near the level of two million shares.

The market continued its steady climb in January 1951 and then flattened out over the next few months; it rose again in April but came right back down in May. There were still concerns over the Korean War, and it began to become a very unpopular engagement. Also, new tax rate hikes were introduced on the corporate side, raising the top rate to 52% from 47%. Finally, a new Federal Reserve chairman was named — William Martin. He vowed to fight inflation, and he pursued implementation of a much tighter monetary policy. Though inflation during most of the 1950s still only managed to rise to low single-digit levels, inflation was a concern (as opposed to not being much of a part of the American economy in the early part of the

20th century) and was starting to generate much more attention and concern as the years moved forward. Even with all this, the economy continued to grow as GNP hit $329 billion (up from $285 billion) and before-tax corporate profits hit $42.2 billion. The market traded basically flat up until the middle of the year. A short three-month rally until September lifted the market higher, and then a gradual decline and flat December left the Dow with a decent 14% gain for the year.

The year 1952 basically continued with the market moving in a fairly narrow range during the first half of the year. Volume was declining as the market stalled, which is basically constructive action. One thing the 1950s exhibited up to this point was a total lack of any prolonged and intense selling pressure on the market. Instead it seemed to take more of the negative issues in stride and just moved along at a fairly steady pace. More gradual up-and-down movements ruled the days until late fall. Some economic figures up to that point were showing signs of slowing. Most of the slowing was attributed to the new tight monetary policies being implemented by the Federal Reserve and continued high tax rates. Corporate profits before tax fell in 1952 to $36.7 billion. GNP actually rose to $347 billion from $329 billion the year before, signaling a somewhat mixed picture on the economic front. The market responded favorably to an Eisenhower presidential victory and surged higher during the latter two months of the year, as it gained 8% and registered its fourth straight winning year.

Darvas Begins His Quest

In November 1952 we are also introduced to Nicolas Darvas, featured in my first book "Lessons from the Greatest Stock Traders of All Time." It was then that Darvas was given shares in a small Canadian mining stock in exchange for a dancing engagement (his main profession) he was going to perform at in Toronto. He received 6,000 shares of a $0.50 penny stock called Brilund. Speculation in Canadian penny stocks was actually gaining popularity back then, and when Darvas checked the price for the first time in early 1953, he was amazed at the appreciation to $1.90 per share. He sold at once and retained an excellent profit. It was from that experience he would develop an insatiable desire to learn more about the stock market. But he soon found out just how challenging the task at hand was going to be. He made many mistakes along the way in trying to find out how the stock market actually worked. But Darvas had one thing going for him — a trait that is found in all the other successful traders that preceded him and one that will also embrace the great ones that would follow him — perseverance. Darvas would refuse to give up even after many long years of trial, error and frustration. His commitment to study and learning from his mistakes are vital traits to success in the market. Remember it took him nearly six years before he would really start to succeed. We saw nearly the same learning curve in years with Bernard Baruch already. Jesse Livermore commented once that it usually took an average of five years of a man making the same mistakes before he would finally begin to honestly learn and cause positive change. We also saw how long it took Richard Wyckoff, who was much more patient than many others, to get on the right track. And soon enough we'll see that it took Jim Roppel approximately seven years to become profitable in the market. Trying to gain consistent success in the stock market is a difficult endeavor, and it takes many years of learning, but those who stuck it out, refused to give in, and kept to their studies were rewarded.

Jack Dreyfus Outperforms

Another important figure to consider when discussing stock market history and success is that of Jack Dreyfus. Dreyfus was born in 1913, and his father got him started in the brokerage business when he helped Jack land his first job. This first job had Dreyfus working for a supervisor who was a chart reader. His responsibilities were to update, by hand, each chart for its changes in price and volume. This chart work fascinated him, and the more time he spent doing this work, the more he recognized certain chart patterns occurring. This is a bit similar to young Jesse Livermore who constantly watched the tape in his early days and would jot down notes in a journal, noticing that many stocks' prices would follow certain and similar patterns. As Dreyfus continued doing his chart work he was convinced that the stock patterns created through their trading behavior were repeating themselves. When he was 24 years old, he landed a position as a stockbroker with E.A. Pierce & Co., which was the predecessor to Merrill Lynch. While he was in that position, in 1937, the chief economist for the firm came out with a published document titled "The Third Great Boom." The market had been strong during the middle 1930s, and this document tried to predict even better times just ahead. Young Dreyfus, who had been studying his charts, thought the market was heading down, as he no doubt was seeing classic topping action in many stocks, as the market had staged an incredible run already up to that point (refer to Chapter 4). He also, through his chart study, didn't see any quality stocks setting up in proper basing patterns, as many were already extended due to the fast-rising market. He therefore went to a 100% cash basis, against the advice of the prominent voice within the firm he was employed with. This happened to occur one day before the beginning of the 1937–38 bear market that would send the Dow spiraling down 50%. Here we see a young aspiring great market operator heeding one of the golden rules for success in the market — don't listen to others' opinions. Dreyfus focused on his own meticulous research of the facts and history and ignored the opinion of even a respected analyst within his own company. This is quite impressive considering the reputation of the firm Dreyfus was with and the fact that he was still very young and somewhat inexperienced at the time. Remember, when everything seems as perfect as it can be, the market may be headed for a change. And just when many give up, the market may be ready to turn around and head higher. We've already seen this occur numerous times, and we'll see it again as we move forward. This knowledge is valuable for all, as the cyclical fashion of the market will keep occurring in the future as well.

As Dreyfus kept learning and succeeding in his career he would eventually open his own firm, and in the 1950s and 1960s he ran the Dreyfus Fund (a mutual fund). As a chart reader and a tape reader he would focus on strong fundamentals, and he combined that with his chart reading skills. He favored weekly charts, and he focused on earnings history and projections on the fundamental side. (We'll see this combination of fundamental and technical analysis with Nicolas Darvas and William J. O'Neil as we move forward.) For Dreyfus though — just as the other great traders discovered — the first key was to determine the trend of the market. Everything else comes from that, he thought. If the trend was strong and upward, that gave him the confidence to begin purchasing stocks. His purchase points would be when a stock would bust out of a trading range it had currently been in and move upward in a strong manner, making a new high in price. This was the ultimate conviction that there was strong demand from others for this stock and its upward momentum would probably continue. It was important to him that a new high price be established. He would watch stocks, and when they surged through these patterns to new highs he would buy into the stock. This is the same strategy that Darvas and O'Neil would discover as well. In fact, Dreyfus was whom O'Neil studied in his early days (along with Livermore and Loeb) to help develop some of the traits of his now-popular CAN SLIM™ method.

Dreyfus was also not afraid to sell stocks quickly if their chart action warranted it. He had strict loss-cutting policies, though they were not based on some percentage method. It was totally derived from the action of the stock and how it looked on the chart to him. His loss-cutting policy and his ability to quickly get out of positions that were no longer working was one of the main reasons he outperformed all other mutual funds when he was activity managing. He stayed attuned to the action of the market and its trend. When he saw the trend change, he would act. All the greatest traders followed this same principle, and it was a key strategy that led to their incredible returns.

From late 1953, when the market started moving higher, Dreyfus became fully invested. He saw, through his intense chart reading study, that many stocks were forming the exact basing patterns he was looking for. These were the same chart patterns he had seen in prior market uptrends, and he knew that stock patterns repeated themselves. During the strong run-up in the mid-1950s he stayed fully invested, and his positions moved up with the market, as many of his stock picks turned out to be the true leaders of that market upward cycle. By the time September 1957 rolled around, Dreyfus had been selling stocks and was 75% in cash, as he was cashing in his hard-earned profits that he had realized over the prior several years. The trend of the market had changed after a strong run-up, which can be seen clearly in Figure 6-1 on p. 81 (similar to what he noticed in the 1937–38 period mentioned earlier). The Dow ended up declining 20% from July 1957 to October of that year. In October 1957, when a sharp break hit the market, Dreyfus was sitting mostly in cash. His ability to study the market diligently, move with the trend of the market, make strategic buying decisions based on price and volume action with stocks hitting new highs in price during a strong market, and sticking to a loss-cutting policy, enabled

Jack Dreyfus to return 604% over the 12 years he ran the Dreyfus fund in the 1950s and 1960s. The next best performance was 502%, or 20% less than Dreyfus over the same time frame. The Dow returned 346% over that same time frame, showing just how much Dreyfus clearly outperformed both his peers and the market. One of his best performers was Polaroid, which earned him over an 800% return by the end of 1957. It was his largest holding.

With a new president in the White House and new promises, there seemed to be more optimism around in early 1953. But once in power, Eisenhower became focused on balancing the budget, and he put off promised tax cuts. The Federal Reserve was also still under a tight monetary policy rule in order to contain inflation. Some of these policies would become drags on the economy, and as the market drifted slightly lower throughout the first half of the year, it again seemed to anticipate slower times ahead. A new recession began in July, and just like the few prior ones, this one would be short-lived as well. A few things did happen right after the recession started that would breathe new life into the market, though. In August the Korean War came to an end, and peacetime issues again ruled the day. A short time later the computer began to be mass-produced and to change lives in many ways. It was truly the beginning of the technology age. The stock market reacted positively to these events and began to resume its steady climb in September. The Dow would finish the year slightly less than where it began, down 4%. As the war ended there was pent-up demand for many items especially homes and consumer-oriented goods. Though the economy was still in recession at the end of 1953, the declines in production and the market were very mild.

The year 1954 started with the economy still in recession but with renewed optimism. With the growing influence of mutual funds, many more from the general public would begin to get involved in the stock market, even if only on an indirect basis. As mentioned, one of the most successful fund managers at that time was Jack Dreyfus. His growth-stock strategies were being recognized as he began to discover new companies that were reaping the benefits of a demand economy. This involvement by more mutual funds would expand the power of the institutional investor in the market. Pension funds at the time also became more involved participants as well. In fact, the total percentage of trading by individuals when measured by total net purchase transactions was 61% in 1951. It would steadily decline and gave way to institutions as the decade wore on. By the time 1959 came around the percentage for individuals' trades had been reduced to 35%. So the impact big traders, such as institutions, can have on the market is quite clear (we'll see more of this when we get to O'Neil and his analysis a bit later). The mutual funds and some larger brokerage houses, mostly Merrill Lynch, would cater to the smaller investor and that would help bring more people into the market as more from the middle class would participate. The market rose steadily during the first five months of 1954, and as seen before, this rise occurred before the official end of the recession, which ended in May. The steady rise was solid and was very broad-based. The market was being led by many different industries, a signal indicating a very healthy market. Industrial stocks were still leaders (railroads and energy), many benefiting from an improving economy, but there were many other new industries from technology and pharmaceuticals as well as population growth that was strong, which just fueled more demand.

Loeb Profits Again in an Uptrending Market

In March 1954, the Dow had just passed the 300 level for the first time since late 1929. As the market kept moving higher back then and people bought more goods on credit, and so forth, new industries were where the new opportunities could be found. It's important to remember how these great stock operators would change their views as the market landscape changed. New opportunities created by new industries and new companies always present themselves in prosperous times. Loeb also reiterated at that time that not only was it important to focus on newly energized consumer-oriented companies but it was important to understand that the expectation of coming events, rather than the events themselves when they materialize, is what moves the markets. This solidifies the forward-looking and forecasting ability of the market. Loeb would go on to do extremely well during the rising market of the mid to late 1950s (there was a clear uptrend in 1954). His biggest winners during that time were Warner Brothers and Chrysler, and he utilized his experience and judgment in another market cycle to reap profitable returns.

In early 1954 President Eisenhower was promising a balanced budget and tax reform, which increased the good mood of the country. Even though economic numbers fell slightly that year, the economy was showing signs of improving. GNP actually fell to $363.1 billion from the 1953 figure of $365.4 billion. Corporate profits before tax also declined to $34 billion from $38 billion. But optimism seemed to rule the day. Mutual funds and other institutions were heavy buyers of stocks, and they helped propel the market forward as many continued to view stocks as a good hedge against inflation. The institutional participation was also driving up trading activity, a key component to rising stock prices. The average daily volume for 1954 would come in at 2.2 million shares, as total yearly volume on the NYSE would be 573 million shares, the highest in 23 years. It was clearly becoming a classic case of supply and demand, which is exactly how the stock market works. Other countries around the world were also experiencing rising stock markets. Only two normal pullbacks occurred in 1954 as the market continued marching higher. On November 17 the market finally reached the 381.37 level, which turned out to be the high it had obtained just before the Great Crash in 1929. It only took 25 years for long-term holders to get back to this point. The Dow finally ended the year up an impressive 44%, its best performance since 1933.

Interest in the rising stock market continued growing as 1955 began, and the market continued its upward trend after a short pullback in January. Strong earnings growth and the broadening out of many other industries continued. Optimism was still present, and President Eisenhower's popularity was rising as he gave investors and the general public confidence in America and its future. The market followed a stair-step trading pattern upward (spurts higher followed by slight pullbacks that were then followed by more rising action) from February up to September, as it pierced the 450 level. On September 24, Eisenhower suffered a heart attack and there was concern for his health and the leadership of the country. On September 26, the market fell 31.89 points as volume surged to 7.7 million shares. It was quite a scare for the country and the market, but it soon recovered, as did President Eisenhower. After regaining that sharp loss, the market flattened out in November and December and ended the year up with a strong 21% gain.

With two-plus strong years behind it the market would find 1956 to be a bumpy and challenging year. As we've seen already more than a few times, after an almost uninterrupted climb, the market many times consolidates its gains as some traders sell stocks to lock in profits and many others find that there are just not many attractive buys after prices have climbed for an extended period. This lack of buying power slows down the market. Thus the market began the year by dipping slightly in January and then traded flat during February. A sharp rise on increased volume occurred in March as the Dow pierced the 500 level for the first time in history. This level would serve as a ceiling and resistance point for the market over the next two years. It almost seemed as if there was some sort of psychological block at that level. A sharp drop back downward in May preceded the Highway Act, which was passed. This act would drive construction of the nation's highway system. Auto stocks rose on this announcement as it was viewed as positive for future auto demand. Loeb was right there again reaping gains from Chrysler, as he was an intense student of the auto industry and he knew who the leaders at that time were. Other leading stocks during this time that were consolidating their gains came from the defense, computer, technology, and pharmaceutical industries. After the passage of the Highway Act, the market moved higher and then flattened out again in August. At that time the Federal Reserve raised interest rates again in order to keep inflation down. The discount rate was increased to 3%, twice the level it had been at in 1954. This continued tightening of monetary policy was beginning to have an effect on the economy. With rising interest rates and a perceived slowing ahead, sellers knocked the market lower in September. For the rest of 1956 buyers and sellers battled each other as slight choppy action prevailed. The market ended a bumpy year up 2% for its third straight positive year.

The year 1957 started off with the market falling sharply in January and early February, as the recent bumpy ride continued. There were two scenarios playing out that were most likely the leading causes for the market bouncing back and forth. On the positive side there was still healthy growth and new industries, an overall sense of optimism, and institutional investors (mostly mutual funds) playing a much larger role in the market. On the cautious side there was still concern regarding inflation and a tight monetary policy that was driving up interest rates. Once the market fell back and touched the 450 mark in February, it rebounded and moved higher until July. It was a nice rally as the market rose steadily for five straight months. It would not last too long, though, as a tight monetary policy, reduced government spending and delayed tax reductions were taking their toll. Business began to slow further, and the market, as it always does, looked ahead. In

July the rally stalled as many leading stocks topped and began to pull back. In August a new recession set in as business conditions continued to slow. The market then began a steep decline, and it wiped out the nice five-month rally that had occurred earlier in the year. Many times we've seen, and we'll see again, how fast selling can hit a market, as fear leads to a much faster reaction than hope. Also in October, which didn't help things much, was the surprise news of Russia's successful *Sputnik I* launch. While losing the space race to communist Russia was a blow to America, it would wake the sleeping giant to move forward and respond. It would also spur more government spending, which would be positive for the economy, as government spending in the 1950s continued to comprise a large part of the economy. The market then returned to its choppy ways during the remainder of the year but would finish 1957 down 13%, snapping the three-year winning streak for the Dow.

While the market was bouncing back and forth in late 1957 looking for a bottom, there were some positive things working in select areas. For one, a tobacco company called Lorillard was introducing a new cigarette to the market. And as we've seen before and we'll see many more times to come — new product and/or service introductions that are widely accepted are major reasons why some of the best gains in history come from innovative companies. There had been many health concerns regarding cigarettes, and when the filter cigarette was introduced, many were relieved, as they thought the filtering mechanism would significantly reduce the health hazard of smoking. Lorillard was at the forefront of the filtered cigarette movement. It could also charge a premium price for these new products, even though the production costs were the same. This was a powerful combination of increased product demand at a premium price with a low cost of production. The market responded as Lorillard began its incredible run. Another area beginning to show strength was in space-related issues, resulting from the space race that would begin due to *Sputnik I*. From October to mid-December alone, there were five issues related to the space industry that increased over 20%. One of those was Thiokol Chemical, which rose 21.6% in that short span. Thiokol was coming out with new rocket fuels that would be used for missiles. Here is another company introducing a new product that would be in great demand and would drive its revenues and profits higher.

Darvas Finally Makes His Efforts Pay Off

Nicolas Darvas, who had spent the prior six years (beginning in late 1952 with his profitable Brilund transaction) studying the market and putting together his strategies, began watching Lorillard in late 1957 as price action in the stock had caught his attention. (His strategies were called the Box Theory and the Techno-Fundamentalist approach — please refer to his publication "How I Made $2,000,000 in the Stock Market" or my book "Lessons from the Greatest Stock Traders of All Time" for details.) He was an avid market student by that time, reading *Barron's* and watching the stock tables for price action and volume in leading stocks. He had also spent the majority of the prior six years making all the mistakes most do in the market and losing money. His perseverance though was quite impressive, and as he kept learning from his mistakes, he felt he was finally on the road to improvement. His strategy of watching the general trend of the market and leading stocks with price and volume action and utilizing a strict loss-cutting policy alerted him to a change in the market's trend by August 1957. As his holdings began to decline, his loss-cutting rule forced him out of all his stocks. He also noticed that there were no good stocks to buy as none were coming up through basing patterns (he called this "breaking through boxes") on increased volume. This was also when Jack Dreyfus starting moving mostly to a heavy cash position. These two experienced market operators started making prudent decisions in order to not get hurt in the market. Sure enough, that was just when the market would start a serious downtrend. They were both listening to the actions and the trend of the market, the leading stocks of the time, and discovering that there were no new good buying opportunities. When those conditions occur, the best traders usually go to a cash position in order to protect prior gains made and to avoid major losses to their portfolios.

During this downtrend Darvas continued his study of the market, and he also noticed that the stocks that would decline the least and also possessed strong fundamentals would probably be the best candidates to lead the market when it would turn around. This was exactly the case with Lorillard. He began watching this stock in the fall of 1957 as it jumped from $17 per share to $27 per share. Institutions were beginning to take positions in this leading stock due to its hot new product. He bought this stock after it had pierced the $27 level, as he made a pilot buy of 200 shares at $27½. He was quickly stopped out of his position, as the strong prior run pulled back some and triggered his short loss-cutting order. He kept watching this even though he suffered a small loss. This is another trait of the successful investor — never give up on something just because it may not have worked out for you the first time. Lorillard then continued its run upward as more volume and demand drove it higher. He bought back into the stock at $28⅜ with another pilot buy of 200 shares. Notice how he kept his initial buys small in case they didn't work out. This was another one of his smart money management rules that he would implement. This latest buy worked out, and the stock sprinted higher. He then would make add-on pyramid buys as the stock kept getting stronger, as we'll see when we get to 1958.

With the economy still in a slowdown recession period the market started off 1958 where it left off in late 1957 — continuing its choppy trading range. But things were starting to look up. Because of the space race with Russia that was just beginning, government spending would begin to increase again. Also, general business conditions also began turning upward after their brief decline. In March, the market rose sharply higher just a month before the recession would officially end in April. There were also more stocks finding bottoms during this latest correction as selling seemed to have halted. Electronics stocks started to rise and generate interest from the growing mutual fund industry. This is near the time that Jack Dreyfus would notice the market beginning to turn up. During the prior few years many stocks had been working on classic basing patterns. Flat and downtrending periods in the market are what create sound basing patterns in stocks. That is why it is important to always study chart patterns, no matter what cycle the market is in. We'll see when we get to O'Neil and Jim Roppel how they never got discouraged, but instead kept up their studies during bad market periods in order to make determinations of what cycle phase chart patterns were in or were forming, so they would always be in tune with the current market action and what may be about to come. Dreyfus would watch the fundamentally strong leaders and wait for their price action to be accompanied by strong volume as they moved to new higher ground. In fact, Dreyfus would become quite active during the last few years of the 1950s as the market took off on a strong upward run. He would buy many stocks breaking out and hitting new highs in price, and he added more profits that just increased the results of his fund.

During this early time in 1958 many industries perked up. Older industrial companies were gaining strength along with newer innovative industries. There were many new technologies coming to market that were in high demand. Some of the demand was coming from industries that produced armaments and materials, and some was coming from defense contractors. This combination of a strengthening in a broad range of industries builds a solid base for an uprising market. Darvas in early 1958 noticed how Diner's Club, another new emerging stock pioneering a new service in its field that was generating strong earnings for the firm, performed well in the slow market period of 1957. Notice how Darvas would watch certain stocks for long periods of time and not act on them until just the right moment. Diner's Club did well in 1957 while the market bobbed up and down, but the volume on its increased run was not that strong — the market just lacked strong buying power during that time due to the many factors that were mentioned above when analyzing that period. The market started to stabilize in early 1958; after Diner's Club suffered a pullback and then announced a two-for-one stock split, its stock started to move up again, but this time there was a marked increase in volume with the rise. This was a clear indication to Darvas that big buyers were accumulating the stock. His first buy was for 500 shares at $24½. The stock kept moving higher, and he then made a pyramid buy of 500 more shares at $26⅛ a few days later. As the price kept rising, the volume action in the stock was rising as well. Darvas knew he had a strong stock, and his newfound strategies taught him to hold on to it until it gave clear signals to sell. The stock soon zoomed past $30, and Darvas kept lifting his stop-loss order behind the stock as it kept rising. He did this in order to not give back profits he had already earned, but he left enough room for it to make normal pullbacks that occur in the market. The market was picking up in April, and Diner's Club continued to lead the market. It quickly crossed the $40 mark and then hit a high of $40½. At this point the stock seemed to have stalled, which is not unusual considering its rapid rise up to that point. To protect himself from a larger pullback than normal, Darvas moved his stop-loss order up to $36⅜. By the last week of April, the market started moving higher and Darvas began noticing some other strong stocks starting to make moves. Diner's Club seemed exhausted, and it did break down, triggering his stop-loss. He sold out for a $10,000 profit and now had more capital, along with his Lorillard profit that was still working, to move into some other new leaders.

One important item to point out concerning Diner's Club was that shortly after the stock corrected, it was announced that American Express was set to enter the credit-card field that Diner's Club had pioneered and American Express would go into direct competition with those in the field. Diner's Club would not follow the market higher during its strong run in 1958 and 1959, and by the end of 1959 it was trading in the mid $30s. Here we see Darvas moving with the market's action, protecting profits and moving on to other strong stocks when the market surged higher. Diner's Club had its run, but its stalling action gave an alert market operator the cues he needed to move on to something else.

While Darvas was watching his position in Diner's Club, he still had his initial position in Lorillard that he took in late 1957, as mentioned earlier. As Lorillard kept acting well and moving up, the volume activity really spiked in early 1958. Darvas, seeing this increased demand, followed up with a pyramid buy of 400 additional shares at $35 per share, and then he added another 400 shares at $36½. The stock then quickly shot up to $44⅜ but then pulled back just as fast, and Darvas raised his stop-loss order to $36 in order to protect his profits. He held on to this winner as it continued rising higher in heavy volume while the market surged higher as well. By early May 1958, Lorillard had reached the high $50s, and Darvas wanted to cash out, realize his profit, and buy into another stock he had been keeping his eye on. His profit was $21,000, good for a fairly quick 68% return.

Darvas Realizes His First Big Profits

The main reason Darvas sold both his holdings in Diner's Club and Lorillard was he wanted to put more capital into an even better investment. He had noticed that E.L. Bruce was generating quite a bit of interest. Its stock price rose from $18 to near $50 very quickly in early 1958 — up 177% in only seven weeks. Darvas watched this move but didn't act upon it yet, mostly because he had his capital tied up in the other two stocks. Once he had more capital he would use margin to leverage his purchase in E.L. Bruce. As the stock pulled back to consolidate some of its huge run and build a classic high-tight-flag pattern (more about those when we get to O'Neil), it fell back to the low $40s but on lower volume. This meant that many who had accumulated the stock recently were still holding on and did not want to sell. Darvas kept his eye on this unique leader and thought if it bounced back up near $50, it would regain its momentum, especially if volume exploded to the upside. That is exactly what it did, and he took a position of 2,500 shares that he purchased in 500-share lots at an average price of $52. From there the stock shot straight up to $77 and then was suspended for trading by the exchange. With the stock suspended from trading, many short sellers had to go to the over-the-counter market and bid for shares so they could buy them back to cover their short positions. After refusing to sell for $100 per share initially, Darvas held on as he saw the tremendous demand for the stock. He eventually sold out near an average price of $171 per share. This 228% gain, off the high-tight-flag pattern in just two months after his purchase, resulted in a profit of approximately $295,000. This would now establish Darvas's confidence in his long, painstaking efforts to establish market strategies that would result in the positive results he had been working so hard to attain.

As markets begin to make major moves to the upside many leaders step up front. In early to mid-1958 there were more than a few stocks vying for leadership. Another stock that caught Darvas's attention was Universal Controls. He was watching this stock in July 1958 as it broke through a basing pattern to clear $30 per share on huge volume. The $30 level seemed to have been an area of resistance prior to its breakthrough. After it formed a fairly short flat base, Darvas made a pilot buy of 300 shares at $35¼ in August as the stock resumed its upward trend. The market at that time was also strengthening. As the stock kept moving up he made more pyramid buys. He bought 1,200 shares two weeks later at $36½. Four days after that he purchased 1,500 shares at $40, as the stock was exhibiting the strength he originally thought it might. The stock then split two-for-one, so he now held 6,000 shares. As the market kept moving higher that year he held on to this strong leader. Not following the rule of "hold your biggest winning stocks" is one of the key reasons why so few have ever made big money in the stock market — they simply sell too soon and hold on to their losers hoping for a comeback. Recall Jesse Livermore's words of wisdom: "The big money is made in the big swings ... and it's not the thinking that makes the money, it's the sitting."

Darvas, during this time frame of 1958–59, is one of the most important stock traders to study as his persistence, patience, and strict discipline displays in detail how a great stock trader controlled his emotions and how he did many things right in reaping huge gains. He even made some serious mistakes (as we'll soon see), but he corrected them quickly, before they got totally out of hand. And while it is more important in the stock market to study one's losses in order to not repeat them in the future, this textbook, real-world study of Darvas's winning positions is one that every aspiring trader needs to read over and over again to see how the big money is made in the market. Regarding Universal Controls, Darvas would continue holding this winning position as it experienced an incredible upward move during the latter part of 1958 and into the early part of 1959. It then went into a classic climax run in the spring of 1959. The stock shot up from $66 to $102 in just three weeks on the biggest volume yet of its upward run. It then started to collapse as the smart money was taking the incredible profits that the stock had already presented. No stock keeps going up indefinitely as we've already seen and we'll see many more times. This topping action that is displayed by price and volume action can be worth many dollars to someone who studies how these best stocks in the past have topped and start to turn lower. For Darvas, he waited to see if the stock would bounce back, but he also raised his stop-loss order so that he would protect most of the profit he had accumulated. As the stock kept falling, he was stopped out at between $86¼ and $89¾ per share. This was nearly 12 points off the high, but it still netted him a substantial profit of $409,000.

As for Thiokol Chemical, mentioned earlier, Darvas was watching the action in this leader as well. When you are committed to being a serious student of the market, many years of study will alert one to the real leaders of the day by their actions. Darvas saw the initial spurt in Thiokol in late 1957 and early 1958, but he didn't act yet. He did however keep watching it as it consolidated its gains throughout the first half of 1958, basically trading in a flat basing pattern, which was mirroring the general market's action. As the market started picking up in late July, Thiokol would soon follow. Darvas was watching this, and he thought that if it rose out of its current box (pattern) past $45 per share, on strong volume, it had a chance to be a big winner. It did just that as it broke through $45, and Darvas made a pilot buy of 200 shares at $47¼ during August 1958. After that, it traded in another classic three-week tight pattern (named by O'Neil) until the end of August. This sideways pattern with no real up or down movement indicated that big investors were sitting tight with their initial positions. Thiokol then jumped out of this pattern, and Darvas bought right into its strength. It's important to note that he waited until the demand moved the stock first — he didn't move forward based on his own thoughts — he waited until the stock's action confirmed its own strength. Darvas then purchased 1,300 additional shares at $49⅞ on September 2. Thiokol quickly rose to over $50 per share on increased volume, as demand kept coming into the stock. Then, during the second week of September, Thiokol issued stock rights. Stock rights were given as a bonus to shareholders at one right per share. The rights allowed one to use 12 rights to purchase one share of stock for $42. You had a choice to either exercise your rights or sell them on the AMEX where they would trade for a limited amount of time. If you exercised the rights, your broker could lend you up to 75% of the current market value of the stock. Darvas took full advantage of this unique opportunity. After a complex transaction in which he actually purchased additional rights and exercised those rights, he sold his original 1,500 shares at an average price of $53½ and used those proceeds to buy yet another block of rights. Then he exercised those rights, and along with the unique loan arrangement, he ended up with 6,000 shares at a cost of $350,820. By mid-December, Thiokol moved to the New York Stock Exchange (from the AMEX), and it shot up immediately by eight points. The stock then kept rising, and it hit $100 before year-end. The market at that time was in a very strong uptrend, Thiokol kept increasing in price, and Darvas knew he had a big winner and now knew what to do with it — hold on to it until it gave him the signal to sell.

These solid stock opportunities were presenting themselves due to the extreme strength of the market during 1958, and Darvas was right there taking advantage of a positive market environment. In fact, the Dow would gain a solid 34% during the year. There was basically only one major break, which occurred in late November, but the market quickly recovered and moved higher. It was also in 1958 that we get introduced to O'Neil, featured in my first book "Lessons from the Greatest Stock Traders of All Time." O'Neil would begin his career in the brokerage business as a stockbroker for Hayden, Stone & Co. in California. As a young aspiring market operator O'Neil would lean heavily toward the research side of the business, which would benefit him greatly in the future. He spent these first few years in the late 1950s studying the market and other great traders and making most of the same mistakes that the others before him made when they started out.

The year 1959 started off with the market continuing its rise and momentum from 1958. The Dow sprinted up in the first few weeks of the year from the 580 level to just over 600. But then it fell back and quickly retraced that gain, and by February 9 it was at 571. From there the market picked back up and would again follow a stair-step pattern upward until June. Each strong rise would be met with mild and normal pullbacks, but then it would pick up again and resume its rise. Speculation and interest in the market was gaining popularity and more attention, as trading volume was picking up rapidly. Many began to get concerned about how far stock prices had risen. The Dow had risen from near 435 just over a year ago to near 635 by April 1959, or over 45%. Stock splits were becoming more plentiful, which is always a sign that things may be getting a bit out of hand. In May 1959, the margin requirement was raised to 90% in a bid to slow down the speculative nature of the rising market. Many were reminded of the 1920s, and they didn't want a repeat of those times. As the market marched higher many leaders showed impressive price appreciation. But one positive, up to the point in early 1959, was that the rise in stock prices seemed greatest for those with the strongest earnings growth, which was more than one could say about the late 1920s.

Darvas Makes a Mistake

Because of his recent success, Darvas, in January 1959 while the market was in a choppy trading pattern, decided to move closer to the action. He moved to New York City. His overconfidence was clearly going to cost him, as his over half a million dollars in profit swelled his head. While there he lost his focus, deviated from his rules, and started listening to others and their opinions — basically doing everything that he learned not to do during his intense and long training period up until his first few big gains. During January's pullback he kept trading short term, sometimes trying to turn trades in just a few hours. He took many losses, and he didn't cut them short like his rules had taught him. All his prior hard work in refining his skills, discipline and rules was ignored. He ended up losing $96,000 in just a few weeks. He experienced 14 losses, one of which was Haveg Industries, in which he suffered an $18,000 loss on 2,500 shares. He lost $11,000 on 2,000 shares of

Sharon Steel. But Darvas finally came to his senses and discovered he had abandoned all the proper tools that finally gave him his first real profits. He quickly made a change and moved away from New York and decided to go back to his successful strategies. The other positive during that time was that he left his Thiokol position alone, as it continued to do well for him. He also didn't touch Universal Controls during that time, as it was also doing well. He eventually sold it and retained an excellent profit as was detailed earlier. It's important to study one's mistakes in order to constantly strive to do better in the future. Here we see a trader, after many years of hard efforts, finally realize the profits he had been seeking. But he became overconfident, which happens to many when they get the results they have worked so hard for. But Darvas learned what he did wrong and corrected it before it really cost him.

As the market moved higher during February and March, Dravas came right back into the market, and he made sure he stuck to his rules. He made $12,000 on a fairly quick trade in General Tire & Rubber, as he bought 1,500 shares at $56 and then sold it on the way up at $69½. He then made another $3,500 on 500 shares of American Photography (bought at $71½ and then sold out at $79). He was gaining back confidence in his system that had produced positive results. He had many losses too, but he went back to his strict loss-cutting policy, and it preserved his capital. Most of the losses he kept under or near $2,000 each (Cenco Instruments at $1,544, Reichhold Chemicals at $1,024, Fansteel at $2,295 and Philadelphia & Reading at $1,088, among others). Notice how he contained these losses as opposed to the bigger ones mentioned earlier from Sharon Steel and Haveg Industries, when he abandoned his successful strategies.

While the market stayed strong, Thiokol continued to work well for Darvas. He still maintained his stop-loss order, but again he trailed it back in order for it not to be triggered during normal minor pullbacks. The stock did pull back sharply during the first week of April 1959, following a three-for-one split, but it still did not hit his stop-loss limit. Thiokol then quickly rebounded and exploded upward in a classic climax run on very strong volume. By the first week of May, Thiokol hit $72 (split adjusted). Volume for that week was huge at 549,000, and the stock shot up 13¼ points for the week. This action, when a stock has a long advance and then suddenly explodes in its most powerful move accompanied by its greatest volume, has happened in many leading stocks when they finally hit their peak price. We just saw the same thing happen with Universal Controls, and we'll see this same action occur many more times as we move forward. It is during those climax runs, when the excitement is at its peak, that it is the right time for the smart money to sell. Recall that Baruch, Livermore and Loeb all liked to sell their big winners on the way up. They all saw the same things happen in their day, and it was happening right here again with this strong leader. What did happen to Thiokol was that the New York Stock Exchange suspended all stop-loss orders on the stock. Since that was Darvas's protection and a major strategy for him, he finally sold out. It was a wise move, and he netted a profit of $862,000, his biggest gain to date.

With the markets still rising during the spring of 1959, even after the Federal Reserve had raised the discount rate in March to 3%, Darvas now had much more capital to put to work in this fast-rising market. His keen eye alerted him to Texas Instruments, a leader in the hot electronics field. This stock was a leading price gainer during 1958 that Darvas had initially missed out on. As it pulled back during the first part of 1959, Darvas kept watching it carefully. Then in April 1959, Texas Instruments suddenly surged upward again on massive volume. Darvas made an initial buy of 2,000 shares during the second week of April at an average price of $94⅜ per share. As the stock kept advancing, he made a pyramid follow-up buy of 1,500 shares at $97⅞. With the market still moving higher and electronics stocks leading the way, Texas Instruments just kept climbing. Darvas would make one more pyramid buy just a few days later of 2,000 more shares at an average cost of $101⅛ per share. He now held 5,500 shares of a strong market leader. By July 6, 1959, the stock was up to $149½, and Darvas kept raising his stop-loss order behind it in order to protect his profits. He would end with another substantial profit when he was finally stopped out of the stock.

An Expert Shows How It's Done

During early May 1959, Darvas made four new initial buys into other leading stocks he had been watching. He took positions in Zenith Radio, Beckman Instruments, Fairchild Camera and Litton Industries. Once he established his positions, he set stop-loss orders on each one of them at 10% below each one's purchase price. On May 18, he was stopped out of Beckman Instruments, as it pulled back in price and triggered a 10% loss for him. The very next day, Litton Industries fell to $106¼ per share from Darvas's buy point of $112. Even though it had not yet reached his stop-loss order yet, Darvas sold out and took a 5% loss, as he didn't think it was acting correctly. This is another great skill that comes to the best over time — their ability to trust their judgment when things don't seem right and they then cut their losses even smaller than their original strategies allowed. Then Darvas, after those two positions had been closed, took that capital and moved it into his other two holdings, which were acting well and displaying strength. He followed up with his initial purchase of 500 shares in Fairchild Camera with a pyramid buy of 4,000 more shares ranging in price from $123¼ to $127 per share. He then made a follow-up buy to his initial position in Zenith Radio with a 5,000 share purchase, ranging in price from $99¾ to $107½. These two stocks ended up contributing to the millions he made during the strong 1958 and early 1959 market. This is classic stock trading skill at its finest that is never taught in any textbook or classroom. Darvas, with just those four transactions, can teach one plenty about the stock market. He stayed in tune with a strong market and bought into four leading and fundamentally strong companies that were initially moving up in price. He then took small positions initially to test his investments. He set strict loss-cutting strategies in place to control his emotions and limit his risk. He took his first loss in stride and then cut his second loss even smaller, without getting angry or hoping for comebacks. He also experienced the average 50% win/loss ratio that even the best traders throughout history have experienced. The difference is that the best traders keep the losses small and let the winners ride. Darvas then took available capital and piled it into his other two stocks that were moving up in price. Pyramiding winning stocks is what leads to big profits. He then held those two stocks until they showed selling signals or forced him to sell them. That is how legendary stocks traders make millions.

In late May 1959, *Time* magazine ran a story in its business section called *Pas de Dough* about Nicolas Darvas and the incredible profits he had retained during the prior two-year period. The article generated much interest, which led to a book deal from a publisher. In the *Time* article Darvas summarized many of the strategies he utilized to finally stay on the positive side of the market. He also mentioned that his main resource for decisions was to study the stock tables in *Barron's* (rumor was that subscriptions to *Barron's* doubled after this article and after Darvas's book came out) and his study strategy to stay focused was to reread his "bible," Gerald Loeb's classic "The Battle for Investment Survival," every two weeks. He did this to stay disciplined, to never give up, and to keep extremely focused on the task at hand. What we see here is a successful operator learning from one of the best by constantly reminding himself of the proper and disciplined ways to act while being active in the market. Darvas looked to Loeb's experience and success to help himself succeed. This progressive learning from the great traders that preceded them allowed the next era of great traders to continue. Livermore and Baruch knew each other and shared common principles about the market. Loeb learned things from Baruch, who would remind Loeb to always study the facts and not become prejudiced in one way or another. Darvas then learned from Loeb through his book as Darvas kept rereading it to constantly stay in focus. O'Neil also learned from Loeb as well, along with Livermore and Dreyfus. Jim Roppel, who we'll meet later, is one of the newer generation of great traders to follow the practices learned from O'Neil and all the other great traders that will be featured or mentioned in this book. It's learning from the best that helps one move forward.

While the strong fundamental leaders were rising and leading the way, there was one disturbing trend that was beginning to occur in the market. As the year went on, many new issues were coming to market in order to try and take advantage of the favorable market environment. Many of these new issues were in the hot new electronics field, and they used the words "trons" and "electros" in their names. Many had no earnings at all and no prior experience. But that didn't seem to matter. The prices of their stocks would shoot up when they came to market due to the rampant speculative nature of electronic issues at the time. This is exactly the same thing that would happen in the late 1990s and in early 2000 when anything with the words "dot-com" in its name would come public — history just keeps repeating itself. Many of these new electronics stocks in 1959, and the lucky ones that would show earnings, would have their PE ratios quickly rise to within the 100-to-200 range due to the excitement. There were also other established companies that were trying to diversify into the electronics field due to the frenzy that was taking place. One example was a company called Farrington Manufacturing. This was a small credit card company that also made handbags. This company had lost money consistently. It then tried to introduce a new electronic device to the market. The hype of the product and its tie to the electronics field drove the stock quickly higher. The stock then split four-for-one. It would finally reach an adjusted price of $57½. When the hype of these new small issues faded, the price of Farrington fell all the way back to under $2 per share. There were more than a few stories like this one back then. Jack Dreyfus was one who commented about the mania that was surrounding these stocks, and he warned about the excesses that were occurring in the summer of 1959.

By August the market was up nearly 18% for the year and there were many predictions of all-time highs to come. It seems whenever the market explodes upward, like we've already seen many times, human psychology just keeps causing the same behaviors to be repeated. A major steelworkers strike hit the market in late summer of 1959, but leading stocks were already starting to weaken, which again always foretells what the market may do. The market quickly corrected from early August to late September as the Dow fell 10%. But underlying strength came right back into the market, and over the next three months the Dow would regain back its 10% loss and finish the year and decade right near where it started its 1959 summer correction. The Dow finished the year up 16%, and it had now put together two strong years of gains. The year 1959 also witnessed a marked rise in trading volume. Average daily volume exceeded three million shares, which was the first time that had occurred since 1929. With the strong market, of course, PE ratios were up. From a PE average of 6.6 in 1950, the ratio stood at 17 in 1959. The dividend yield also fell, which stood at 3.25% in 1959 down from 6.5% in 1950. Growth in stock prices always results in higher PE ratios and lower dividend yields.

The 1950s would turn out to be a great time for opportunities in the stock market. Only two years experienced losses — 1953 and 1957. These were the only years of the decade that experienced recessions. New innovations were introduced, and the market responded with great profit opportunities. Jack Dreyfus and Nicolas Darvas proved once again how staying in sync with the market's trend and implementing successful strategies can produce profits that well outperform the market average.

7

A "Go-Go" Bull Run Puts Profits in Pockets That Studied History (1960–69)

Jack Dreyfus Followed Historical Stock Price Patterns to Reap Huge Returns

The beginning of the 1960s didn't start off where the 1950s ended. Mounting concerns regarding high unemployment rates and general stagnation at a higher level began to weigh on the market. During February

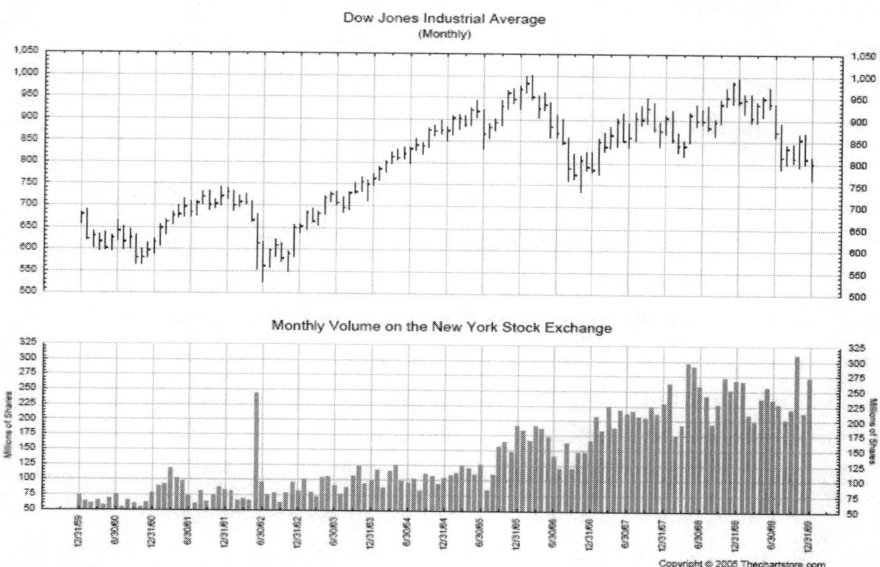

Figure 7-1 The Dow Jones Industrial Average 1960–69.
Source: *www.thechartstore.com.*

the market was selling off, and by the end of February the Dow had fallen nearly 50 points in the first two months of the new decade to close near 620. On February 29 the market fell on very heavy volume, and two weeks later the Dow was at 609. It didn't stop there, as by the end of the first week in March, it had fallen under the 600 level. And just as we've consistently seen how the market always looks ahead, a recession began that year in April. The market whipsawed up and down in April and May. By the end of May the market seemed to settle down, and then it traded flat. Then, during the early part of June the market shot upward for four straight days registering very strong gains. It was one of the biggest rallies up to that point, and the Dow crossed over the 650 level again. It seemed a strong uptrend was just beginning. But it didn't last long as the market started pulling back right after that fourth day. As the market could not regain that high and then began gradually slipping back, it was a strong warning sign to the astute trader that buying power to continue driving the market higher was clearly short-lived. By the last week of July the Dow had retreated all the way back to under 600. A quick round-trip from 596 on May 2 to 663 (up 11%) on June 9 and then back down to 597 (down 10%) on July 25 was whipping traders around with no clear trend in its actions. Many great traders have seen how frustrating this whipsawing action can be and decide to stay out of the market until a clear trend is established. Remember, as we've seen before, the very best traders decide many times that the safest way is to be out of the market completely. They use downtime to increase their study while never losing their observation skills.

August continued the seesaw action as the Dow shot back up to 645 by August 24. Then, again and just as fast, it dropped back, undercut the 600 level and was at 565 by the end of September. A slowing economy and other uncertainties, especially Russia, were heavy burdens for the market, and there wasn't enough strong buying power to keep any of these short rallies moving forward. Just as soon as it looked like an uptrend would gain strength, the sellers would pound the market lower. This is the environment of the ever-challenging market and reiterates the reason why Loeb always considered it a battle. This action in 1960 was clearly a battle between the bulls and the bears. By the end of September gold stocks had been rising while most others were in decline, and many feared inflation problems. We'll see this repeatable pattern happen again, and if one remembers this action from prior history, it could make for a profitable opportunity. One bright spot began to emerge and that was the campaigning of John F. Kennedy for president. Kennedy was touting a stronger administration to get the economy moving again. He campaigned that a gross national product (GNP) growth rate of 5% was achievable and sustainable. GNP had been averaging around 2.5% per year for the prior eight years up to that point. A young and aggressive presidential candidate thought that a doubling of the production and output of the nation could be possible. The market then began to march up off its bottom, and by the end of the year it finished just over 600 and down 9% for the year breaking the strong two-year uptrend that ended the 1950s.

O'Neil Gets His Start

Also in 1960 we see a young William J. O'Neil studying hard, just like the many great traders before him, in order to try and succeed in the market. While a young stockbroker with Hayden, Stone & Co., and still making many amateur mistakes and not much money, he began to research the Dreyfus Fund and discovered that it was significantly outperforming all other funds during the rising market of the mid to late 1950s. In January 1960, O'Neil was so intrigued, passionate, and hungry to succeed in the market that he sent away for every quarterly and prospectus report on the Dreyfus Fund during the 1957–59 period. We mentioned earlier that Jack Dreyfus was running this fund and that he attained superior returns in his fund that dwarfed all others. O'Neil wanted to understand how Dreyfus did it. It was meticulous work, but O'Neil researched over 100 purchases that were made by Dreyfus during the strong market period of 1957–59. O'Neil then marked on charts, using the average purchase price in the reports, of every stock that Dreyfus had bought in each quarter to determine the price and timing of each stock. What O'Neil discovered changed his views on the market and led to the building block of his highly successful CAN SLIM™ method. O'Neil also discovered that Dreyfus would only take on a new position in a stock once it broke through a certain chart or basing pattern and would then hit a new high in price. This didn't just happen randomly, it happened on every single one of the over 100 stocks that O'Neil researched. Remember what Dreyfus said, "… I just saw the same patterns occurring over and over again." Obviously when he saw these leading stocks breaking out, Dreyfus would act and jump on board as well. Also, Darvas was using a very similar strategy, as he would only buy into stocks that would break through his boxes (from his Box Theory) and move to higher ground on strong volume. He was probably seeing many of the same stocks that Dreyfus would be purchasing. Dreyfus was purchasing stocks based on price action, volume and strong fundamentals.

From this study O'Neil would now focus on certain chart patterns, and he would only buy stocks when they would break out of those patterns and hit new highs in price. This meant that the demand was building and was strong for those issues at that time. With O'Neil beginning to build on his newfound strategy the first stock he purchased following this method was Universal Match in February 1960. The stock went on to double in price in only three months. But O'Neil sold out quickly, and he didn't make much due to his limited capital and position in the stock. During the latter half of 1960 he also purchased small positions in Proctor & Gamble, Reynolds Tobacco and MGM. He did well with these issues even during a choppy market. At about that same time he was accepted to the Harvard Business School's first program for management development (PMD). While at Harvard, O'Neil kept up his study of the market and great stock traders, and he learned through reading Jesse Livermore's book "How to Trade in Stocks" that the pyramiding strategy was the key to large gains in the market. He then began to utilize this strategy on his strongest stocks. Also in 1960 Nicolas Darvas's first book, titled "How I Made $2,000,000 in the Stock Market," was published. The book was an instant success and sold over 200,000 copies in its first eight weeks and over 400,000 copies by 1964. The book still today commands a large demand and has been reprinted many times. It is one of the most inspiring books on the stock market in that it shows the perseverance of Darvas and his willingness to never give up. It also details his successful methods of his Box Theory and Techno-Fundamentalist approach. It is highly recommended reading for all who decide to participate in the stock market.

Experienced Experts See the Market Trend Change

With a new president in the White House and renewed optimism in the country, even though unemployment was still high and the country was still in a recession, the market began sprinting higher as 1961 began. Investors and the market seemed to have left behind the shaky market of late 1960 and focused on the future, which they believed showed promise. Kennedy was talking of stimulating growth through tax incentives, and mutual funds were still growing rapidly, which provided buying power in the market. Gerald Loeb became very bullish at this time. He noted, while following the market's action, that a group of leading stocks possessed very strong fundamentals and the majority of the up days in the market were accompanied by heavy volume. He also viewed the relationship between new price highs (over the past year) against new price lows as a clear indication of the strength or weakness of the market. During this early time in 1961 he noted many days when the new high list would dwarf the new low list. For example, on the day he announced that the market was ripe for him to become very bullish, the new highs that day hit 193, while new lows were only 33. O'Neil was also more confident as he now had a few small gains under his belt and was following and developing a market strategy that was beginning to produce positive returns. As the market continued rising in early 1961, O'Neil's best picks were Great Western Financial, Crown Cork & Seal, Kerr-McGee, Brunswick and Certain-teed.

In February the recession would officially end as business began to pick up. The market reacted in kind as it followed a very bullish stair-step progression on the way up. Strong bursts of rising prices would be met by shallow and short pullbacks. This is constructive action during a rising market, and it continued from January through May of 1961. There was however one detail that was a bit disturbing during this run in the first half of 1961, and it was starting to draw some attention. Many very small issues, which did not exhibit earnings or any other strong fundamental traits, began surging as well. This happens often when the market begins to look exciting to everyone. Caution, as we've seen in the past, seems to get swept aside. This is a great lesson for many traders to look for in future markets, as we'll see it does occur again after this point in time more than once. Understanding how history has worked in the market is very valuable knowledge to have as many behaviors keep repeating themselves.

While the market kept moving higher, more low-priced electronics issues along with other weaker industries such as vending and savings-and-loan stocks were registering strong advances. From late 1960 to early 1961 many new low-priced issues would hit the market and rise 20% to 50% on their first trading day. Again it sounds a bit like the late 1990s and early 2000 with the dot-com stocks. In fact, in 1961, seventy percent of the new issues that came on to the market were from companies that never had sold securities to the public before. These less-than-stellar stocks were fueling a purely speculative frenzy, and they started to become the new rage on Wall Street. Many were being listed on the American Stock Exchange and the over-the-counter market. There were a few exceptions though. Control Data Corporation came public in 1958 at $1 per share. Within three years it had advanced to $120. But it had a great product in the hot technology arena, and it was reaping the benefits of the high demand for its product through increased revenues and profits. There were also many large, more-established stocks that were very highly profitable then such as IBM, Polaroid and Xerox. But these small more speculative issues, which seemed to rise more on a promised future story than on realized profits were of more concern. A few of them were Mother's Cookie (up 63% in 5 weeks), Nytronics (up 180% in less than a month), Bristol Dynamics (up 157% in only three weeks) and Packard Instruments (up 118% in only 10 days).

By May 1961 speculation in lower-priced stocks was still sizzling. Even the failed invasion of Cuba couldn't seem to slow the market down. By this time many people were getting excited about the market, and it seemed to be the main talk from everyone. The market had come off the bottom in late October 1960 and moved up to hit 714 by late May. It was a strong 26% upward move in less than seven months. Bernard Baruch, then 91 years old, even commented that it looked very similar to other previous wild speculative times that he had gone through. Here was a very experienced operator using his knowledge of prior stock market cycles to inform others of what may be about to happen. How wise would many have been had they heeded the advice of one of the greatest stock traders of all time here at the twilight of his career when he again would end up being correct about the market.

While O'Neil was seeing gains materialize in his account, he applied his newfound pyramiding strategy, which he had learned from Livermore's book would work well in a strong market, just as Livermore had done many times in his day. But O'Neil was still young and inexperienced, especially in a fast-moving market like early 1961. For example, his position in Certainteed was correct on the buying side, when he purchased it in the low $20s. But he made a mistake and was shaken out when the stock pulled back in a normal fashion and he quickly sold. He realized a quick two- or three-point gain, but it turned out he sold too early. Certain-teed later went on to triple in price. It first ran up 20% in two weeks, ended up surging 100% in five weeks, and then formed a classic high-tight-flag pattern and blasted off from there to run up 482% in 12 months, just like E.L. Bruce, which Darvas had latched on to, did in the late 1950s. This is just another example of what Livermore and Dreyfus used to see — the same stock patterns keep repeating themselves over and over.

O'Neil Learns a Key Market Rule for Success

The other mistake O'Neil made in his early days was he didn't pay enough attention to the movement of the general market. By the summer of 1961 many of his holdings began to top and then turn down, and he ended up not selling correctly. The market fell back more in June and July than it had on its previous run upward. O'Neil ended up giving back all the profits he had accumulated in these positions during the first half of the year. He became so discouraged that he spent the remainder of the year reviewing every transaction he had made and viewing those against the action of the market. This was when he discovered how important it was to first study the general trend of the market and then move with the market. He also noticed that he had not developed any selling rules. He had the basic buying rules down, and they worked out well for him. But without proper selling rules he was just spinning his wheels and knew he'd never make any real progress. One sell rule he established then was to hold leading stocks that surged 20% or more during the first three weeks after breaking out of a proper basing pattern. These, he would discover, usually turned out to be the biggest winners. Another important selling rule he implemented was to sell and lock in profits when the market begins to turn down and head for a major correction, as he discovered that even the best leading stocks succumb to hard breaks in price when the market falls. We've already seen that occur many times in prior cycles when tops in the market have occurred. O'Neil would later add many more selling rules to his models, as his continued study of prior market leaders would alert him to create time-tested strategies in order to lock in profits and not give them back. Also, his meticulous historical study of the market would later help him create and pinpoint key turning points in market tops and bottoms, as he also proved that the market's cycle activity just keeps repeating itself over time. We'll see much more of that as we move forward.

In late July 1961 the market shot higher, and it looked as if the rally would continue after a choppy prior few months. It was here, though, that Gerald Loeb remarked it might be a better time to do some short-term trading. This comment came from his extensive experience about how market cycles behave. He knew that without a clear trend in place it would be a more challenging environment. His comment turned out to be correct. From August to the end of the year the market whipsawed up and down and then finished flat in December. Many leading stocks were teetering at year-end, and most were well off their highs reached earlier, while many of the lower-priced speculative issues were even further off their highs. The market would end up 19% for the year, though the majority of that gain was made in the first half of the year.

When 1962 began, it seemed the market knew of only one way to go and that was down. Many mutual funds were in liquid positions by the start of the new year, but they were not in a buying mood. It seemed like their tactic was to raise more cash. The Dow, which had started the year at 734, undercut the 700 level by midmonth and fell to 686 by month-end. There were many outside influences going on at the time that may have caused some concern for investors. The Kennedy administration was involved with the steel industry in trying to control price increases, which caused tension there. The SEC was investigating mutual fund activities and the New York Stock Exchange. Capital spending was down and declining. And though Kennedy's administration was good at controlling inflation, unemployment was still over 5%, which was holding back economic growth.

Nicolas Darvas had been active in the market from May 1961 to this point on a limited basis. Even after the millions he had made in the market, a feature story in *Time* magazine and his best-selling book on the market, he was having difficulty in a choppy market. It just goes to show how challenging the market really is and that it requires one to always be in a constant learning process. Darvas did however keep his losses small, as he always did after he refined his rules. He was so frustrated with the market and the fact that there were no new good buys being offered up that he quit trading the market at that time. His rules forced him out of the market. Darvas was like Loeb in the sense that he did not feel comfortable shorting stocks. Darvas's system was based on being in long positions with leading stocks when the market was in an uptrend. His timing here in early 1962 turned out to be excellent, as the market had already hit its high for the year during the first week of the first month. Here is an example of the market giving off vital signals well in advance of a decline by not having any leading stocks moving up from strong buying power. The market just continued to weaken, and here we see an experienced market operator watching and listening to what the market was doing and then acting properly, instead of relaying on other opinions or even his own. This objective behavior allowed him to stay safely in cash and preserve his capital when market conditions were not ripe for strong opportunities. Patience is just another key skill and trait of the best market operators.

O'Neil was also back in the market and active in early 1962. On April 1 all of O'Neil's newly formed sell rules kicked him out of all his holdings, without him knowing there was about to be a serious break in the market. He didn't argue with these new rules; he just followed them, which in turn were reflecting what was happening in the market. This is exactly what Darvas had just done as well, and also what Darvas and Jack Dreyfus did in 1957 just before that market cycle went into a correction. O'Neil here in 1962 was sitting in 100% cash when the market was just about to begin its downfall, which can be seen clearly in Figure 7-1 on p. 105. It shows how important continued study in the market can be. Recall he spent the last half of 1961 studying his prior mistakes to implement those new sell rules. Had he just brushed it off instead of learning from those mistakes, he would have surely been hurt again in the spring and summer of 1962.

O'Neil's Continued Study Leads to Big Gains

Showing just how astute a young trader he was at this time, O'Neil was just finishing reading "Reminiscences of a Stock Operator" by Edwin Lefevre. Recall that this classic was originally published in 1923 and was actually out of print in the early 1960s. O'Neil had to pay $50 to get his copy of this investment classic that profiled the life of Jesse Livermore. As I mentioned in the Introduction, here is another example of a great stock trader learning from history to profit in his current market time. The 1907 market that Livermore was so successful in when he took short positions in stocks due to the fact that many leaders of the prior uptrend had topped out and began to decline and did not bounce back, began to look eerily similar to the spring of 1962, according to O'Neil. Many leaders, which had been teetering for months, did not come back up, and many started breaking down. The market was clearly beginning to weaken, and O'Neil would use history and the experience of one of the most successful traders to profit from his current situation. He then began to short Certain-teed, one of the strongest leaders of the uptrend, due to its weakness as it began to turn down with the market. In fact, Hayden, Stone & Co. was still recommending it to their clients while it was falling, and O'Neil was criticized for shorting it in his own account, as he was still employed by the firm at that time. This flexibility to change course on a stock when the stock does change course was one of the biggest reasons why Gerald Loeb was so successful. Loeb was flexible to change course (for him it meant selling and going to cash) and that allowed him to retain many of his profits. O'Neil would also short Alside at this same time. A few months later he shorted Korvette at just over $40 per share. The profits he realized on these short sales were significant, as the market was now in a clear downtrend and then had trouble sustaining any upward moves throughout the summer and early fall.

It was in late spring of 1962 that the market really broke hard. But remember that a few of the successful traders saw the warning signs well before late May. Darvas was out of the market a full four months before as his system showed him there was nothing good to buy and he got tired of taking small losses. O'Neil was out and 100% in cash more than six weeks before the late May severe drop. We saw in earlier decades Livermore, Baruch and Loeb mostly out of the market months before the 1929 crash. We saw Dreyfus and Darvas mostly out of the market well before the 1957 break. All of these instances happened because the great traders took the cues from the market and the leading stocks of their time and acted appropriately. Here is a look at the action of the Dow average in late May 1962, when Darvas was in cash and O'Neil had cashed out of his long positions and now held short positions in a few former leaders who were headed lower:

Mon. May 21. Small decline on the Dow on slow volume.

Tue. May 22. Market down 12.25 points (worst drop in over a year) on heavy volume. Volume picked up as the decline worsened (over one million shares traded in the last half hour). Gold stocks also rose.

Wed. May 23. The Dow fell 9.82 points to 626 (lowest level in 16 months). Volume jumped to 5.4 million shares. Leaders IBM and Xerox sold off at $19¾ and nearly $10, respectively. There were 460 new 52-week lows and only 5 new highs.

Thu. May 24. Dow was up in the morning, and then fell and ended lower.

Fri. May 25. The Dow sank 10.68 points, or 4.2%, as 6.4 million shares traded. There were 695 new lows. It was the worst week for the Dow since 1929, as the index shed 38.82 points. IBM lost 53 points for the week. Because of the volume, the tape was running a half hour late.

Mon. May 28. Selling intensified as the Dow fell nearly 35 points, or nearly 6%. Volume was huge at over nine million shares, the first time since 1933 and this also delayed the tape.

Tue. May 29. The market opened lower on heavy volume (down 2%) but reversed late in the day as mutual funds stepped in. The Dow recovered much of the prior day's loss and finished 4.7% higher as volume hit 14.7 million shares, the most since October 1929.

The mutual fund buying that finally came into the market late on May 29 helped slow down the panic in 1962. There were no major increases in margin calls, mostly due to the fact that the margin requirement had been raised to 80% that year. Also, corporate profits remained fairly strong, and many mutual fund managers were willing to pick up former growth stocks at perceived bargain prices. While the GNP of the country rose 20% from 1958 through 1961, corporate profits had increased only 3.3%. Whatever the reason for the decline, which brought the Dow down 25% from December 1961 to May 1962, those watching the action of leading stocks and the general market, like a few of these experts did, could have avoided some serious damage to their portfolio, especially if they held many of the hot new small issues, as some of them declined 90% and never came back to their prior levels.

One of the other important lessons that O'Neil followed in 1962 was to always remember the oft-quoted statement from Bernard Baruch, "… even being right three or four times out of ten should yield a person a fortune if he has the sense to cut his losses quickly on the ventures where he has been wrong." One of the accounts O'Neil was managing was actually ahead at the end of the year, while the Dow fell 29%. How did he do that? He was right in only one out of every three stocks he bought that year for that account. But recalling Baruch's statement, O'Neil limited his losses in a dangerous market. The profits he attained on the 33% of the stocks in which he was right were twice as large as the average losses he took on the losing positions. Discipline can pay off when the market falls hard, and here is another example of someone adhering to a strict loss-cutting policy and producing overall profits.

The month of June in 1962 was actually no better as the Dow kept falling further. The market hit a low of 524 on June 25. In only six months the Dow was down 29%. Those market drops, if not properly avoided, wreak havoc on portfolios and the confidence of traders as many stocks usually fall farther than the averages when major corrections occur. The market would gain nearly 100 points during the next two months on a short-lived rally, but that didn't last as it pulled back 9% in September alone. By October, O'Neil was once again 100% in cash and protecting his capital. The choppy market offered no new buy candidates up to that point, and his sell rules forced him out of any holdings he had. Then in October, President Kennedy demanded the Soviets remove their missiles from Cuba. The end of the Cuban missile crisis boosted confidence in America as it started to look as if the cold war was leaning in our favor. The market soon sprang higher on a classic follow-through day (market up higher on significantly higher volume), and O'Neil was right there watching the action. He soon bought into Chrysler at $58 per share just as it launched higher through a base as the market confirmed a change in its trend. This would turn out to be a huge winner for him. Gerald Loeb was also right there, and he noticed that the late-1962 rally was now being led by more investment grade–type issues, rather than the smaller speculative stocks, which were mentioned earlier that caused concern for Baruch. This gave Loeb confidence that the initial advance of this new trend would probably be strong, as it was now being led by more strong fundamentally solid leaders from blue-chip industrials to railroads. One other observation that Loeb had made when he looked at the parallels and the differences from 1929 to 1962 was that the earnings power and dividends of most businesses were still actually growing after the decline of the market in 1962 as compared to 1929, when profits and dividend payments declined fairly quickly across the board after that market break.

In the last two months of 1962 the market actually recovered over 100 points to end the year at 643. Helping push stock prices higher was an announcement by President Kennedy on November 15 that a tax cut was coming. Despite the strong finish, the Dow still ended up losing 11% for the year. The year would turn out to be one of the widest in terms of price spreads on the Dow as it would fluctuate from 525 to 735. The year 1963 started off where the market left off 1962 and that was riding a new uptrend higher. As the market moved higher led by older and more established industrials, some of the growth stocks began to move higher as well. These were the more profitable and established firms, again solidifying underlying strength to the market. Other groups showing strength were in the consumer industry. Bank of America established Visa that year, and it provided more buying power to the consumer, as consumer finance would begin to take off. During this market uptrend O'Neil would stick to his newly established and tested rules and would profit significantly. One industry that was leading the market higher was the airline industry. Orders for jets were increasing, and Boeing, benefiting from the increased orders, would be one of the strong leaders throughout 1963 and for the next several years. Another firm, Monogram Industries, which supplied special toilets for airplanes, reaped the benefits of the increased demand that airliners were experiencing, and it also became a huge winner that year. Monogram's earnings would surge 200% in 1963, and its stock price soared 1,000%. Throughout the first half of the year the upward trend of the market was marked by only one correction in late February. Other industries that were strengthening were cyclicals and turnarounds. It usually takes several industries moving forward to create a very strong upward-moving market.

O'Neil Profits Handsomely

From the beginning of March through the end of May the market made a solid move forward. O'Neil was very active in his own account and managing accounts for others in his role as a stockbroker with Hayden, Stone & Co. As the market began to flatten out in June, O'Neil kept his eye on one stock in particular. Syntex, which introduced a new product to the market, was generating heavy interest and moving up rapidly. Its introduction of the birth control pill was met with increased demand, which in turn drove revenues and profits up significantly. By June, Syntex had already risen 104% in just two months. O'Neil missed this first opportunity, but he kept watching it, just as Darvas had done with Lorillard in the late 1950s. When the market flattened out in June, as mentioned before, so did Syntex. After its quick spurt, it needed time to consolidate its gains. What Syntex was doing was actually forming a new high-tight-flag pattern. Since O'Neil was seriously studying charts and he had seen this same pattern form with two other prior leaders, he thought this could occur again and present an opportunity for him. Both E.L. Bruce, which paid off well for Darvas, and Certain-teed, which O'Neil missed earlier on in its greatest upward run, had formed the exact same pattern that Syntex was now forming. Here again it pays to study past leaders and their charts, which just reflect the supply-and-demand price action within the market. O'Neil also knew from his study of Jack Dreyfus that the same types of chart patterns keep repeating themselves. As Syntex then shot up higher through its high-tight-flag pattern, O'Neil bought the stock in June 1963 from the profits he attained on the Chrysler stock he bought off the bottom of the 1962 market in October. The price he paid for Syntex was $100 per share and the PE ratio at the time was 45, after it had already doubled in price during the prior two months. How scary would a transaction like that seem? And to boot, the market had trouble going higher and it actually pulled back for its second correction of the year in July. But O'Neil saw the tremendous strength of this stock and its solid earnings growth. The excitement and demand for its new product propelled this stock even higher, and it rose 40% in just 8 weeks from O'Neil's first buy point. He ended up riding the stock out over the next six months and then sold it near its top of $570 per share. The stock had surged 470% in just six months and Syntex earnings were up 300%, as the market turned up from its July pullback and bolted higher until the end of the year, registering a 17% gain.

Even the assassination of President Kennedy couldn't bring down the market. On that tragic Friday, Nov. 22, 1963, the market sank over 20 points when word of Kennedy's death came public, as within 25 minutes over 2.2 million shares changed hands. The market would close early that day at 2:00 p.m. On Monday, November 25, the market was closed out of respect for Kennedy. But by Tuesday, November 26, with newly appointed President Johnson in place and the public feeling somewhat unnerved, the market rose a strong 32 points, or 4.5%, to regain its traction.

Throughout the healthy market of 1963 O'Neil did very well by sticking to his rules. Many of the accounts he managed were up several hundred percent for the year. His worst-performing account that year was up 115%. Though his returns were exceptional, he proved he was human as well. He suffered many losses that year, but he kept them small at between 5% and 6%. He recalled what Jesse Livermore had learned from his experience and also what the other great traders had discovered — when you're right, have the patience to be right big, and when you're wrong, have the discipline to be wrong small. Here we see a still very young market operator not straying from time-tested market rules and being extremely disciplined and unemotional. His rewards came to him as his own personal account grew from $5,000 to $200,000 in 18 months. He used margin fully, and with mainly three very strong trades he grew his capital to a point where he would become one of the youngest ever to purchase a seat on the New York Stock Exchange. Being short Korvette, long Chrysler off the market bottom in October 1962 and long Syntex from June through December 1963 would turn out to be just the beginning of successes for a truly great stock operator. He would quit the firm of Hayden, Stone & Co. and venture out on his own, just as we saw Baruch and Wyckoff do when they experienced their first successes. O'Neil would start the firm of William O'Neil + Co., Incorporated, the next year in 1964, and it was then that he really decided to do some in-depth analysis of stock action. He bought an IBM mainframe computer, hired a few engineers, and then set out to build the first daily stock database.

This was also an active time for Jack Dreyfus. With the market moving higher and many stocks breaking out and registering new highs, he bought into these emerging leaders. Recall that he was a tape reader, similar to Livermore and Loeb, and he was a chart reader. This combination of stock price study and action was the leading reason that he was able to outperform all others during this time. Mighty rewards can be had by an avid observer with experience and a keen eye who sees the repeatable action in stock charts and takes the time to understand these patterns and history.

As 1964 began, the market just continued its upward trajectory. From 760 on January 2, the market marched almost straight upward to hit 831 on April 17, for a solid and quick 9% gain. After some choppy trading from April through August, but holding up well overall, the market sprinted higher throughout the fall, even despite the beginning of the Vietnam War, and it hit a high of 897 on November 18. It pulled back a bit over the next month and then finished the year at 879, good for a 15% gain and its second straight solid positive year. O'Neil continued to do well in the market, and he also concentrated on his new firm and the creation of his historic stock database. Gerald Loeb also did exceptionally well during this bullish uptrend. He was now later in his career, and his experience continued to pay off well for him. He also did well with many different companies and in many different industries. His best returns throughout his career came from the automobile industry (he traded Chrysler probably more than any other stock), railroads, motion pictures (he did exceptionally well with Warner Brothers numerous times), oil companies, and electronics. He wasn't right all the time, as no one is, but one of his biggest reasons for his success was implementing the same thing that rewarded O'Neil already a few times. That was to keep the losses small and hit it big with the winners, compounding those with margin and a pyramiding strategy. Loeb would say, "One of the most important factors with stock people is that they have more money on when they're right and less money on when they're wrong." It was here that he told of a friend of his who was a great market operator with a net worth of over $100 million. Loeb described his friend's approach to the market this way. He said this friend would have handwritten notes on oversized paper with many different columns on it, but he would only hold four stocks at a time. He would list details of the prices and transactions week by week. One particular time period looked like this:

Bought 10,000 shares one week — increased this holding to 40,000 by month-end.

Bought 10,000 shares of another stock — still held those 10,000 at month-end.

Bought 10,000 shares of another stock — sold them all by month-end — down in price.

Bought 10,000 shares of another stock — held only 5,000 by month-end.

These transactions show how this wealthy stock operator would sell off the stocks that quickly didn't work out and add to the ones that were still promising. Loeb stated that he would sell when the stock no longer did what he originally bought it for. This would be one of his "ruling reasons" for exiting a position, as all the great stock operators had valid reasons and rules, before they ever occurred, to exit their positions if things did not go as planned. Also, notice how Loeb's wealthy friend concentrated his holdings in only a handful of stocks — another great trait and skill of the greatest traders.

The first part of 1965 continued the upward trend of the market, now over two years in the making. A few minor pauses in February and March turned out to be normal breathers as the market surged higher in April and through the first half of May. Huge tax cuts in 1964 were passed affecting both the personal and corporate tax rates. These cuts were fueling much of the increase as business kept improving and both consumers and corporate America took full advantage of the reduced burden of tax. These middle years during the 1960s would also never experience a recession. The earlier recession that ended in February 1961 would not give way to another one until the very end of the decade. But the Vietnam War was looming, and American troops would first start moving in 1965. Jitters occurred again of course with this uncertain situation. The market took a rather steep fall in late May and June as it dropped nearly straight down by almost 12%. It would have been a scary time for active investors, and that's why a strict loss-cutting policy acts as insurance. No one knows how bad it can get, but with discipline one can at least protect themselves. The market bounced back somewhat in July, and it seemed to have steadied. The Vietnam War and concern was growing, and it was turning out to be an expensive campaign. Heavy demand for electronics and military applications would fuel a rally for some industries and stocks. We've seen this same type of action occur before when war breaks out. Here again is an example of the benefits of learning from history. These war issues just keep repeating themselves. Demand for certain war-related products picks up, and it benefits those firms that produce those products. Here in 1965 many aerospace and semiconductor industries were leading the market. At home the introduction of the first home VCR would fuel TV sales and provide a solid foundation for TV stocks.

The market bottomed in late June and then in July followed through on a classic upward confirmation, just as we have now seen numerous times, O'Neil bought Fairchild Camera as it blasted up through a classic cup-with-handle formation soon after the market turned around. (Please refer to O'Neil's publications for detailed explanations of the stock price patterns that will be mentioned throughout the remainder of this book.) He waited for the market to lead him in and latched on to a leader (one that paid off well for Darvas a few years back) as it broke through to the upside (just like Darvas and Dreyfus would do). Fairchild climbed 25% in a quick three weeks, and O'Neil knew what that meant. Strong stocks that rise that much and that fast should be held, as many times they turn out to be the biggest winners. Fairchild kept the tradition going, and in five weeks it was up 50% as the market surged higher. It did experience a sharp fall, but it never violated one of O'Neil's sell rules when he was up that big already in a stock. Polaroid was another huge winner in 1965, with big money funds powering this stock higher on heavy-volume days as the stock kept rising. This was one of Dreyfus's biggest winners, as he held on to this leading stock that would produce an 800% profit for his fund. The market put together one last sprint in 1965 to end the year at 976, up 11%, and recording its third straight double-digit gain for the Dow, which was only the third time in its history it had accomplished that feat up to that point.

The market moved slightly higher to begin 1966, and after three strong years of gains, it looked like it was getting tired during February. The Dow flattened out and had a hard time gaining ground. Also, many leading stocks, which had staged incredible runs already, began to look weary. In February there were many factors that were beginning to weigh on the markets, and astute traders like Loeb and O'Neil were watching for danger signals. American troops began heading into Vietnam at a steadier pace, causing much uncertainty, as Vietnam was becoming a very unpopular engagement. Civil unrest and social issues were increasing. Interest rates were continuing to rise, and inflation began to increase as well. From the first week in February 1966, in which the Dow pierced the 1,000 mark at 1,001.11 to the middle of March, the Dow sank nearly 100 points without bouncing back. At 915 on March 15 the Dow put together a suspect comeback as it rose to 961 by April 21. It wasn't a very convincing rally, and many leading stocks began to show classic topping signs that have been seen in many of the other preceding market cycle tops.

O'Neil Sees a Topping Market

Watching the market and especially how leading stocks act with price and volume action is the key to staying in sync and in rhythm with the market.

This pattern has occurred over and over again in the market, especially when the market has staged a very strong uptrend for an extended period of time and then other conditions begin to weigh on the future outlook of corporate profitability and the ability for sustained increases. Here are just a few of the early warning signals that occurred in 1966 that may have meant that the market was probably about to enter a major correction. O'Neil would notice these through his intense study and observation: He in fact was trying to get all his institutional clients to sell stocks and raise cash.

Boeing. From near $20 per share in January 1964, Boeing was the leader riding the increased demand for aircraft manufacturing. The stock moved up strong throughout 1964, 1965, and the very beginning of 1966 with no major breaks in its run. By April 1966 the stock had reached $91 per share, or up 350% in just over two years. After topping with the market and forming a classic head-and-shoulders pattern (see Figure 7-2 on p. 124), Boeing started to break down and sell off on heavy volume. Many who had gained strong returns on this leader were cashing in their profits. The stock had undercut previous levels of support (50-day moving-average line), and it was accompanied by heavy volume. The stock continued its downward trend with the market, and by October was trading under $50 per share, or 44% off from its top.

Motorola. Another leading stock that broke out in early 1965 near $70 per share, Motorola, would follow nearly the exact same pattern as Boeing. After a strong rise through 1965 and early 1966, it would top in April near $220 per share, or up 215%. Motorola topped in the same head-and-shoulders pattern as Boeing at about the same time. Volume increased noticeably on the downside, the stock broke through areas it had not violated before, the market's trend had changed, and other leading stocks were following the same pattern. By October 1966 Motorola was trading under $100 per share, down 55% off its high.

While many readers may point out that it's easy to pinpoint tops and bottoms and calculate percentage ups and downs when looking from a historical perspective, as compared to making the proper decisions in the market at

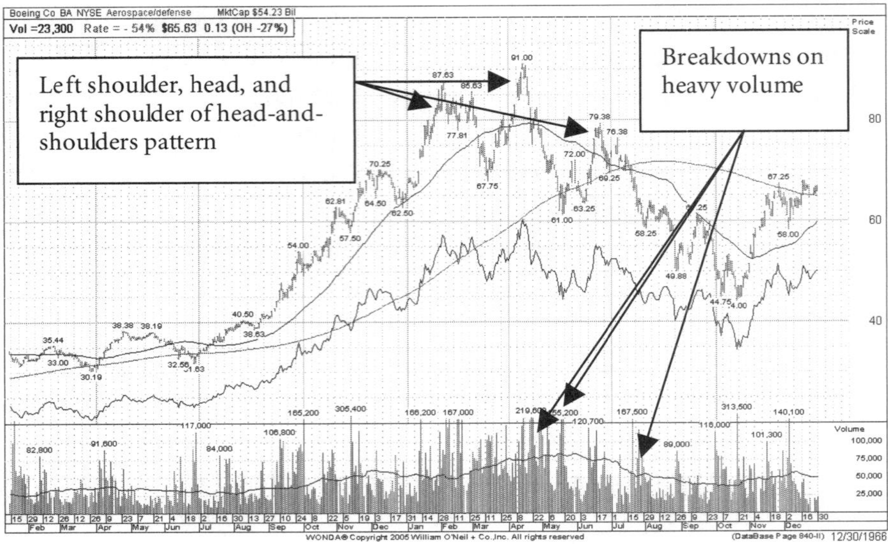

Figure 7-2 Boeing 1965–66 Daily Chart.
Source: © *William O'Neil + Co., Inc. All rights reserved. Reprinted with permission.*

that exact time, it is important to learn that many of these same patterns in the market and in stocks do occur over again. Also, many of these great traders understood this, and this is how they made decisions that led to their incredible gains. Nobody is ever going to be able to buy at the exact bottom and then sell at the exact top. But the best traders used signals like these to at least help increase the returns when the market would turn upward and then lessen the damage when things turned the other way as they did in early 1966.

By late April with many leaders topping like we saw earlier, the market would begin its downtrend as the direction of the market had clearly changed. There were other leaders topping as well, so it would have been somewhat clear to an experienced stock market operator that things had turned. Simmonds Precision, which was in the aerospace computer market and was one of the best-performing groups of 1965, also topped. It peaked in April 1966. It had blasted off from a classic cup-with-handle basing pattern in October 1965 at $24 per share and shot up an incredible 650% in just seven months when it peaked near $180 per share in April 1966. Xerox, which was one of the top leaders of the mid-1960s, topped a bit later, in 1966, as it clearly had started to lose momentum as well. It surged 700%

from March 1963 until its peak in June of 1966, while its earnings were growing a solid 32% per year.

With Vietnam growing to be more of a concern and the market topping out, the Dow headed lower throughout the spring, summer, and early fall. The Dow hit 735 in early October, down nearly 27% in just under six months. It was a major correction in such a short period of time, and those market breaks can cause monetary and emotional damage to a trader unless the trader heeds the market's signals and takes appropriate action. No one knows just how bad a correction can get, as we've seen a few already that were quite substantial. The best thing to do in a topping market is to sell stocks and go to cash or short former leaders if you're experienced enough. That's what the best traders did, and that's what the next great traders will do as we move forward. That is the strategy that all the individual market operators adhered to in order to profit and protect themselves from bad market periods.

Words of Wisdom from a Legend

While the market was falling, Gerald Loeb would discuss some of the more challenging aspects of battling the market for profits. It's important to listen to an experienced professional who succeeded in the market over many decades. Loeb would have been investing in the market for nearly 45 years by this time. One thing he cautioned about was that many leaders, but probably not all, may never come back in price when the market recovers. He pointed out such names as New York Central, Consolidated Edison and Western Union, all of which were crushed during the Crash of 1929 and never came back. Also, many of the hot new issues that helped lead the market in early 1961 were devastated in the 1962 market decline, some losing more than 90% of their value, as most never recovered. We'll see the same thing occur again as well, as market history continues to repeat itself. To this end, Loeb would continue to state how important flexibility is to a stock market participant. He said, "Only the professional market man knows how to move from stocks to cash or cash to stocks, or long to short or vice versa." He would add, "Only the pro knows how to go from certain groups to others such as gold which will rise when the market falls. But nobody can always pick tops and bottoms.

'Buy low and sell high' is one of Wall Street's rainbows that many chase and nobody completely catches." Loeb would also talk about selling, to which he would say, "Selling is the hardest decision to make." He didn't have certain fixed percentages, though he would almost always seem to be out before any position would fall greater than 10% from his buy point. He didn't like to lose more than three points if he was in a trade for the short term. Ten points would be a maximum if he was trading longer term. The trick, he would remind, would be to not lose good positions on temporary declines but to get out of the ones that continued to fall. The first key he would emphasize was to cut all losses short. On winning positions he held, if they fell by 10% off a strong peak, he would sell a portion of his holding. He would also sell more if the market was acting right but that particular stock was not following the upward trend of the market. Finally, he reiterated that he would use his ruling reasons — write down the reasons for the trade — before he entered the trade. This helped him control his emotions, which is needed due to the fact that the market is the most inexact science because public psychology is its greatest single shaping factor.

While the market was falling and looking for a possible bottom, many leaders that fell hard began slowing down their declines. The market also seemed to exhaust its selling, and by mid-October, even with the war worries present, there seemed to be a change in the trend of the market. Keen observation pays off if when things get so bad that they couldn't seem to get any better. Remember we've seen that occur many times in the past as well. After hitting a bottom on October 11, the market followed through in classic form on the seventh day of a new rally attempt. The S&P 500 surged 1.6% in heavy trading on October 18. On October 19, the Dow shot up 1.7% on higher volume confirming that the market was beginning to change its direction. One of the upbeat items helping propel the market forward was the promise of the personal computer and how it could impact growth. This new technology began to generate excitement. We'll also continue to see how the market begins to move up off of declines to begin new uptrends. Again, O'Neil's meticulous detail of how this has occurred is important information that will benefit all future market operators. This type of action has repeated itself over many decades, so it's important to note when these events occur. From mid-October's follow-through to mid-November the market moved higher and then bounced around in a choppy pattern until the end of 1966. It would have been a rough ride had one not heeded the markets and the leading stocks' cues earlier in the year. The Dow fell 19% that year, ending the three-year double-digit winning streak it had put together from 1963 through 1965.

The year 1967 started off with the market bolting higher at the start through to the end of January. From there the market would trade in a very choppy fashion, almost rising strong for one full month (March, April, July and September) and then falling back for a full month (February, May, June and August). The full-month increases, though, would be somewhat stronger than the declines allowing the market to rise over the first nine months of the year. But it was quite a choppy ride and was better suited for more short-term trading like Loeb would do. When the trend is not as clear, many of the great traders would either sit out until a clear trend was established or shorten up their trading time frames. Or, if you're extremely focused and observant, you can find the small majority of stocks that break through bases and rise steadily without flashing major selling signals. There are always a few of those in every market cycle, though they are extremely challenging to find and hold. This also means that strict loss-cutting would not change, but because the market is whipping up and down more often, trading may increase due to many trades triggering the loss-cutting policy in order to protect capital. To profit in those types of markets requires experience and judgment.

During this challenging market O'Neil noticed one stock, Control Data Systems, was acting well during one of the down days on the market. The Dow had dropped 12 points one spring day in 1967, and O'Neil noticed that Control Data had surged 3½ points that day on heavy volume. He bought it at $62 per share. He knew the company well, and its prospects and fundamentals were then top-notch. Also, computer-related groups were one of the strong ones at that time. Control Data later went on to reach $150 per share. A few of the other strong groups along with computers at that time were hotels and conglomerates. Hotels were reaping the follow-on benefit of the airline industry from the prior few years. As more people traveled there was more demand for hotels across the country. A few of the winners during that time were Hilton Hotels and Loews. The Loews stock would rise 819% from April 1967 to its peak in February 1969. Hilton began to franchise hotels, and its earnings growth took off. The stock soon followed as it broke out of a basing pattern on huge volume at just over $20 per share on March 1, 1967.

It quickly ran up 25% in just two weeks. From there it would nearly double as it approached $40 by the summer. During the choppier part of 1967, Hilton would stay contained in a flat base for nearly three months. It then broke through that base on October 5 and sprinted up another 20% within two weeks. Patient investors could have held on to this winner as it followed a fairly steady rise up until the latter part of 1968, where near its top it was up 560% from the proper buy point in March 1967. Holiday Inn was another lodging stock that did well. It broke out of a base in late 1966 and soared 151% to its peak. Other strong stocks at the time included General Cinema, Milton Bradley, MGM and Digital Equipment. All of them posted triple-digit gains from when the Dow bottomed in October 1966 to December 1968, which saw the Dow rise 35%.

Other groups and stocks that did well were smaller stocks again, like we saw in 1961. Many of the glamour growth stocks that did well in the early to middle part of the 1960s were not the leaders of this later uptrend. That may be why it was a bumpy ride as well; the leaders were more mixed and some were more speculative too. After a sharp drop in October and most of November the market moved back up to finish the year just over the 900 level. The Dow registered a solid 15% gain for the year, though it was somewhat of a rough ride.

The year 1968 would continue the choppy trading from the prior year. A steep drop in January, February and March brought the market down to the low 800s. Then just as quickly, it rose strong during the latter part of March and then through April to regain all that lost ground plus a few points as well. Vietnam and civil and social issues continued to cause concern for the country, and the market seemed to reflect the ups and downs. One group that did well in 1968 was mobile home stocks as demand began to increase for mobile homes. There will always be leading groups in a market cycle, and if you're experienced and disciplined enough, like many of the traders so far mentioned in this book, you could profit. One of the best in 1968 was Redman Industries, which was a mobile home manufacturer. Just about all mobile home stocks soared during this time, and Redman broke out of a cup-with-handle base in March 1968 near $12 per share. The stock would rocket up nearly 900% by December when it hit $110 per share. O'Neil though missed this one. He did buy it properly when it broke out, but due to the shaky market, he sold out and took a small loss. He therefore missed its big move, but he did remember this stock and its action. Redman created a 12-week ascending base pattern after it initially took off from its original base, and it then would blast off from there and gain 503% off the ascending base (an ascending base has three sharp pullbacks in price) en route to its huge gain. O'Neil, as mentioned, would remember this same pattern nearly 30 years later when he was watching America Online (AOL) in the late 1990s. He scored a huge gain on that stock as he remembered Redman, and he held fast to AOL, as it had three price pullbacks, instead of selling out. Here again we see O'Neil using prior history to learn from in order to profit in the future. These lessons are critical if one is to score big gains in the stock market.

A flatter pattern to the market took place from May through the early part of July. Then the market fell back again, and by early August the Dow was at 863. The whipsawing continued as the market shot nearly straight up from early August to the third week of October. A slight dip in early November led to a rally the last two weeks of November as the market peaked on December 2 at 994. Activity was picking up as small-cap issues again were out front leading the market. This was beginning to look a lot like the 1961–62 market period. Trading volume was increasing, as the average daily trading volume in 1968 would finally exceed the 1929 level for the first time.

After the market peaked on December 2, many warning signs began to show up. Just like we've seen many other times, leading stocks stalled and selling hit the market with volume increasing. The Vietnam War was becoming a very expensive campaign, and the government levied a 10% income tax surcharge to help pay for the war. The war was having an effect on inflation too as the consumer price index (CPI) began climbing to levels not seen in nearly 20 years. As the market peaked, the S&P 500 began to show signs of topping that we've seen before. This meant that institutions were unloading shares. Starting on December 2, the S&P 500 registered five days of selling on heavy volume and churning (no price progress but heavy volume) in a seven-day stretch. By late December the selling intensified, and the S&P 500 would cut through its 50-day moving average, a sign of technical support when the average stays above this line. The Dow ended the year at 936, or up 4% for the year, but there was clear selling pressure as the market entered 1969.

With inflation continuing to rise, much social unrest due to the war and civil rights issues, and the market showing topping signals late in 1968, it looked like a dangerous market when January 1969 rolled around. The Dow slid during the first week of the year and then shot back up to its starting point of the year by mid-February. From there it would be more whipsaw trading as the index fell hard in late February and then traded choppy until it rose higher by mid-May. But there were more signs of a teetering market. Many smaller issues, which had led much of this run, were beginning to break down, reminding some of the 1962 market decline. By this time in May, the market also began to show heavier selling, as down days started to dwarf up days and volume signs were clearly indicating that mutual funds and other big traders were selling stocks.

During May, O'Neil's attention to the market was clearly signaling to him that selling had overtaken buying in the market. He was aggressively trying to get his institutional clients to sell stocks and raise cash. We've now seen O'Neil in more than a few instances following what the market was actually doing and responding to it. And his experience now was also proof enough that he knew what proper disciplines and actions were required. These signals have always occurred, and we'll see him do this again as the decades move forward. Needless to say, he was out of the market in mid-1969 and avoided most of the damage that was to come. The market headed sharply lower until late July. From there choppy trading led to a feeble rally attempt in October, but the market crumbled again and finished the year and decade at 806. It was a losing year for the Dow, which ended 1969 down 15%. The 1960s basically started off strong and were mostly recession-free. Unemployment remained low, and inflation was well contained for most of the decade. The Vietnam War then began to weigh on the market as inflation rose steadily and other social issues raised concerns. Many astute traders profited handsomely in the first half of the decade (Loeb and O'Neil), and they also reacted to the market's action when it was time to sell and raise cash in order to protect most of their hard-earned profits.

8

Most Get Whipped Up and Down Except the Best (1970–79)

William J. O'Neil Knew That Flexibility Was One of the Keys to Success

The new decade of the 1970s didn't start off so well for the economy and the stock market. A slowing down in business conditions that ushered in a recession just as the 1960s were ending greeted the new century and its president — Richard Nixon. The unemployment rate would begin rising; it had actually fallen in a tapering fashion throughout much of the 1960s. Also, American troops would begin marching into Cambodia, which just kept raising antiwar sentiments and concerns about this very unpopular and expensive (in terms of both dollars and, much more importantly, lives lost) campaign. Interest rates were also moving higher. The Dow basically slid

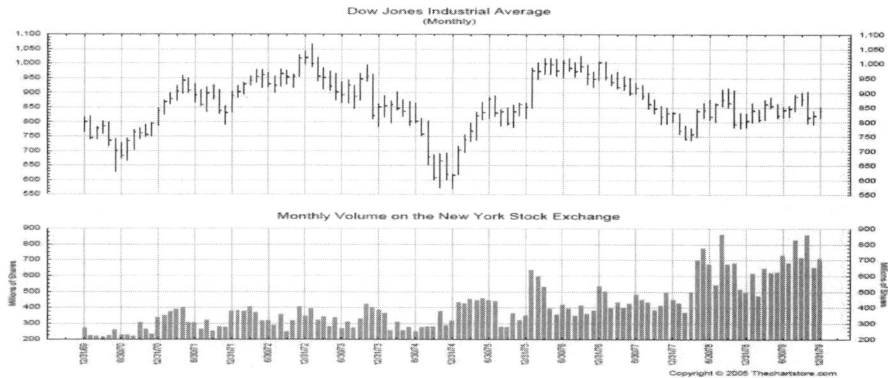

Figure 8-1 The Dow Jones Industrial Average 1970–79.
Source: *www.thechartstore.com.*

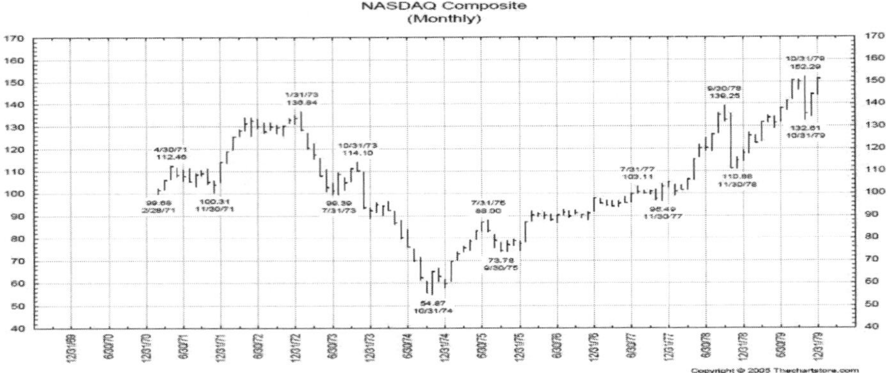

Figure 8-2 NASDAQ Composite Average 1971–79.
Source: *www.thechartstore.com.*

straight down during January. After a flat February, the market was somewhat choppy through March. Many leading stocks were still sliding downward, and some of the best performers of the prior run-up had already started showing signs of cracking as there was a clear lack of buying power in the market to support these former leaders. A few of them were:

Radioshack Corp. A huge winner in the late 1960s. It started topping and heading lower in early 1970 on heavy volume.

Hilton Hotels. Another huge winner mentioned earlier from the mid to late 1960s. It started breaking key support areas in early 1970 that it had never violated during its huge run-up, also on huge volume. The stock fell from near $60 to under $30 by the summer of 1970.

Control Data Corp. Another former big winner mentioned earlier. This stock made a huge run-up in the mid to late 1960s that William J. O'Neil did well with. It however flattened out from June 1968 to the end of 1969 at near $150 per share. It really began to break down in early 1970, undercutting key support areas it had held up during its run. By the summer of 1970, it was down to $30 per share, or one-fifth of its high.

These examples prove that it's critical to keep watching even the best stocks that produced the best returns at some prior time. O'Neil made great profits on some of these stocks, but he also knew how to sell them correctly when they broke down so he would retain his previous profits made. Great stock traders don't ride their gains all the way back down — they listen to the action of the market and their holdings, and they act appropriately. They try to master the art of holding on long enough to big winners in order to get the most of their gain but also try to sell them on their way up after a prolonged advance. This skill comes from many years of experience in the market. They also know that most stocks follow the market (since they together make up the market), and they reduce their holdings when the market turns and begins to trend in the other direction. Former leaders that begin to break key support areas, especially when the general market starts to experience heavy selling, are actually the best stocks to possibly become excellent opportunities for taking short positions and profiting when the market is clearly headed in a downtrend. We saw that this was the case in earlier periods, when Livermore, Baruch and Wyckoff would take short positions when the markets of their eras had topped and started downward. They all did well on the short side by shorting the former big winners that led the prior uptrends in the market. Many of the stocks I will mention that follow this pattern are shown as examples in detail in O'Neil's recent book "How to Make Money Selling Stocks Short."

Selling really picked up during April and May, and by May 26 the Dow had already fallen 23% for the year. It was quite a panic scene on the street as many started laying blame on reasons why the market fell so far so fast. Some blamed performance fund managers, while others pointed to higher interest rates as corporate bond rates were nearing 9% and 10%. Again, whatever the reasons, and there were plenty back in early 1970, many investors just didn't like what they saw as they looked ahead regarding solid corporate performance prospects, with so many uncertainties hanging over the markets. Selling is what many big traders were doing, and when selling takes over and the trend is clearly heading down, the best thing to do is either get out of the way by going to cash or to start selling short.

As inflation and interest rates were rising, stocks began to be seen as not quite the hedge against inflation they used to be. With inflation growing steadily, it was thought that the Federal Reserve would keep increasing interest rates in order to try and head off inflation. With rates rising, many would view alternative interest-rate-paying investments as better hedges against inflation than stocks. From June through August the market began to recover from its early sell-off. It was another choppy ride, but the market finally settled down in the fall, as the Dow traded flat until mid-November. During these choppy market environments there are always a few opportunities available, but it takes an experienced eye and extreme discipline. O'Neil would notice one exceptionally strong stock in 1970, which was Levitz Furniture. Levitz had introduced a new shopping concept as it related to furniture. Their strategy was to build giant warehouse discount-furniture outlets. The idea caught on, and the company reaped the benefits to its bottom line. Revenues and profits would soar, and the stock would reflect this hot new concept. Levitz would turn out to be one of the best performers in early 1970, as its stock price surged 660% from its correct buy point to its peak in 1971. We'll see another retailing concept similar to this in the 1980s relating to home improvement. Home Depot, as we'll see, would turn in a stock price performance that would rank with the very best ever. It pays to know these superstars from the past, and some shrewd market operators who made it big with Levitz would no doubt see the similarities with Home Depot just a decade further down the road. Other strong stocks coming up off a bottom in the market during the spring of 1970 included Disney, Sony, Winnebago, Amerada Hess and McDonald's. All of these would record triple-digit gains as the market moved generally higher until January 1973.

The Dow would actually sprint toward the finish in 1970 as it shot up nearly 100 points during the final six weeks of the year. As it had done numerous times before, the market seemed to have anticipated better times ahead. The recession that began at the end of 1969 would officially end in November 1970 as business conditions began picking up. A few new groups also started to exhibit some strength just prior to this renewed strength in the market during the latter part of the year. Building-sector stocks became hot, especially stocks within the mobile home group again. By the middle of August many groups in related industries to the building sector began making their initial moves to the upside. Masco, which hailed from the plumbing group; Kaufman & Broad, a homebuilder; Scotty's Home Builders, a materials retailer; and MGIC, a mortgage insurer, all became leaders and stayed in leadership positions until mid-February 1971. It should be noted that many of the traditional home-building stocks did not participate in this leadership move. Instead, the real price leaders came from more specialized or related groups. Also, the mobile home stocks became the real price gainers during this time, so one would have had to do one's homework and be alert to the fact that certain specific stocks were standing out while others were not. It was still a choppy market in the early 1970s, and having a keen eye for strength, like O'Neil exhibited, would have allowed opportunities for the observant and serious market operator. As for the market, the Dow ended up closing the year at 848, good for a 4% gain and quite impressive considering it had fallen so quickly early on. By the end of the year the trend had definitely changed, and it looked as if the market had some strong momentum behind it.

The market was in a buying mood as 1971 began. The Dow moved up steadily higher during the first six weeks of the new year to hit almost the 900 level by mid-February. On Feb. 5, 1971, the Nasdaq Composite average was introduced and began tracking at the 100 level. This composite would include a broad range of younger companies that would trade not on the New York Stock Exchange but rather on the over-the-counter market. It was actually the automated quote system of the NASD, rather than the specialist and floor traders that worked the New York Stock Exchange. This new technology in quoting stock prices would be viewed as more efficient and fair to many who would participate in the markets. The idea was to also better capture the activity of the newer and more innovative companies that were being created at the time. The listing requirements for firms to trade on the Nasdaq were not as stringent as for the NYSE, and so younger companies would list their shares on this new and innovative marketplace.

Interest rates actually fell back a bit in early 1971, as the Fed had eased off on its tight monetary policy, mostly in response to the Penn Central Railroad bankruptcy in 1970, and gross domestic product (GDP) improved greatly. The market responded favorably to these economic occurrences for the time being. The Dow surged right from the start, and it hit 958 by the end of April, up from 826 at the beginning of the year, or a strong 16% in only four months. The newly introduced Nasdaq average would follow suit, moving up from its inception level of 100 in early February to hit 112 by the end of April. But there seemed to be just too many outside factors that created many uncertainties for possible unfavorable business conditions in the future. High inflation mostly caused by the Vietnam War and a tight monetary policy continued. The other major issue facing the U.S. economy was the outside influence of many international markets. The dollar was beginning to decline, and many foreign influences would soon hold sway over the U.S. economy, which was really the first time in history that these outside influences would have such an impact on our domestic economy. Budget deficits were also rising, just adding to the many factors that seemed out of place when trying to supply a steady growing and healthy economy. The factors were all heading in the wrong direction. The market, sensing many of these uncertainties, fell from May through July. On August 15, with the Dow having given up all the gains it had made during the first four months of the year, President Nixon delivered his message to the public about ways to turn things around. He announced wage and price controls to fight spiraling inflation. He then stated that he would devalue the dollar by cutting its convertibility to gold. The next day the markets rallied on the news as the Dow surged 32 points on 31 million shares, a record high in trading volume. It would turn out to be a short-lived rally, as many foreign investors would soon thereafter begin selling off the dollar.

As the wage and price controls began to take effect many tariffs were also put in place. The dollar continued to weaken, and the stock market fell nearly straight down from early October until late November as the Dow lost over 100 points in just six weeks. But then almost just as quickly the market turned around and sprinted higher. Even though there were many factors that looked to spook the market as mentioned previously, the economy was still growing, and the CPI was actually falling. It was clearly turning out to be a volatile battle between the bears and the bulls. The Dow would quickly regain the 100 points it had just lost in a little over a month, actually faster than it had lost them during the prior few months. The Dow would end the year 1971 at 890, or up 6%, though it was a whipsaw ride. The Nasdaq would end its first year at 114, or up even greater than the Dow, as it surged 14% from just November 23 to the last day of the year.

The momentum from the end of 1971 carried over into the early part of 1972. While the Dow shot up nearly 11% in the first 3½ months of the new year, the Nasdaq climbed over 18% during the same stretch. Xerox and Polaroid were just two of the biggest gainers and leaders that stepped out front. The last two weeks of April experienced a sharp pullback on both indexes, but a rebound during May recovered those losses. These market periods that whipsaw back and forth can become extremely frustrating. Remember that when a clear trend is not established, it's better to either sit the market out or trade in shorter time frames, like Loeb and Wyckoff would do. That takes extreme discipline and a keen experienced eye to the market. With many uncertainties whipping the market up and down most find it best to just sit it out until a clearer direction establishes itself. The choppiness was not quite over yet, as trends usually persist for many months or longer. A sharp drop occurred in June as the Watergate break-in made national news. That was just one more item to add to the fire that was already simmering. After hitting 900 on the Dow in mid-July, the market then traded in another choppy pattern until mid-October.

A few positives were occurring in the economy near this time. The CPI was falling back, which eased a few concerns. Also, the unemployment rate seemed to level off instead of worsening. From mid-October to mid-December the Dow surged higher, broke through the 1,000 barrier and rose 13% to hit 1,042 on December 12. The Nasdaq lagged as it rose nearly 8% over the same time frame. A sharp pullback for both and then a sprint near the end left the Dow higher by year-end, good for a 15% gain and its third straight positive return despite a very choppy market. The Nasdaq also finished higher, up 17% in its first full year of activity.

While the end of 1972 looked like a new uptrend had been set in place and the 1,000 barrier on the Dow had been broken and left behind, more negatives were soon about to hit the market. Many topping signals began creeping up in some of these leaders just as we've seen many times before. Recall that way back in the late 1920s was when Gerald Loeb saw these same topping actions among leading stocks. Price action just keeps repeating itself, and that is the main reason why he cashed out of the market well in advance before the real damage hit the market in late October of 1929. As for 1973, there was heavy volume on down days in the market and among leading stocks and a slowdown of the upward momentum was becoming clearer. A few of the leaders during that time that were showing these classic signals were:

Walt Disney Company. This stock topped right near the first of the year in 1973 near $120 per share. New highs on low volume were then followed by the highest weekly volume in over a year as the stock broke its 50-day moving average. By December 1973, Disney had fallen to under $45 per share.

Kaufman & Broad, Inc. Mentioned earlier as a strong leader in the early part of the 1970s it struggled to make new highs during the latter half of 1972, and then in early 1973 the selling really picked up. Heavy volume reigned as the stock fell from near $22 to near $5 per share by the end of 1973.

Also in early 1973, OPEC announced a sharp rise in the price of oil. With the dollar still in decline from late 1972, oil would double in price very quickly. This would be a huge hit to the already wobbling American economy. The market reacted by falling in a stair-step fashion on the Dow and an even steeper similar pattern on the Nasdaq, which can be seen clearly in Figures 8-1 and 8-2 on pp. 131 and 132. Remember many times we've seen charts of healthy markets rising in a positive stair-step pattern. During those strong markets the market would rise up and then pull back mildly in smaller steps to consolidate its gains. This case was clearly the opposite. Steep falls would be followed by mild and weak upward rally attempts. This is something the reader definitely needs to be aware of as these patterns clearly repeat themselves as well. In early 1973 it was selling time, and the market and the leading stocks were screaming that loud and clear.

The new-issue market also seemed to dry up totally, which is always a bad sign for the stock market, as many companies that have planned offerings will usually delay them if market conditions don't seem ripe enough. With inflation already a major concern, the higher oil prices would just add fuel to the fire. The recently retreating CPI would not head down much longer. A look at the bigger picture at this time revealed a bleak future ahead. High oil prices, high interest rates, rising inflation, a falling dollar, budget deficits, wage and price controls in place, the Vietnam War still raging even though peace pacts were near, and a possible presidential scandal taking place all made for a lot of uncertainties. There were however a few safe spots in the stock market for the brave and experienced. Because of oil's higher price, oil producers would benefit from the escalating price of the commodity. A few companies in this industry would go on to score huge stock price gains. Houston Oil & Gas was one of them. From late 1972 through 1973, its stock would rise 968% in 61 weeks. Those who learned from history would have seen a parallel to the market in 2003 and 2004. Higher oil prices led many oil service and oil producer stocks to triple-digit gains in the 2004 market, while the general market languished for the most part.

The market began a steep stair-step pattern to the downside, one we've seen a few times in the past already. Steep declines on heavy volume would be weakly supported by mild short-lived rallies on weaker volume. This classic action almost always results in major corrections. In February 1973 the gold group would move up into one of the top-performing groups in the market. Gold stocks have historically been a weak defensive group that tends to move in the opposite direction of the general market. This was an observation that Gerald Loeb would also look for, and he mentioned that the very flexible trader would rotate into gold stocks when the general market would begin a downturn. Silver issues, in February 1973, also began moving up with the gold stocks as the market was heading lower. From January through July the market followed a declining pattern and the Dow lost nearly 20%. The Nasdaq featuring its smaller-cap issues declined nearly 27% in just six months. Many leading stocks were cracking and had broken major support areas. Some of the hottest groups from the prior few years, which included mobile home and other building-related stocks, began topping to end their strong runs. Kaufman & Broad, a building stock, began to weaken in February 1973 along with MGIC, a mortgage insurer, which had a great run in the first years of the 1970s. We've seen this play out before. When the strongest leaders of the prior uptrend start breaking down and no other new leaders, except for maybe just a few defensive groups, come to the fore, the market is in for a major correction. It just cannot sustain an upward trend with no buying power coming in from new leadership. The economic and political shocks of the times were really starting to weigh heavily on the stock market.

During July and August the market bounced up and down in a choppy fashion, but it at least seemed as if the selling had subsided for the time being. September actually witnessed a rally, but it would be short-lived as on Oct. 6, 1973, a coalition of Arab states suddenly attacked Israel. In order to weaken the American support for Israel during this time, OPEC would impose an embargo on oil to the U.S. This would be just one more major hit to the current fragile American economy at the time. The embargo would kick off a severe energy crisis that would drop the economy into recession, cause long lines at the gas pumps, and further weaken prospects for an improved economic future. Near the end of October the market dove nearly straight down. The Dow would lose over 20% in just about five weeks, and the economy would begin its longest recession in nearly 40 years starting in November. As oil prices surged due to the embargo, they just added pressure to the rising interest rates already in place. Inflation would now begin to spiral upward. When the year finally ended, the Dow would close down nearly 17% for the year, but the Nasdaq would take the hardest hit as it lost 31% in only its second full year.

The year 1974 at least started off lacking the intense selling that ended 1973, though the Dow dropped nearly 100 points from January through mid-February. Then just as quickly it added those 100 points back in about four weeks. The choppy and bumpy ride continued. From there, though, the peak of the market for 1974 would hit in mid-March as another steep drop occurred from mid-March through the end of May. This was another one of those stair-step declines we've seen before. When the down days continue to outnumber the up days and those down days occur with heavier volume to the downside, the market keeps repeating that pattern of a downward trend. Adding to the negatives was the fact that oil prices had already doubled from October 1973 to January 1974, interest rates kept rising, and production was falling. Adding fuel to the fire was that the unemployment rate was rising as well. Leading stocks were hard to find during this time, and one of the leading groups became coal industry stocks. Again we see a defensive group with positive returns, another sign of the continued weakness in the overall market. By early spring it was clear by the market's action and that of the former leading stocks that things were getting worse. Here again are a few examples of prior leaders breaking major support lines on heavy selling. These are also listed in O'Neil's book "How to Make Money Selling Stocks Short," as many of them created the classic topping chart pattern of a head-and-shoulders top. These examples should be studied well as we'll see many more former leaders fall hard in future markets that showed the same topping signals and chart patterns, as these did in 1974:

Rite Aid Corp. While this stock fell hard during 1973 after being a leader in the early 1970s, it really fell apart in 1974 after forming a head-and-shoulders top. When former leaders can't get back up and continue falling hard, it's a bad market environment. From near $55 in

March 1973, it fell with the market to hit $16 by the end of 1973. In 1974 it continued its fall, and by the spring of 1974 it was trading under $5 per share.

Clorox Co. This prior leader fell during 1973 from a peak near $50 in January 1973 to near $15 by January 1974 as it formed a classic head-and-shoulders formation. From there it collapsed to under $6 by December 1974 on heavy volume all the way down.

Coca-Cola Co. After a steady climb to near $150 per share by late 1972 and then holding within a fairly tight trading range during the brutal decline of 1973 in the $130 to $150 range, Coke finally fizzled with the market in 1974, proving that even some of the bluest of the blue chips eventually fall when markets sell off hard. Near the end of 1973 Coke was selling off as high weekly volume escalated. By early 1974, Coke was down to near $110. The selling really hit home in late summer and fall of 1974 as institutions were unloading the stock. By year-end 1974 Coke was trading near $50 per share. This example alone should be a lesson to all that believing any stock to be immune to declines due to its reputation no matter what is happening in the market is a dangerous mind-set. We've seen others in prior market periods (RCA, Xerox, etc.), and we'll see others in future cycles (Cisco, Lucent, etc.) that were thought to be immovable on the downside prove to be just like all other stocks — they tend to move with the market, even if they sometimes seem to delay the inevitable. As O'Neil has said many times, "… when they raid the house, they usually get them all."

By the beginning of June the Nasdaq had already slid nearly 14% since the start of the year and the Dow had dropped nearly 11%. With the market still very weak and economic conditions continuing to deteriorate, William O'Neil + Co., Incorporated, put Xerox, which had been one of the most reliable and stable leaders of the market, on its institutional sell list at $115 per share. Many were amazed that his firm was recommending a sell on one of the most popular stocks of that era. But O'Neil had already learned from experience that when the market is in a serious selling mode that even the best stocks eventually fall and follow the market's lead, as we just saw with Coca-Cola. O'Neil had been selling many stocks, and his firm was trying to get larger institutions to see just how bad the market was getting. Needless to say, Xerox soon thereafter collapsed along with the rest of the market. This goes to show how an experienced and disciplined trader can avoid many bad market periods, which always arise. O'Neil would follow his market-tested trading rules. His strict loss-cutting rules kicked him out of bad markets early on as he would avoid at least part of the large losses sustained by many who refused to sell their holdings when conditions would weaken. His strict buy rules would allow him into the market only when accumulation by big traders would drive up strong fundamentally sound stocks through proper buy points after a stock had formed a sound basing pattern. These basing patterns have repeated themselves over time, and he would be patient to wait for just those right times. His discipline and intense study allowed O'Neil to not be whipped around during choppy markets as much as others. Though he did still make plenty of mistakes, as all the best traders did, he would limit them to numerous small losses and then step back and away from the market when it was wise to do so.

After a short bounce back in early June, it would be all downhill from there. For the next four months the market would create a very steep stair-step decline pattern that would send the Dow down under the 600 level or 36% lower than where it started the year. The Nasdaq would fall to the low 50s, or down nearly 43% in just 10 months. Adding to the selling pressure during this time was the untimely resignation of President Nixon on August 9 due to the Watergate investigation. The collapse of Franklin National Bank in October didn't help things much either. Franklin National was the 20th largest banking institution at the time, and it would be the biggest banking failure up to that point.

With economic conditions worsening, uncertainty from foreign affairs and even our own internal political problems mounting, the market was buckling under the current state of affairs and the many problems that had led up to that point. The steep drop in 1973 was something to heed, as the market, with its ability to look forward, always seems to sense when there's trouble ahead. Business conditions just couldn't withstand the many negatives that were occurring. As a result real GNP would decline in four successive quarters in 1974 just worsening the current recession. Consumer buying was drying up as unemployment nearly doubled from 1973 levels. By 1975 the unemployment rate would reach 9%. As a result of high inflation and weakened consumer demand, inventories grew to very high levels. For the prior few years, as inflation kept increasing, many companies would stock up on inventories fearing they would have to pay higher prices in the future to restock goods as continued increasing inflation rates were expected. When the recession hit and unemployment rose, and then consumer demand waned, many companies were now stuck with high inventory levels. At this point in October 1974 with the S&P 500 down 50% since January 1973, the Dow down 46% during the same span, and the Nasdaq falling 60%, many members of the NYSE were predicting that the stock market would not survive as a viable institution. Many former leading stocks crashed 70% or more. We've seen that happen before, and we'll see it again. If only one could remember some of these extreme events in the stock market and understand that they can and will happen again in the future, then maybe more people in the future can protect more of their hard-earned money.

O'Neil at this time was visiting many money management firms, and he remarked that he never saw so many scared and worried expressions. While O'Neil had been trying to protect his portfolios, many others felt the world was about to end. And as we've seen many times before, when many give up and give in, the bottom may be just around the corner. As many indexes hit lows in early October, the S&P 500 would also hit a low on October 4. Three sessions later on October 9 that index would bolt up 4.6% on heavy volume. The very next session it climbed another 2.9% on the heaviest volume in more than a year. These strong index price gains on very heavy volume indicated that the selling had exhausted itself and that a new trend in direction was beginning.

It many times takes courage to buy when things have looked so bad for some time. But O'Neil's study and analysis of past market bottoms over many decades shows how the market behaves and acts with its price and volume interrelationship. These recent powerful advances on the broadest index gave at least some comfort that maybe the worst had finally passed. A rally in the markets occurred off this bottom and would last for five weeks until mid-November. There was still one more scare left though as the indexes came back down from mid-November through the first part of December. The Dow actually undercut its low in early October, but the broader Nasdaq and S&P 500 did not. They both actually rebounded during the last week of the year. It was still a rough year for the markets as the Dow declined nearly 28% for the year and the Nasdaq fell 35%, its second straight year of over 30% declines. It would be the worst bear market since the Great Crash of the 1920s and early 1930s. It was also in December that the market rebounded and moved higher off its sell-off on the seventh day of its attempted rally on huge volume. This would be the second confirmation of a bottoming market within a few months. Some leaders began breaking out of basing patterns at that time. Tandy, Northrop and United Technologies all moved up and scored triple-digit gains from that point, as the Dow would increase 80% in less than two years.

As 1975 began, a few things started to change that would bring more confidence to the markets. The Federal Reserve began to ease up on its tight monetary policy in early 1975. Bank strains due to failures, a struggling economy, and high unemployment had finally gotten the attention of the Fed to ease up on rates. In January, banks lowered their prime rates four times. The market liked this action, and the Dow shot up 14% that month alone, which was the largest monthly increase in 35 years. Cyclicals and turnaround stocks began to lead the market, just like they had in the 1963–65 market that was coming off the severe decline of 1962. They also led in the 1953–55 market rally. Newly enacted legislation regarding retirement accounts drove more participants to the market indirectly through the usage of various saving and retirement accounts.

As the market kept moving up in early 1975 the economy began to strengthen. Earnings per share for the Dow stocks had declined 24% in 1974, so comparisons to the prior year were showing a move up for many. And being consistent with history, the market showed strength before the recession officially ended, which happened in March. It ended up being a long recession for its time, and its effects were severe. Industrial production declined 15% from 1973 to 1975, which was the worst performance since World War II. Inflation and recessions together can cause severe damage to an economy. Aggressive inventory reductions along with interest rate decreases would begin to bring inflation down. Inflation still rose 1.5% during the first three months of 1975, but that was a sharp reduction from the 2.6% increase from the last three months of 1974. But two other events would really propel the market higher. The Vietnam War ended in the spring, and in March the government passed a $22.8 trillion tax cut. Small-cap stocks then started to lead the market as well. By spring the Fed started to ease up on interest rates. This positive move was welcomed, as the discount rate was 8% in November 1974, still historically high. The market rose in early 1975 off the bottom of the 1974 bear market. A key to remember for the future was that Bernard Baruch made most of his fortunes in the stock market during periods just like this. Recall that he would wait for those times when the market would turn around to the upside after a prolonged downtrend. In fact, the market in 1975 was following the exact same pattern that the market followed in 1907 and 1908 right after the Rich Man's Panic — just another example of how the market's cyclical rotation repeats itself. O'Neil did the same thing in 1962, when he pyramided Chrysler, which turned out to be a big winner for him as it came up off the bottom of the bear market, when a new uptrend was confirmed during that market period. Big progress is made buying new market leaders as a key index has a volume follow-through day — usually on the fourth to seventh day of a turnaround rally.

As the market kept moving higher many stocks broke out front to lead the market. One group that did exceptionally well was coal producers. Because the price for oil was still high, many firms would begin to look at and invest in alternative forms of energy. Mutual funds and other big traders would pile money into these stocks, and this is where astute investors should have had their focus. O'Neil was right there seeing that this industry was becoming one of the standout performers. Some of the stocks within that group would go on to rack up impressive gains. Falcon Seaboard was one of the strongest, surging 997% in three years after it broke out of a basing pattern. Elgin National was another leader as it gained 371% in just over one year, and Carbon Industries rallied 283% in fewer than just two years from its breakout. These returns show just how large the gains can be if one buys at the right time and has the patience to ride out a stock until it flashes price and volume warning signs that it's about to top and turn lower. It is important to learn how to sell leaders correctly, because when they turn, which is usually with the market, they tend to fall the hardest as well. If one is very experienced and alert, these are usually the best candidates to make big money on the short side of the market when a major correction sets in. By the early summer of 1975 the Dow and the Nasdaq had both increased over 40% for the year. In July the prime rate was actually raised in two steps to 7½%. This along with some profit taking and consolidating of the huge gains already made slowed the market down. A sharp drop from mid-July to mid-August pulled the averages back.

From October though the end of the year the market traded in a mostly choppy fashion, and the trading range was fairly tight. Other groups that began to spring up included catalog showroom retail stocks. Service Merchandise was the standout performer in this leading group. Its stock would rocket 586% from its breakout in September 1975 to September 1978. Best Products would gain 467% during the approximate same time. Oil stocks also did well along with auto stocks. General Motors nearly doubled in 1975 from $29 to $59 per share. The Dow would rise 38% for the year, its best showing since 1954, and ended its two-year severe decline. The Nasdaq rose 23% for the year.

The year 1976 started off with a flurry of buying. The Dow shot up 16% in January alone. Oil stocks continued to rise, and health care stocks started to lead as well, especially hospital and nursing home issues. But persistent inflation and unemployment would still be major challenges for the market. From February through the beginning of summer the markets traded in a choppy tight trading range making basically no progress even though the Dow would pierce the 1,000 level several times and come back below it over the next several months. It had been nearly three years since the Dow had seen this level. As always, there were some opportunities for the experienced eye. O'Neil, in June 1976, made a presentation to Fidelity Research and Management where he recommended Sea Containers. The company possessed solid fundamentals as quarterly net income had just soared 192%, and it sported a 54% earnings growth rate. The stock broke out of a classic cup-with-handle basing pattern in mid-1976 at $22.50 per share. It would soar 554% in the next two years even despite a very tough market ahead. As the summer months wore on, heavy spending for oil along with continued high inflation created an environment called "stagflation," which signifies high unemployment along with high inflation.

By late September the markets were wobbling a bit and heavy volume on down days began to show up. Experienced market operators know what that means, and soon enough the market pulled back fairly quickly. The Dow lost over 100 points, or 11%, from September 22 to November 10. However, the Nasdaq only lost a little over 5% over the same span. While many of the bigger blue chips fell hard, some of the smaller and faster-growing stocks held up better. One example was Waste Management. Its group also did well in 1976, and in September, Waste Management broke out of a cup-with-handle pattern and soared 1,100% in just over one year. The markets made a sprint to the finish in 1976 as the Dow regained most of its prior loss, and it ended up finishing the year just over the 1,000 level. The Dow registered an 18% gain for the year, with all of it made in the very first part of the year. The Nasdaq however turned in a much better performance, as it gained 26% for the year and actually finished at its high for the year.

The beginning of 1977 did not start where the end of 1976 had left off. Both the Dow and the Nasdaq started off trading lower. The S&P 500 actually produced three straight sessions of losses on heavy volume starting on January 3. Then on January 11, the market fell hard again on heavy trade. That marked four heavy selling days out of seven trading days. We've seen that type of heavy selling before, and it almost always leads to a change in trend in the market. The Dow fell nearly straight down from 1,007 at the start of the year to 926 by February 11. The Nasdaq continued to outperform; it still traded lower, but it followed a choppier pattern. From mid-February to June both indexes traded with a choppy pattern and with a slight declining downward trend. The economy was still teetering, and inflation and interest rates remained high. But in the summer a divergence was beginning to show up. Those experts who study the market closely would have seen this. We know O'Neil did. As the Dow continued to trade lower it hit 892 on the last day of May 1977. This would put the index at a loss for the year of 11%. The Nasdaq however, which had been outperforming the Dow for quite some time now, was at 95 on the last day of May, or down only 2%. This was telling investors that small-cap stocks were continuing to outperform large-cap blue chips. By the end of June, the Nasdaq had actually risen past the level it had started the year at. The Dow however continued to trade in a choppy pattern and slightly downward. By the third week of July the Dow was down 8% for the year, but the Nasdaq was up 6%. One of the smaller stocks that was beginning to show some strength was Pic'N Save. In July, O'Neil was recommending this new innovative stock to institutions. None of them would buy it, mostly because it had traded only 700 shares a day on average at that point. But it possessed strong fundamentals and its innovative concept of retailing was intriguing to O'Neil. He also used history again as a guide. He went back and discovered that a few other innovative retailers started out with very low trading ranges when they came on the scene. Kmart was one of them, when in 1962 it only averaged about 2,000 shares traded each day. Jack Eckerd was another, which in April 1967 also averaged just 2,000 shares of trading each day. Both of these stocks went on to become huge winners. Even though the institutions at first would not pick up Pic'N Save, O'Neil did for his own personal account. He actually kept purchasing this stock on the way up, buying more shares every one or two points when the stock would rise. He did this for several years. In fact, he made 285 different buys on this stock in a span of 7½ years. This is probably one of the most masterful examples ever of how to pyramid a winning position. At one point he actually owned 4.99% of the total stock outstanding (if you own more than 5%, you must register with the SEC). This stock would turn out to be one of his biggest winners ever, with some of his initial positions up 20-fold when he finally sold out, and his profits were a main funding source for starting the newspaper *Investor's Business Daily®* a few years later.

The months of August, September and October were losing months on the Dow and Nasdaq. The Dow had dropped 21% from the beginning of the year by late October, but the Nasdaq continued to hold up better. A new product that William O'Neil + Company came out with in 1977 was called *New Stock Market Ideas (NSMI)* and *Past Leaders to Avoid.* These publications came out each week for his institutional clients. His meticulous study and detailed research of the market would provide valuable information to his client base. How well has this service performed? From its inception in 1977, *NSMI*'s new ideas have outperformed the S&P 500 by 30-fold up until 2000. One of the first new ideas of this publication in 1977 was Dome Petroleum. O'Neil was trying to convince money managers to buy this stock at $48 per share in November 1977. Its energy group was very strong, and Dome possessed solid fundamentals and its outlook was strong. Not many managers jumped on this one, but O'Neil did personally. Dome turned out to be one of the biggest winning stocks of the 1970s. In just a few short years it gained 1,000%. Dome was a stock listed on the young Nasdaq, and in November 1977 that index started a strong run that would take it up 9%, in still a mostly dangerous market environment, in just the last two months of the year. The Dow however continued to lag behind and actually closed 1977 down 17%, basically giving back all the gains it had made the previous year. The Nasdaq though registered a gain for the year of 7%; it now had three straight positive-return years since the brutal bear market of 1973–74. It showed that any strength in the market was clearly focused on the smaller and faster-growing stocks.

As 1978 began there were still many problems from an economic standpoint. But the economy was picking up a bit. The markets headed lower in the first part of the year. The Dow continued to lag behind, and it plunged to the low 700s by March 1, or down 11% already in the first two months of the new year. The Nasdaq was down just 2% during the same time, quite a small decline given its sprint at the end of the prior year. The market looked like it had bottomed, but on the fifth day of an attempted upturn the indexes rose strongly on heavy volume. Then the S&P 500 rose a strong 1% on heavy volume on March 10, the eighth day of an attempted rally. We've seen how the market usually behaves when it rises 1% to 1½% or more on heavy volume between the fourth and tenth days of a market bottom. This timing is critical because it usually takes a week or so to get more heavy investors buying stocks and convinced of an upturn in trend to really make a new rally sustainable.

O'Neil Sees the Trend Change Again

Just before this confirmed upturn in the market, William O'Neil + Company placed a full-page advertisement in the *Wall Street Journal* in March 1978 called "Now's the Time to Grab the Bull by the Horns." The ad actually helped turn around the market and pessimistic views because it predicted, based on market action of the Nasdaq, that a new bull market in small to medium-sized growth stocks was probably imminent. His timing couldn't have been much better. Here was an experienced and successful market operator not listening to any other opinions but rather paying attention to the price and volume action of the market and individual stocks that were breaking out and starting to lead. This is how a master operator outperforms the market averages and profits in stocks.

Over the next three months the Dow rose 19% and the Nasdaq jumped over 20%. The groups that stood up to lead this uptrend were mostly in electronics, oil and energy and small computers. The dynamic leaders hailed from these groups. Wang Labs, with its new word processing office machines, broke out of a cup-with-handle base with the market in March and shot up

1,543% over the next 36 months. Prime Computer, which was actually an early leader as it broke through a base in February 1978, rocketed up 1,595% over the next 40 months. Many of these new technology stocks came from new groups within the computer industry. The mainframe computer stocks underperformed during this time. New industries such as minicomputers, word processors, software, graphics and microcomputers created new and exciting companies. In addition to Wang Labs and Prime Computer just mentioned, there were Commodore International, Datapoint, Electronic Data Systems (EDS), Rolm Corp., Tandy and Cullinane Database, to name a few. Many of these stocks would increase five to seven times from their early 1978 prices before they would top and begin to seriously turn downward. They would pull back just like all stocks do, but they wouldn't exhibit the strong selling signals that leaders had displayed in past market tops. This is very important to understand and learn.

After a slight pullback from early June to early July for the Nasdaq, but a more pronounced pullback for the Dow, which fell 9% in one month, both indexes returned back to the upside and resumed their advances. O'Neil's firm was recommending to several of its money management clients the purchases of M/A-Com and Boeing. Both stocks broke out off of base-on-base patterns and ended up surging 180% and 950%, respectively. Both indexes rose steadily until mid-August when the Dow ended up flattening out, while the Nasdaq kept chugging higher until September and then paused to consolidate its gains. Then in mid-October both indexes took a steep dive. This was still an uncertain time as far as many factors were concerned. Interest rates started rising again, and the economy was still experiencing stagflation. In just a few short weeks the Nasdaq plunged nearly 18% from mid-October to the end of that month, while the Dow fell nearly 14%. It was a scary drop and continued the whipsawing action that dominated much of the 1970s. The averages managed to stabilize and then traded in a slightly choppy pattern up until the end of 1978. It would turn out to be another losing year for the Dow, as it declined for its second straight year, losing just over 3%. The Nasdaq however continued to outperform the Dow with a solid 12% gain, good for its fourth straight positive year. Smaller and more nimble profitable stocks continued to perform reasonably well despite much of the whipsawing action that continued in sections of the markets.

The year 1979 started off with the markets moving higher and seeming to leave behind the prior October slump. January was especially strong as both the Dow and Nasdaq recouped some solid ground. Many of the small computer stocks that led the market for much of the Nasdaq's rise in 1978 continued to move higher. Another new name was Computervision, which in February 1979 broke out of another classic cup-with-handle basing pattern and shot higher. This stock would rise an outstanding 1,233% in just over a year. Since the Federal Reserve's discount rate had hit an all-time high in late 1978 at 9.5%, a few months without an increase seemed to get Wall Street a bit excited. After a short but somewhat meaningful pullback in February, the markets turned right around and began climbing higher in March with the Nasdaq out in front again.

The market was also seeing some of the same leading groups and stocks adding to their prior uptrends. Oil stocks and oil service firms were still on the rise. But in the early part of 1979 it was still smaller technology stocks mostly from the computer groups that were really supplying the biggest returns. Keeping in line with the volatile 1970s patterns the markets rose solidly until late April 1979 and then pulled back in another sharp correction. But many leading stocks, even though they had pulled back with the general market, were still not displaying many of the major selling and topping signs that had occurred in a lot of the prior market environments that had displayed heavy-selling action. Actually a couple of positive economic figures may have prevented more heavy selling from occurring. Unemployment began to improve a bit in 1979, and the economy was growing and not falling back into a recession or downward trend.

While the industrial stocks from the Dow were trading in a fairly tight range and not making much headway during the summer months of 1979, the Nasdaq resumed its advance. By late August the Nasdaq had already gained 28% for the year and many of the small technology issues were up by far greater amounts. Even the Dow finally took off a bit in August and climbed higher and made a new high for the year. As the markets continued a slow upward trend in September a new Federal Reserve chairman was named. President Carter had chosen Paul Volcker to head the banking industry and try to reign in inflation, which was still a major problem facing the U.S. economy. Volcker announced a rise in the discount rate, and that is exactly what Wall Street did not want to hear. After many years now of rising interest rates, the last thing the markets wanted was another round of tight policy and increasing rates. The markets fell nearly straight down after that announcement. The Nasdaq lost nearly 13% in just fewer than three weeks, and the Dow nearly 12% after being down 10% in just two weeks following that announcement. As the Dow was falling it reminded many of the 1920s, since the 50th anniversary of that decline was being touted. With the discount rate now at 12% and heading higher, the dollar still weak, and budget deficits looming large, many money market rates were now higher than long-term bond rates. What did happen though was the market recovered within months, and the Nasdaq actually ended up surging higher right up until the end of the year and finished just about one point less than where it had been before Volcker made his announcement. The adage of holding stocks as a hedge against inflation seemed to persuade many to continue buying stocks. The Dow didn't fare as well; it ended the decade less than 50 points from where it was on October 5, before Volcker's announcement. Other major issues facing the country at the time were another oil shock from OPEC and the Iran hostage crisis late in the year. While the Dow would eke out a 4% gain for 1979, the Nasdaq continued outperforming and staged an impressive 28% gain for the year. It was the indexes' fifth straight positive year following the brutal bear market of 1973–74.

The end of the 1970s marked one of the most volatile and challenging decades the market had ever been through. Political instability, foreign influences and stagflation would mark the decade. High inflation was something the markets didn't quite have to deal with much before the 1970s as inflation rates for the preceding decades were as follows: –1.1% (1920s), –2.0% (1930s), 5.4% (1940s), 2.2% (1950s), 2.5% (1960s) and 7.4% (1970s).

Leading mostly to this high-inflation environment was the high price of oil. By 1978 a barrel of oil was going for $30, almost 15 times higher than the price it had been in 1970. With so many unbalanced economic and other influences going on, the markets were whipsawed up and down for most of the decade. That didn't mean there weren't profitable opportunities to be had.

O'Neil was now very experienced, successful, and building his firm, and he did well in the 1970s. He landed one of his best performers ever — Pic'N Save — and kept adding to it as the decade was closing. He did extremely well in oil-related stocks, especially three Canadian oil stocks, because he saw the increased rise in oil prices as being a huge benefit to many of the firms that use oil as the lifeblood of their business. Many oil-related firms would go on to double or triple in price from 1979 to 1980. The best ones increased five to seven times in price as they broke through proper basing patterns. He also would follow the action of the market and leading stocks, and he sold plenty of times when things began to crack and looked bad. This he learned from his prior experiences in the 1960s and his constant study of how the market actually behaves through price and volume action. We'll see as we move along that O'Neil's good and bad experiences would only benefit him more as new opportunities would present themselves in the upcoming decades.

9

A Great Trader Outruns the Bull *and* Avoids the Crash (1980–89)

William J. O'Neil Follows the Actions of the Market and Then Acts Appropriately

The new decade of the 1980s started off with hope, and the major indexes climbed throughout January. But by early February it seemed the choppy and whipsawing 1970s market environment was back. The markets fell sharply throughout February and March. Times were still very challenging, and the economy actually fell into a recession beginning in January 1980. The Federal Reserve was still maintaining a very tight control over the money supply, and interest rates kept rising.

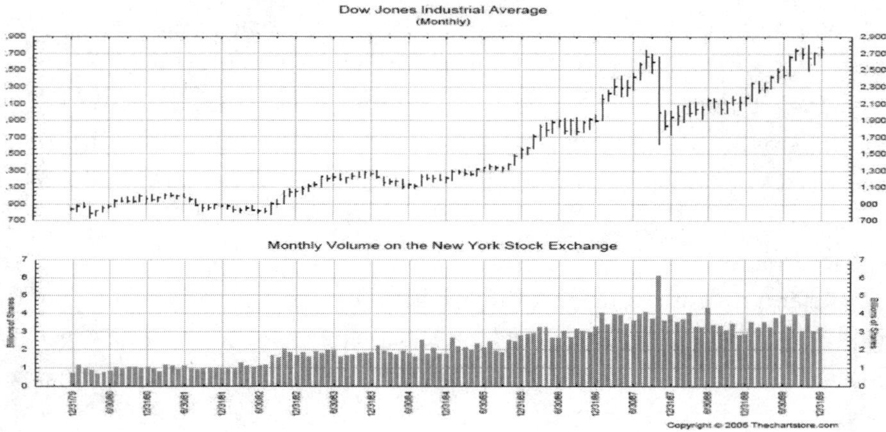

Figure 9-1 The Dow Jones Industrial Average 1980–89.
Source: *www.thechartstore.com*

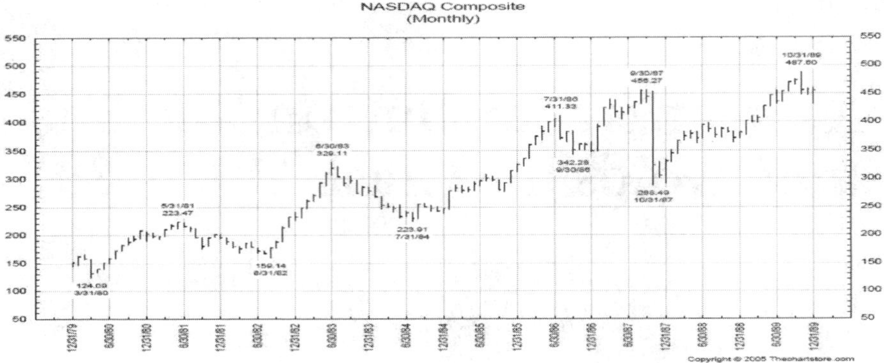

Figure 9-2 The Nasdaq Composite Average 1980–89.
Source: *www.thechartstore.com.*

Unemployment was also rising again. While the market was weak in the very early part of 1980 and not showing too much promise, the decline would be short-lived. In fact, the market and its forecasting ability would soon sense better times just ahead. The third and fourth quarters of 1980 exhibited a very strong surge in real GDP, which brought the economy out of its short recession by September. It was by no means an all-clear signal, as many troubling segments still existed in the economy, but the market's action was signaling at least a temporary change in direction to the upside. In fact, the Nasdaq would explode to the upside, starting near the beginning of April and climb strongly with no major pullbacks for the next six months. The gain was approximately 57%. The Dow shot up as well, lagging behind the Nasdaq but still up a very strong 33%. With the expansion of the personal computer catching on, many of the best returns were found in the smaller and faster-growing computer stocks that were mentioned in the previous chapters, as they kept their upward moves intact.

After a decent strong run, the markets began consolidating their gains by mid-August for the Dow and by late September for the leading Nasdaq. Just as it looked as if things were really turning around, the Federal Reserve began to raise interest rates again in another aggressive move. Another oil scare prompted the Fed to begin a round of tight monetary policy in order to head off another possible spiraling of inflation. Memories of the early

1970s quickly surfaced. On September 26 the Fed raised its discount rate. Then again on November 17, it raised it again. A few weeks following that, it raised the rate a third time on December 5. These three rapid-fire rate increases slowed the market down again just as it had in previous periods similar to that. The markets actually responded better than many may have anticipated as the Dow and Nasdaq basically traded flat, without giving up most of the previous gains made, until the end of the year. The Dow would finish up 15%, and the Nasdaq again scored the best gains by more than doubling the Dow at 34%, registering its sixth straight positive year. The broad market clearly outperformed the industrials as the S&P 500 also scored a very strong gain of 32%. Staying with this recent uptrend and especially in the leading groups that included technology stocks and banking and retail would have scored big gains for one's portfolio. Meanwhile, William J. O'Neil was still adding to his stake in Pic'N Save and using the strategy of pyramiding a winning position as his profits continued to grow and compound.

The year 1981 began, and a new president took office — Ronald Reagan. Reagan had campaigned for tax cuts as a big agenda item for his administration. His supply-side economic ideas would be viewed as ways to stimulate the stagnant economy. After a brief dip in January, the markets moved back to the upside and seemed to ignore the higher rates and other negatives in the economy. A strong rally again led by the Nasdaq stretched out until late May. One of the standouts at this time was a new innovative telecommunications company called MCI Communications, which broke out of a basing pattern at $15 and would propel upward to $90 in just 21 months, despite a rocky market ahead. The Fed, also at this time, then raised interest rates one more time on May 8 bringing the discount rate to a historic high of 14%. Short-term rates then exceeded long-term rates, inflation was spiraling upward again and would reach 15%, and the IPO market was drying up as well. The high interest rates seemed like the straw that would break the market's back, just as it had in the early 1970s. After a solid run for the first year and half of the new decade, these historically high rates would begin to choke the economy. Starting in June the market would wobble and then begin to turn in its direction and trend. Leading stocks would start to crack and selling would begin to take over the market.

O'Neil's Warning Is Correct Again

Some of the best performers of the prior several years had been stocks from the oil and oil service groups. While they provided shrewd investors with great returns from the late 1970s to the very early 1980s, they were beginning to show signs of weakness. As with almost all market cycles, former leaders of prior cycles do fall and take a backseat to others at some point. O'Neil made some great profits in the energy groups during their run, but his experience and the market's action was telling him that things were changing. In fact, he had been trying to get many of his institutional clients to get out of the oil and oil service groups starting in November 1980. All the way up until June 1981 he kept advising that big investors start realizing that these groups were topping and heading down. Oil prices stabilized somewhat, and many of the leaders from this group looked tired after such tremendous run-ups. Stocks don't keep going up forever. It's the ability to change when the stocks begin to change course that really separates the experts from all the rest. One energy leader that began to crumble was Helmerich & Payne, Inc. This stock had a nice run-up with many of the energy leaders in 1979 and 1980. That stock showed many strengths — a steady rise, strong volume supporting a rising stock, and support as it would bounce up off its key 50-day moving-average line, when it would pull back.

But by late March 1981, Helmerich & Payne formed the right shoulder of a classic head-and-shoulders topping pattern, and then higher-volume days on down days would overcome up days and weeks as the months passed. There was clearly a change in trend for this stock as profit takers overpowered holders and future buyers. By the fall of 1981 support areas were broken for the first time during its run-up. Things would get worse from there as sellers overtook the entire industry group. Helmerich & Payne would then use its 50-day line as a resistance area instead of a support area. Volume on the downside really picked up in the summer and fall of 1982 as the stock fell to under $15 (adjusted for stock splits) per share by August 1982, or down from over $50 per share at its head-and-shoulders peak. O'Neil notices these price and volume actions in a stock's chart pattern, and that is a key reason why he has been so successful over many decades in the market — the same patterns keep repeating themselves over time. Some of the other stocks that O'Neil was trying to get many of his institutional clients out of were Standard Oil of Indiana, Gulf Oil, Mobil and Schlumberger. The oil service company Schlumberger was one of the biggest winners from this group, but O'Neil noticed the stock had begun to top out in classic form. When he had noticed that the best leader was about to turn over, he knew it would be just a matter of time before the whole group would crumble. This is similar to what happened with Union Pacific in railroads in late 1906 and early 1907 and Crucibal Steel in the metals group in the early 1920s. This is due to the fact that stocks tend to follow each other in packs, but the leaders usually set the pace. O'Neil then advised that other stocks such as Hughes Tool, NL Industries, Rowan Companies and plenty of others would probably all come down as well. When the market broke hard in June 1981, the oil and oil service firms came tumbling down. It was a wise call and one of the best up to that point for O'Neil. It would actually propel the reputation of his firm and earn him accolades.

How did he do it, and how did he seem to have the insight into this? He just followed the actions of the general market and kept a close eye on the leading stocks. He knew from experience that when the general market seemed to top out and begin to show distribution that it was time to look for volume selling signals in your holdings. The leaders who usually bring the market up during uptrending markets are also the ones that bring the market down if no other strong leadership is there to keep the uptrend intact. Many times there are sector rotations during strong markets when one leading group will pass the leadership on to another strong up-and-coming group or groups. But in this case oil and oil service firms had risen very far already over the prior several years, mostly due to the rapid increase in oil prices and how those higher prices were a benefit to those firms. With oil prices steadying a bit, but still high, many would think the oil companies would keep on increasing in stock price with no end in sight. Remember the market *always* looks forward. Here, the smart money was just starting to take the great profits they had earned already during these stocks' spectacular run. O'Neil's experience, rules and judgment were all telling him the top was near for these leaders. He therefore cashed out of them, retained profits and avoided the misery that many would realize who refused to sell stocks in that group. We'll see O'Neil do this many other times as we go on. Experience and objectivity can pay huge rewards in the stock market. One needs to assess volume action in a chart. Schlumberger, the industry leader, had shown several weeks of heavy-volume distribution in its weekly chart before it really broke down.

By the end of May 1981 other problems began to surface in the economy as well. New initial public offerings (IPOs) coming to market began to dry up, even though the market was fairly strong for the first part of the year. Capital investments were declining, and research and development projects at many firms were put on hold. Industrial production also began to fall. In June another recession would begin, which was not even one full year since the prior recession had ended. June and July 1981 were down months for the markets as the trend had clearly changed directions. After a flat August, the markets resumed their sell-offs throughout September. By the end of September both indexes of the Dow and the Nasdaq were showing double-digit losses for the year. To show just how far many of the prior energy leaders fell we can look at Dome Petroleum. This stock was mentioned earlier as one of the best performers in the late 1970s. Its days at the top were over though, and by September 1981 it had fallen from $16 (adjusted for stock splits) to $12 per share. Months later it would trade for $1. It pays to recognize when these former leaders top and turn down and then take the appropriate action so one does not give back all prior profits gained and then possibly turn that into a substantial loss as well. Nothing hurts worse in the stock market than having a solid profit at one time and then watching it whittle away and then turn into a large loss. Great traders don't let that happen — they take action and protect themselves.

A few changes at least brought some comfort to the markets in late 1981. Congress passed the Economic Recovery Tax Act, as Reagan kept his campaign promise of tax cuts to stimulate the economy. Long-term capital gains rates were slashed, and depreciation expense as a short-term write-off was enacted to help spur the economy forward. Also, with the higher interest rates, many foreigners accelerated their investments in the U.S. The dollar then began to climb for the first time in quite a while. As the market somewhat stabilized, it traded in a more choppy pattern until the end of the year. The Dow lost 9% for the year, and the Nasdaq gave up 3% as its long winning streak of positive up years would end.

The year 1982 began with the economy in recession, unemployment rising, and high inflation and high interest rates. The deficit was also high. The markets headed down during January and February, as gloom seemed to take over again. First-quarter real GDP dropped by over 6%, and with unemployment rising and corporate profits down, the future looked bleak. But there were some changes starting to occur. Oil prices continued to recede, and as we look back at the decline of the formerly strong oil and oil service firms, we again see the forecasting ability of the market's action from that group. In February 1982, William O'Neil + Co., Incorporated, placed another full-page ad in the *Wall Street Journal.* The ad stated, "... inflation's back is broken and its time to invest for the recovery ahead." This ad stressed that the tax cuts that were recently passed were beginning to kick in even though many were unable to see their effects just yet. It also suggested that the decline in oil prices was reducing the historically high rate of inflation. The ad also mentioned that defense electronics and consumer growth stocks would be groups that would possibly benefit the most from the ensuing recovery. More interesting was how the ad referenced other periods in market history that looked similar to the current time in 1982. It mentioned the low PE numbers the market was currently at and how historical lows in the past that were near those same levels resulted in market bottoms. With PEs near 7 in 1982, this period looked similar to market bottoms of 1974 (PE of 6), 1949 (PE of 7) and 1932 (PE of 5). It also mentioned how the current psychological mood in the market of 1982 was very similar to the market psychology that dominated the 1947–49 market environments. And we all know by now what an important role psychology plays in the results of the market. This ad would also come out while many were still licking their wounds from a declining market and when pessimism mostly ruled the day. Recall that many times in the past we've seen that when things look like they will never improve, that's when it is most critical to be on the lookout for a possible change in direction.

From early to mid-March the markets did change direction and marched higher. It was a mild rally and would be met by further pullbacks in mid-May that would last for the next three months. I'd like to note, before we move on, a key point — the very best traders didn't waste their time or their money looking for cheap low-priced stocks that were somehow "undiscovered" by everyone else, and they surely didn't mess around with penny stocks. And as O'Neil's studies have shown, the very best stocks — the truly outstanding price gainers over time — usually start out as higher-priced (mid-$30s and greater) stocks before they make their big moves. Many of the examples that are mentioned in this book show or tell of stock prices that may seem like lower-priced issues. But those prices are usually quoted on an adjusted-stock-split basis, which means that they were much higher priced when the beginning of the move actually occurred.

After another pullback in late summer 1982 with unemployment still rising and corporate profits still falling, which resulted in another negative real GDP reading for the third quarter, the market hit bottom in early to mid-August. At this low point in August the Dow was at a level that was 25% less than it was during its high in 1972. Again, how does one know when these bottoms in the market occur, especially when everything seems all gloom and doom at the same time? Recall how Baruch, Livermore and Loeb would always be on constant alert of the market's action, looking for specific turns in a market trend. O'Neil's studies and analysis of past market bottoms is the key today for market participants to study in order to be on alert for these changes. One needs to remember that no single major bull market has ever started without a follow-through day. Back in 1982 the S&P 500 followed through five sessions after it hit bottom on August 13 when it surged 3.5% on very heavy volume. The Dow average had a follow-through day on August 17 on huge volume, which was the seventh day of its new rally attempt. It then surged higher on the ninth and tenth days of its rally attempt on heavy volume as well. What was happening and what caused this sudden change in direction? The Fed was easing up on interest rates, which expanded money supply growth (this would increase by over 13% by early 1983), and big traders were coming into the market buying up shares. This has occurred again and again, and here it was on display for all who cared to do the proper study, homework and observation.

O'Neil and his in-house money management firms went on full margin in late summer of that year, and they would end up producing their best performance ever up to that point. From 1978 to 1991 his firms' account would shoot up over 20-fold. New leaders were taking shape, and many blasted out of sound basing patterns. Many came from the technology groups, which consisted of computer services, software and peripherals. Many of these firms ended up being follow-on leaders from the prior computer and technology issues that led the 1978–80 market. A few others from different groups also sprang forward. When a market confirms its new trend and many leaders from diverse groups start to break out of proper basing patterns, this is the clue that the entire market's health is improving. The more leaders a market displays, the more power it has to keep moving forward. Dollar General came up off a flat base in August, and it soared 705% in just under three years. Price Company was an even earlier leader as it broke out of a double bottom base in June of 1982 and shot up 110% in just 11 months. O'Neil saw this one and bought into it right at its breakout point. He liked its innovative concept of opening up a chain of wholesale warehouse membership stores that would begin in Southern California. From its breakout point in mid-1982 all the way through 1986, Price Company would surge over 15-fold. O'Neil held on to this winner for the entire 3½-year run as the general market would strengthen, and he had learned the valuable lesson of holding on to a winner that keeps increasing in price without showing signs of major selling pressure.

As the buying power began to build in September the market raced higher. Inflation it seemed was now clearly under control, something O'Neil had been stressing for many months up to that point. His ad that had been placed in the *Wall Street Journal* months before was pegging this market right on the button. Corporate profits had also stopped falling and were beginning to grow. The tax cuts from the prior year were starting to really kick in. And just as reliable as before, the market jumped forward before the official end of the recession, which was over by December 1982. The trend was clearly up now, which can be seen in Figures 9-1 and 9-2 on pp. 155 and 156, and October was even better as the S&P 500 rose 11% during that month alone. As this rally was gaining speed in late 1982 consumer spending was rising following the recession. This just fueled more demand. Also, here in the early 1980s stock ownership had been declining as the whipsawing 1970s still lingered in many minds. In fact, only 16% of all households held stock in the early 1980s, which was lower than for the 1960s. By this time in 1982 institutions were dominating market trading, as they would account for approximately 70% of all market activity. And with the market and the economy beginning to improve, many from the middle class would become more involved in the market through participation in mutual funds and other indirect investment vehicles.

While the Dow slowed down near the end of 1982 and began another choppy trading range for the last two months of the year, mostly due to the lagging performance of older industrial stocks, the Nasdaq also consolidated some of its recent gains. The fourth quarter of 1982 produced a slightly positive real GDP number, reversing the negative reading of the third quarter. But the market again was looking well past the fourth quarter and beyond. It was apparently seeing brighter days ahead with interest rates coming down and inflation receding. The powerful rally off the market bottom in August 1982 was a clear signal to the astute market operator that the trend had changed to the upside, and many powerful stocks took off to lead this new bull market. The Nasdaq finished the year up 19%, and the Dow was up 19.6%.

The momentum of the newly formed uptrend from late 1982 would carry over into 1983. With interest rates and inflation continuing to fall and corporate profits growing, stocks were enjoying a renewed interest. Many of the smaller and more innovative companies were continuing their strong runs, and they were reaping the advantages of an improving economy and an improving consumer segment. With the improving economy, business confidence and business hiring began to grow as well. The unemployment rate would finally begin to turn down as more companies hired more workers to keep up with improved demand. One segment of the workforce that was beginning to show great promise was the resurgence of women coming back into the workforce at higher levels. A few companies would reap huge benefits from this surge. Dress Barn and Limited Brands, which catered to women's work fashions, saw their revenues and profits begin to soar. The Limited would actually end up increasing 3,500% from 1982 to 1987, though there were many opportunities to get into this stock properly as we'll see a bit later on. As the months moved on, a stair-step upward pattern was clearly visible during the early months of 1983, just we saw many times before when the market was in a clear upward trending pattern.

As the rally grew stronger many of the best traders were adding to their strongest stocks. O'Neil was still purchasing Pic'N Save as it was gaining more attention and its stock price kept rising. Price Company was another big winner that O'Neil would pyramid up on at strategic buy points and opportunities. By early 1983 the Dow was already over 300 points higher than its 1982 low. First-quarter and second-quarter real GDP numbers were strong, especially the second quarter, which increased near 9%. Solid growth was now reverberating throughout the economy, and confidence was rising. The new-issue market was on fire as IPOs just in the first quarter of that year totaled $8.7 billion, which was up over 350% from the first quarter of 1982.

The market slowed down in the summer but still kept its upward trend intact, and selling would be mostly contained and attributed to profit taking versus topping action that in the past would lead to major sell-offs. It's important to understand the distinction between the two. There was also a bit of a divergence going on in the market during 1983. The Nasdaq ended up nearly 43% from the first of the year to the early part of June as smaller companies were on a tear. The Dow lagged behind but was still up an impressive 24% during the same time frame. When the markets pulled back during the summer and fall, the divergence occurred again. The Dow only retreated 4% from mid-June to early November. However, the leading Nasdaq fell by nearly 18% over that time. O'Neil stuck to his time-tested market analysis, so he knew the difference between normal selling action that always occurs during upward-trending markets and sell-offs and heavy distribution that result in trend reversals that can damage portfolios if proper selling techniques are not implemented. He actually welcomed normal selling as he looked at those pullbacks as opportunities to add to positions he already had a significant gain in. The trick is it has to be conducted based on proper price and volume action and the lead of the market and how it is performing and responding. Certain areas of support can always give the astute trader more opportunities to profit, if done correctly. Again, please refer to O'Neil's publications for a detailed analysis of all his strategic trading principles, especially his many sell rules.

There were many other very strong stocks that year, and one that caught O'Neil's eye was Fleetwood Enterprises. This stock from the mobile home group would turn out to be another huge winner for him. And because of the strength of the mobile home group, other follow-on stocks that supported the mobile home industry would do well also. One such stock was Textone, which made paneling and cabinets for recreation vehicles (RVs) and mobile homes. Another big winner was Franklin Resources, which was a new mutual fund company. Because of the strength of the market and improved involvement from the general public in the market, especially indirectly through mutual funds, Franklin would prosper. The stock was a new issue in 1983, and it would increase 750% in just 15 months. Following a choppy year-end, which featured an up market in November and a down market in December, the Dow would end up 20.3% for the year for its second solid gain in a row. The Nasdaq actually lagged the Dow again for the second straight year as it increased 19.8% in 1983.

The first few weeks of 1984 started off with the advance continuing. But then a few clues started to surface. The Dow, which peaked on January 10 at 1,295, would sell off with three distribution (heavy selling) days that occurred in just five trading sessions. By January 13 there was clear heavy selling taking place. We all know by now what that means to O'Neil. It means he would watch very closely what the market and leading stocks were doing, and after seeing multiple days of heavy selling, he would be quick to start selling some of his holdings, if they started to trigger some of the classic sell rules. One leader that was starting to wobble was Home Depot. After a meteoric rise off its initial public offering in 1981, this stock would run up over 20-fold in less than two years from under $2 (adjusted for stock splits) to over $30 by September of 1983. With the market looking tired and starting to weaken in early 1984, Home Depot began to top by finishing many of its up days on low volume. This lack of buying power, which is what propelled this stock upward the prior two years, had run its course. And with the general market topping, Home Depot would top as well. There was nothing wrong with the company, as growth prospects were still excellent. But when selling hits the market no one knows how bad it can get, as we've already seen throughout history. The smart money in Home Depot was exiting the stock and keeping the strong gains made to date. There is no reason why, when a healthy market appears again, that you can't buy back into a strong stock if it turns out to lead another market cycle. And as we know, stocks don't go up forever, and after such a huge advance Home Depot was ripe for a correction. By March 1984, Home Depot had lost half of its value off its peak price and was trading in the $15 range as the market fell hard through the latter part of January and all of February.

What happened in early 1984 was the Fed raised interest rates as the discount rate went back up to 9%. Fears of more rate hikes and a return to the very early 1980s' high-interest-rate environment started to surface. The 30-year bond rate rose back up to 14% as inflation started to pick up again. The economy was still strong, but it would slow down as the year went on, which again the market had already reflected in its ability to look ahead. From March through July the markets would stair-step their way downward. The Dow's correction would be approximately 17% from its January peak, while the Nasdaq would give up over 20%. Those may look minor compared to the gains made since August 1982, but corrections are no fun when you're in one and not certain how far they may slide. And for only a six-month period, corrections like that can be very damaging and frustrating. The turnaround in the correction began in early August as the Fed then reversed its increasing stance and then began lowering the discount rate. The market responded positively to this change and jumped with strong gains in early August that added back the majority of the losses from the prior few months. From there the markets traded mostly in a choppy pattern and slightly downward for the rest of the year, but at least the fear of increasing rates was laid to rest. There were also a few new IPOs that generated some strong interest. TCBY (This Can't Be Yogurt) generated heavy interest with its franchising concept for the new yogurt food fad. TCBY would zoom 2,290% in just 1½ years from the very beginning to 1985. King World, which was involved with the popular TV shows Jeopardy and Wheel of Fortune, was another new issue that year, and it soared 300% in just one year. Another strong performer that year was Liz Claiborne, which surged 715% to its peak price.

The Dow would end up losing ground in 1984 due to its early correction and ended down 4% for the year, snapping its two-year straight 20% gains. The Nasdaq ended up underperforming the Dow as it fell 13%, also snapping its strong two-year run. Not to be left out, the S&P 500 fell 6%. Another significant event in 1984 was the introduction of *Investor's Daily* (later changed to its current name of *Investor's Business Daily®* in 1991) in April. This new innovative newspaper, founded by O'Neil, would challenge the *Wall Street Journal* and bring factual, historically tested and unbiased data to the general public regarding the market and individual stocks. This newspaper was funded totally by profits O'Neil made in the market, and most of the funding came from only two stocks — Price Company and Pic'N Save. It takes a fair amount of capital to start up and maintain a national publishing product, so you can imagine how profitable these huge winners were for O'Neil.

As 1985 began, many economic factors were falling into place to create a healthy landscape. Interest rates were coming back down, inflation was receding, and unemployment was declining as well. The economy was clearly growing, and quarterly real GDP was healthy. New companies were coming to the market, and mergers and buyouts were growing, which is always a healthy sign for the stock market as it shows that corporations have confidence in their current and future outlooks. So after a short correction, which actually helps build healthy bases for stocks for future uptrends, confidence and the trend of the market were moving back to the upside. After a strong January and February, the markets consolidated their gains and climbed higher throughout the summer in a mild and steady advance. Astute market students were watching active leaders and seeing the healthy market environment offer up some solid opportunities. One other important detail was that the Nasdaq was beginning to reassert itself as the leading market index. After lagging the Dow for the past three years, the Nasdaq had some smaller and innovative companies that were racking up decent gains. New issues are always a sign of a healthy market, especially if they come to market with strong demand and fundamentals for their products or services already in place. A few standouts in 1985 included Novell, with its local area network (LAN) software product, which bolted 100% in just five months from its IPO issue date. Costco, another wholesale membership store concept, was another huge winner, as its stock price would soar 700% in just over three years. The Limited also made another huge run in 1985 as it continued its leadership ways.

After a slow but steady rise up until October 1985, the markets surged higher the last three months of the year. Volume was picking up, and the trend of the market was clearly strong as demand fueled higher stock prices. In October, Franklin Resources would burst out of a flat basing pattern. O'Neil jumped aboard this leader. He was following the strong market's trend and looking for fundamentally strong leaders that were setting up in classic basing formations. This stock would turn out to be one of his best gainers of the decade, as it would run up 3,596% in five years. O'Neil didn't hold it that long, as it did give off sell signals along the way, and he heeded them to retain his profit. But it pays to hold your winners as long as possible, as the big money is made by sitting with the strong leaders until they show signs of serious selling signals. And when they do, as all will eventually, you lock in your gain. That's what O'Neil did, and that's how he has become so successful in the market. Remember that no one ever, throughout the history of the stock market, will buy at the exact bottom and sell at the exact top. It is impossible to do, and don't think that some fancy software program will magically make you the first person in history to do that. Gerald Loeb even stated in his classic "The Battle for Investment Survival" that, "The money that has been lost 'feeling' for the bottom or top never has been generally appreciated. The totals, if they could be known, must be staggering."

As for 1985, in November, Genentech blasted upward and would end up racing 300% higher in just five months. Somewhat puzzling to some at the time was that its PE ratio right at its buy point before the run-up was 200. Great stock traders don't trade based on PE ratio bias — they look for the handful of leaders who outperform financially with new products and/or services only when the market is in a confirmed uptrend. In fact, PEs are usually used by the best as more of a measure of when to sell a rising stock as opposed to when to buy a stock. Loeb and O'Neil both used rising PEs as measures of when to properly take their profits on the way up. The Dow moved up 28% that year, and the Nasdaq regained its leadership with a strong 31% gain.

The momentum of the uptrend kept moving as 1986 began. Interest rates were still falling, inflation was well contained, and the economy was still growing. Volume levels on the markets were growing, and more people continued to enter the market either directly or indirectly through mutual funds, which were continuing to gain popularity. Strong groups leading the market included software, cable TV, supermarkets, food, medical stocks, and especially generic drugs stocks. Genentech was continuing its advance, and O'Neil would buy into this leader as well and hold on to it until 1987, reaping one of his other monster gains for the decade. Reebok International was another big winner when it broke out of a cup-with-handle base in early 1986 on huge volume that was over 100% higher than its then-current average. It would race ahead 262% in just four months. New IPOs were still coming to the market, and a few of the outstanding ones were Adobe, with its innovative printing software. This stock would zoom up 482% in just six months during the strong market. Circuit City, with its electronics stores concept, would turn out to be a huge winner. It electrified shareholders with a 1,971% increase over 4½ years.

The markets were on a tear the first half of the year, rising strongly through March in an almost uninterrupted upward move. From April through June the uptrend continued but was more of the stair-step pattern that we've seen numerous times in the past. It had been quite a climb for the markets. So far, just from October of 1985 to the end of June 1986, both the Dow and Nasdaq were up over 40% in just nine months. But there were some concerns that started to arise. Internal scandals involving insider trading were beginning to surface. Most of these seemed to stem around investment bankers and brokers again. We've seen in the past that when things get almost too good many try to take shortcuts. It wasn't any different in the mid-1980s. Huge trade deficits and budget deficits were also raising some eyebrows. Also, the junk bond market, which began a few years prior, was responsible for some overleveraged deals. Buyouts with firms using heavy leverage drove merger mania ever higher. But the economy was still growing, albeit at a slower pace, and corporate profits were solid. The markets fell sharply in July but then bounced back somewhat in August. As mentioned, it had been quite a run for the averages, so some consolidating of the prior gains made seemed normal and healthy.

O'Neil Locks in a Huge Profit

Starting in September a divergence took place in the market, as the Nasdaq got hit with more selling than the Dow. Profit taking began to take place on the Nasdaq as the prior gains made were being sold off by some of the more astute market operators. O'Neil for one sold off his holding in Price Company. He realized a gain of over 1,000% on this stock. It's important, probably more so than any other strategy, to be able to sell correctly. With the many sell rules that O'Neil would implement from his intensive study of history's best-performing stocks, he would discover common buying rules and selling rules when stocks would begin to top and roll over. Locking in a 10- or 20-fold profit doesn't come from luck — it's hard study and discipline. O'Neil at one point in his holdings of Price Company held 3.6% of all the outstanding shares. When you own a position that large, you had better know how to sell correctly. And O'Neil was one of the first to determine, through extensive historical study, which proper selling rules contribute to the best gains being realized. And he still continues to use the historical data from the very best winning stocks of all time to build his models in which he bases many of his successful strategies.

The quick correction on the Nasdaq brought the index down 17% in just 2½ months. After a strong run-up it's difficult to tell just how far an index can fall. The insider trading scandal would make many nervous. Then on November 17 there was a sharp sell-off when Ivan Boesky made a plea bargain for insider trading charges. The Nasdaq would continue to struggle and underperform, but a few new issues would surface late that year that would add a spark to the market. Microsoft came public in October 1986 and would end up breaking through on huge volume to gain 350% in just 12 months. Compaq Computer came public in December that year and would end up breaking out of a cup-with-handle pattern and soar 378% in just 11 months. Both of these new issues offered up exciting new products that came from young and innovative companies that would enhance worker productivity in great ways for many years to come. However, the Nasdaq just couldn't regain much of the ground it gave up during the second half of the year, but it did end up 7% due to its very strong rise during the first half of 1986. Real GDP also slowed during much of 1986 but was still positive, extending the positive quarters to 16 since the first quarter of 1983.

The year 1987 started off with a flurry as the uptrending market took a strong turn upward following the choppy end to the prior year, which can be seen in Figures 9-1 and 9-2 on pp. 155 and 156. Tax reforms were kicking in, and there was buying power driving up stocks. The economy was rolling along, and the general attitude was positive. New issues were still thriving as more IPOs came to market. It actually seemed similar to the 1950s era as many more were coming in to the market. The Nasdaq, with its many smaller and innovative leaders, shot up over 25% in less than three months early in 1987. The Dow was right there as well, up nearly the same amount and crossing the 2,000 mark for the first time ever. The excitement of the markets rise began to spread, and trading volume increased dramatically.

A well-deserved rest for the market occurred during April and May as consolidation of prior gains allowed for some breathing room. From there though, another divergence occurred in the market. The Dow took off in another flurry of buying but was led by more cyclical-type stocks. The Nasdaq lagged behind as many leaders began to look a bit tired. Now, this is easy to analyze after the fact and very hard to see when you're active at the time and are all excited about a rising market. But we'll see shortly how one of the best removed his emotions and saw clear signals in some of these details along with others. This is also why it is critical to study, read and understand history, especially regarding the market, because the present and the future will look similar to past time periods. It is also important to learn from, so one doesn't repeat the same mistakes made in the past, years into the future. This frenzy buying was very similar to other prior times when this same type of activity occurred, and we'll see it again fairly soon down the road. It's also important to understand topping markets and proper selling rules of leading stocks, which have repeated themselves. O'Neil's study of this is probably one of the most profitable lessons one can learn about the stock market. A few leading stocks did start topping in mid-1987. Adobe Systems, Inc., which was a huge winner from the fall of 1986 to April 1987 as it shot up over 600%, began breaking down. By June, high-volume sessions on down days clearly outnumbered strong up days, which was occurring for the first time during the market's tremendous run. It also then broke through its key 50-day moving-average line on tremendous volume. These are clear signals that big investors are locking in their prior profits.

Reebok International, mentioned earlier as a strong leader, experienced a classic climax top back in March 1987. From April through August it would experience many down sessions on heavy volume. Also, there was virtually no upward progress being made on any rebounds, and volume was very low as compared to when it was racing up in price — now showing virtually no buying power. These are clues that selling is overtaking buying and its time to act appropriately. This stock actually really began to fall apart in September, well before the crash, which occurred a month later.

By late August, as the market was surging higher, the Dow hit a peak on August 25 at 2,746. The Dow had risen another 25% in just the past three months and was up 45% for the year already. As mentioned, the Nasdaq was still rising but at a slower pace by then. It was up 31% for the year at that point. In August of 1987 the volume on the New York Stock Exchange had reached 180 million shares. Another former leading stock was topping as well. The Limited, which had a huge prior run, would top out in August as volume was picking up while the stock began selling off. This was smart money selling and locking in huge prior profits. Another bad sign for the market was that interest rates started rising, which would reverse the trend of lower rates that had been present for the past several years. Also a new Federal Reserve chairmen was named. Alan Greenspan was appointed to head the banking system, and he was determined to stop inflation, which had begun to rise again. Also, long-term Treasury yields began to increase dramatically during the summer of 1987, and Citicorp in the summer announced its largest loss ever due to the Third World debt crisis. These were all signals to the most astute operators that things could change.

During the latter part of August the market started sending off signals, and O'Neil was right there reading them. He already knew how markets seemed to top due to distribution that began showing up in the major averages and the fact that many leading stocks looked like they were topping in classic fashion. He noticed that the Dow experienced five major selling days from late August to early September. In fact, the correction that was about to begin started on August 26. During this stretch of time five heavy sell-offs occurred within 15 trading sessions. Of these 15 sessions only 5 were up sessions and 10 were down. Of the five up sessions, only two of those closed near their highs for the day. Of the 10 down sessions, only one of those would close near the top of its trading range for the day. These are important details to watch for. This was a signal that things were changing as the market's previous uptrend did not show these bouts of heavy selling. The problem is most people ignore them as their emotions take over. When the market has experienced very strong days for quite a while, most just ignore these important signals and get all wrapped up in the current frenzy. But what is really happening is that the smartest traders are taking and retaining their profits. This is classic selling into strength by the best traders and a quite early warning signal that the trend was changing directions. As the days wore on and the market action continued to flash warning signs, O'Neil was one of those smart traders. He ended up selling all his holdings and went to a 100% cash basis. Recall that he remembered how Livermore was doing the same thing in 1907 and that O'Neil used that precedent in 1962 to sidestep the bear market that was just about to occur back then. Here he was again doing the same thing. His experience was telling him that something was about to change, and he wanted to make sure he retained his previous profits and not give them back. And he held some major gains. Imagine how difficult it would be to sell off such huge winners when the majority of everyone is ecstatic and talking up the market. But O'Neil used his experience and time-tested market rules to control his emotions and to reap and keep his gains.

As September began, newly appointed Fed chief Greenspan raised the discount rate to 6%. This would be just another negative for the market. With a correction already under way and inflation and higher-interest-rate worries renewed, there were clear signs that selling was beginning to get stronger and take over the market. After a sharp sell-off in September, a weak rebound up until the early part of October was then met with further selling. By mid-October the markets were all over 10% down from their peaks with O'Neil in total cash watching the action from the sidelines. This is a major skill of the greatest market operators that I mentioned many times in my first book and in this one — having the ability to stay away from the market when it is wise to do so. On Friday, October 16, the market was hit with heavy selling as the Dow lost over 100 points or 4.6%, which followed decent sell-offs on Wednesday and Thursday as well. The loss on Friday was the sixth largest loss on the NYSE since World War II, and volume came in at a record high of 344 million shares. It would be a nervous weekend for many, and when trading resumed on Monday, October 19, many overseas markets had sold off hard. By 10:30 a.m. that morning, 11 of the 30 Dow stocks had not yet opened for trading due to a heavy imbalance of sell orders. By 11:00 a.m., trading volume had already broken the full-day record and was at 154 million shares. Panic selling was hitting the market in a manner that none had seen before. By 2:00 p.m. it was total panic. The Dow would end up losing 508 points that day or a record 22.6% on a record-setting volume of 608 million shares. The backlog of orders from the volume was huge and reminded many of the 1920s and 1960s. The Nasdaq lost 50 points, or 14%. New issues that recently went public were crushed. Overseas markets sold off as well, and many surpassed the losses on the U.S. markets. The Australian market sank 58%. After the close, the Federal Reserve reaffirmed its readiness to serve as a source of liquidity, much the same way as J. P. Morgan did in the panic of 1907, as the Fed lowered the federal funds rate to 6.75% from 7.5%. The next day, Tuesday, October 20, the market rebounded early and was up at one point by 200 points, but by mid-day there was another imbalance to the markets. Mutual funds then stepped in and did some buying, and prices firmed up by the end of the day offering some relief. The next day, Wednesday, October 21, witnessed a solid rally for the markets, but from there through the rest of the year the markets would experience choppy trading.

There have been over the years many who have tried to give specific explanations for the collapse on October 19. Reasons have included index arbitrage trading and portfolio insurance, along with the increased usage of program trading that utilized computerized trading techniques. Many even paralleled the 1929 crash, which caused margin call selling to the 1987 crash, which caused portfolio insurance selling. Whatever the cause, which just may have been an overextended long upward run and then some panic selling, which we have seen occur in decades from the past, it was pretty clear to an experienced operator like O'Neil that selling had changed the trend of the market, and he heeded the signals and acted appropriately in moving with the rhythms and actions of the general market and the leading stocks, which will always signal what lies ahead. One other interesting note about this time period was that David Ryan, one of O'Neil's students, would win the U.S. Investing Championship three years in a row beginning in 1985 through 1987. He utilized the CAN SLIM™ investment method that O'Neil had created when he built models of the greatest stock market winners going back to the early 1950s. Ryan amassed a total return during this three-year period of 1,378% to his personal account to win the championships. Soon after, he became an in-house money manager at William O'Neil + Company. It's just another example of how outstanding returns can come to those who study hard and follow time-proven strategies.

Jim Roppel — The Passionate Student of the Market

During this same time a new trader would appear on the scene. Jim Roppel was born in December 1964 in Illinois outside the Chicago area. While in college he opened two brokerage accounts, one with his college roommate's father acting as his broker. His friend's father was a broker with A.G. Edwards, and he specialized in options. Roppel then started trading options in 1987, and he soon found out just how risky that venture would be. Because of his limited amount of capital at the time, his trades were fairly small. He also had no system in place as he was buying put options (basically betting against a rising market) during the first half of 1987 when the market was in a strong upward trend. Here we see an inexperienced market operator violating one of the major rules of the most successful traders — going against the momentum of the current market. Needless to say, Roppel lost money on those early trades. He had finally given up on put options just before the crash took place. After the crash occurred, he quickly turned around and bought call options (betting for a market upturn) on Chrysler, Paramount and General Dynamics. He lost money on all those trades as the market was not quite in rally mode so soon after the devastating break it had just been through. In fact, Roppel lost borrowed money as well and ended up owing a friend with a note payment over the next year. Roppel's timing with the option plays was totally out of sync with what the market was doing at the time, and he paid a price for those mistakes.

But he wouldn't quit, and here again we see a determined market operator, who would eventually make it big, by starting out with a limited amount of money and making early amateurish mistakes. The events of that year and the October crash had a major impact on his life, and he soon discovered that the market, heeding its challenge and succeeding at it, was to be his calling in life. And just like all the traders whom I have now profiled in my first book and this one, he would soon learn that the road to success was to be a long and sometimes painful journey. But for Roppel, as we saw with many of the others, his passion and determination to succeed would overcome his learning curve. A passage from another excellent book about trading, "Trend Following: How Great Traders Make Millions in Up or Down Markets," by Michael Covel, cites a quote from Brett Steenbarger, Ph.D., an Associate of Psychiatry and Behavioral Sciences at SUNY Upstate Medical University, N.Y., that sums up the insight and vision Roppel possessed in his quest. It concerns passion and states:

> Find your passion: the work that stimulates, fascinates, and endlessly challenges you. Identify what you find meaningful and rewarding, and pour yourself into it. If your passion happens to be the markets, you will find the fortitude to outlast your learning curve and to develop the mastery needed to become a professional ...

Roppel would end up spending the next seven years learning and studying the markets and making many mistakes, including many that were outright devastating, before he finally found the strategy, discipline and patience to reap huge rewards in the stock market. His learning curve would just happen to be about the same length in time as those of Bernard Baruch, Nicolas Darvas and many others, proving that to become a great success in the stock market means many sacrifices will need to made along the way and that the learning process takes time and patience. One of the main reasons for success eluding Roppel during these early years was that he would try many different strategies and switch between many of them when they would not produce the results he expected. He really acted much like Nicolas Darvas did during his early years, which entailed switching from this or that strategy looking for the secret to success in the stock market. His actions were not that different than those of many others who decide to venture into the market.

As the market seemed to stabilize in early 1988, cyclical stocks, which consisted of paper, aluminum and chemical stocks, among others, took the early lead. Their lead however didn't last very long, and soon growth stocks would jump out in front again. A main difference in the market environment after the crash in 1987 and other major drops in the market prior to that time was the economy was still strong in the late 1980s and there was no sign of corporate or economic weakness on the horizon. Many mutual fund managers saw this, and that is why stock prices seemed to recover rather quickly instead of heading into a major downfall like the one seen in the early 1930s. Quarterly real GDP numbers were still positive, unemployment was still declining, and interest rates seemed to level off for the time being. In speaking to many companies following the October crash many mutual fund managers were hearing that business confidence was still strong, and many didn't see a major slowdown ahead. This confidence helped the buying side to increase and probably halted the selling pressure. The Nasdaq led the market back upward as it actually soared from mid-January to mid-March, rising 16%.

The Dow also rebounded but lagged the Nasdaq as smaller issues led this newly revised uptrend. Surgical Care Affiliates broke out of a flat base in February 1988 and would soar 1,833% in just under three years. Health care stocks would be leaders in this new rally. Also in February, O'Neil came out with his first book on the market titled "How to Make Money in Stocks — A Winning System in Good Times or Bad," which took him many years to write. The book became the number one selling investment book of the year, and as of this writing has sold well over a million copies and is in its third edition. It is highly recommended that one study this reference as it is one of the best books ever written on the market and how to apply sound trading rules that work in real-life situations.

While the markets seemed to bounce back fairly quickly from April on, they traded in a mostly choppy and whipsawing fashion until the end of the year. There were still good opportunities in the market as the overall trend was still up, but it was a much more challenging environment, and the indexes still did not recover all the ground they had lost near the end of 1987. The Dow would finish the year up 12%, while the Nasdaq rose 15%.

Roppel graduated from college in 1988, and he landed a job with a small firm, Shelter Rock, which he later discovered was heavily focused on penny stocks. Still young and inexperienced, he would fall for the advice of others, especially those within the firm he worked for. He bought Choice Drugs at $6 per share and sold out at $3, for a 50% loss. He bought Reebok at $27 and held on to it all the way down to $7, good for a 74% loss. He did land a few small gains, but listening to others, doing no individual research, and having no loss control discipline led to another disappointing year for him. He eventually left Shelter Rock, as the firm offered no training and he was only doing cold calls based on the firm's recommendations. He then landed a position with a firm called David A. Noyes, as a broker, where he would stay for the next seven years.

The markets started off 1989 on a positive note. The recent upward trend continued as the major indexes powered higher throughout January. It seemed that the memory of October 1987 was fading away. A new president, George Bush, would follow Reagan, and Wall Street was pleased with the prospect of another Republican in office. The economy was still growing, but other concerns were still present. As the market consolidated its prior gains throughout February and March, many of those concerns were put to rest when the Fed began to reverse its course on interest rates. The Fed, in the spring of 1989, began a campaign of lowering interest rates. In fact, beginning in 1989 the Federal Reserve would cut rates 24 consecutive times until 1992. During that time overnight rates dropped to 3% from 8% and left those rates at lows not seen since the 1960s. This pumping of money into the economy was a positive for the economy as a whole, and the stock market was reflecting this.

The markets responded favorably to the reduction in interest rates, and in the spring the markets were clearly in another upward trend. Many leading stocks were also stepping up. Corrections always lead to base-forming patterns in stocks, and they set up the leaders for the next upturn. Many of the leaders from 1988 and 1989 came from groups in the health care, software, telecom, cable TV and consumer groups, which included jewelry stores and shoe apparel. The markets moved up strongly, offering up many opportunities throughout the spring and summer months of 1989. In fact, the Dow would finally pierce the level at which it was at just prior to the October 1987 crash by August 1989. It still shows that by adhering to the action and signals of the market, like O'Neil would do, one can save themselves a lot of time and emotional stress. Two years to wait for many to get back to their prior levels is time that is wasted. It is better to stay away from a bad market or move into something else that may be working properly.

The markets would receive a jolt in the fall as the junk bond market collapsed. All the major indexes declined sharply in early October. This then led to the savings and loan (S&L) crisis as many S&Ls had bought junk bonds for investments. From mid-October to the end of the year and the decade a divergence appeared in the market again. The Dow recovered from the sharp October sell-off and actually closed the year near its peak just prior to the break. The Nasdaq, however, actually weakened more after this break in the market, and despite a last rush upward during the final two weeks of the year, it would lag behind the Dow. The Dow finished the 1980s with a strong 27% gain in 1989, while the Nasdaq finished up 19%. The 1980s ended a strong period for the markets once it reversed from the recession in the early part of the decade. In fact, the 1982–89 period would experience no recessions and would string together the longest number of growth periods since post–World War II. The 1980s as a whole ended up being the best decade for the market since the 1950s. One big reason was the continued growth of the economy, which was fueled in part by tax cuts that were passed under the Reagan administration. Strong corporate profitability and new innovative companies were coming on the scene. Inflation was also better contained, as the average rate of inflation was 5.1% during the 1980s, down from 7.4% in the 1970s.

As for O'Neil, he proved how an individual can outperform due to his strict loss-cutting policy, his flexibility to move with the markets, and his intense study of the models he had built based on history's actions in the market. He averaged better than a 40% average annual return during the 1980s. He landed some big winners such as Price Company and Pic'N Save, in which he made more money than most ever make in their lifetimes, and especially in the market. But the real secret to his success came from his discipline to cut his mistakes short. While this book does focus on how the greats made the big money, it should not be overlooked that they all experienced many losses along the way. In fact, O'Neil estimates that he is correct only approximately 66% of the time on his initial buys. But with his experience now over two decades in the making, he realizes that the faster you admit and act on the times when you're wrong, the better. That is the single biggest reason why he produces such impressive returns, as this one rule forces him to avoid bad market periods.

Finally, as for Roppel, he was still making the same mistakes he had made during the prior few years. Even with the market in a strong uptrend, he made no progress in 1989, as he basically did not implement any market analysis skills. He was actually active again in options due to his still limited capital stake, caused mostly by him not having a strict loss-cutting policy in place. But we'll soon see his learning curve begin to improve as he starts to study the great traders before him and he begins to implement the necessary skills, discipline and trading rules that led to big profits for the legendary traders. But he would still need a few more years of hard-knocks learning before he really turned it around, as the 1990s were set to begin.

10

New Technologies Produce Unprecedented Opportunities (1990–99)

William J. O'Neil Studies the Best Past Performers to Discover the Next Great Ones

O'Neil Notices a Major Opportunity

The 1990s began by dampening some of the enthusiasm the markets were displaying as the 1980s ended when the Dow had reached and then exceeded its pre-1987 levels. Both the Dow and the Nasdaq indexes fell sharply in January 1990 — both by approximately 11%. For the time being this turned out to be just a rather normal correction as the markets soon

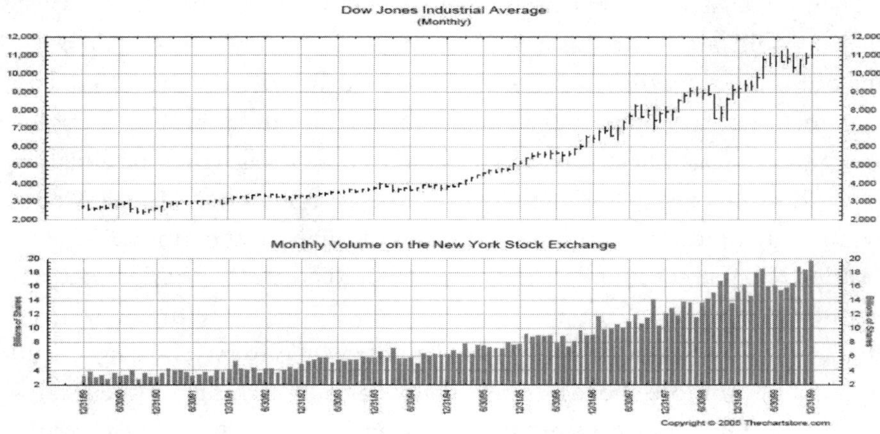

Figure 10-1 The Dow Jones Industrial Average 1990–1999.
Source: *www.thechartstore.com.*

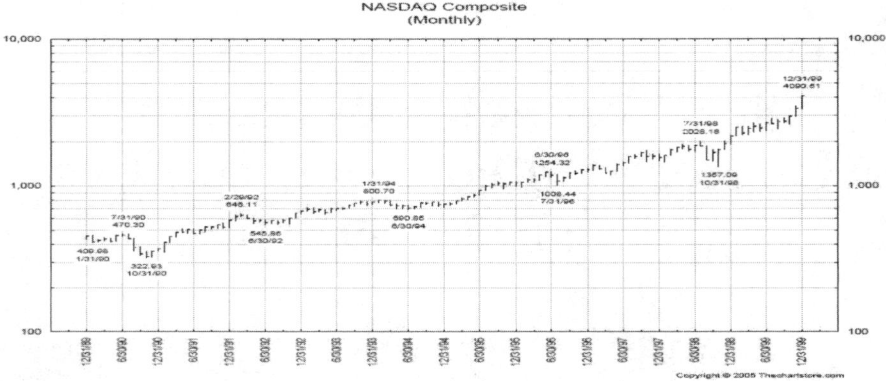

Figure 10-2 Nasdaq Composite Average 1990–99.

Source: *www.thechartstore.com.*

found a bottom and headed back upward. A rebound from this early sell-off occurred over the next several months, and by mid-April the Dow had recouped its entire January loss. The Nasdaq lagged and would not reach its beginning-of-the-year level until May. It began to look as though the uptrend was back, and a few leading stocks began displaying strength again. One stock that showed great strength at that time was Amgen, which was just introducing two new biotech drugs. This stock broke out of a flat basing pattern in May on big volume and rose steadily higher throughout the summer months. Medical-related stocks were leaders during this time, and Amgen possessed excellent fundamentals and a bright outlook.William J. O'Neil would latch onto this new leader, and it would actually end up being one of his biggest winners of the entire decade, in a decade that offered up some of the best possibilities in years. He held on to it throughout some rough patches, as it held up without flashing major sell signals or violating any of his other sell rules, including his loss-cutting policy. He also would pyramid up on this stock numerous times throughout the time he held his position. He bought more of Amgen as it would create new basing patterns on its way up to a 640% gain by early 1992. O'Neil made many pyramid buys on this stock when new breakout points would form, and they would be 20 points or more above his previous average cost. This is another example of a master stock operator adding to a winning position while carefully watching and limiting his risk. We also get a new IPO near this same time, on February 16, from what would turn out to be one of the biggest winners in market history, as Cisco Systems went public.

While the markets were heading slightly higher during the spring and early summer months, there were some worries and uncertainties brewing in a few areas. Economic activity started to slow down. Though the first quarter's real GDP rate for 1990 was solid, it would slow down considerably in the second quarter. There was also some concern relating to the strength of the banking system at that time. July was the month that things began to go astray. A new recession would begin, and it had been a while since many had to get used to a slowdown in the economy and business conditions. Also, Saddam Hussein then invaded Kuwait. The Dow had just passed the 3,000 mark, and many began to think another Vietnam situation would have America engaged in another costly and unpopular conflict. By mid-July the markets began to top along with many leading stocks. A few of those leading stocks that flashed topping signs during this time were:

Computer Associates International. This leading technology stock worked its way higher throughout 1988–89. It then formed a classic head-and-shoulders topping pattern starting in late 1989. During the first part of 1990, it rebounded back to the upside along with the market to near $17 per share by June (adjusted for stock splits), but it couldn't make a new high as it was off from its previous high of near $22. When the market started weakening, Computer Associates broke hard on heavy volume. By September the stock was trading for under $5 per share.

MCI Communications. This was another huge winner during the 1988–89 market period. It soared nearly fivefold during that stretch from near $10 per share (adjusted for stock splits) in early 1988 to near $45 by early 1990. By June 1990 many heavy-volume down days were dominating trading in this stock. By October it had fallen to near $20 per share.

There were also four strong selling sessions that were present in mid-July as distribution days began piling up. These selling days are just like the many we've already seen in prior market cycles, and it meant that big sellers were selling stocks. The few uncertainties that had cropped up had all but dried up the demand and buying power for stocks. Besides, there had already been a strong advance in equities since the 1987 break. And as we've already seen numerous times — stocks don't keep going up forever, as they always pull back and correct at some time. The challenge is that no one knows how severe or shallow a correction in the market can or will be. That's why the best traders turn around when they see these topping signals and learn to implement a tight defensive plan that includes selling and cutting losses short.

The Dow didn't spend much time above 3,000, and by the third week of August it had shed over 500 points. The Nasdaq came down even harder. In a little over a month it fell over 23%. Possible war worries had many feeling a bit uncomfortable, and a slowdown in business conditions was now spreading. Many mutual fund managers were saying that companies that they had big positions in had become cautious and were concerned about their short-term prospects. They had mentioned that business inventories were rising and orders were slipping. This was in sharp contrast to the sentiment that prevailed following the crash in 1987, when many companies still expressed strong optimism concerning their business outlooks. We've also seen many types of hard sell-offs in the past when it seemed the U.S might become engaged in military conflicts. Also, when growth slips and begins to turn down, we've also seen those cycles turn down in the market as well, but usually the market leads first as it always looks ahead. These lessons from prior cycles must be remembered because they'll repeat themselves in the future too. After a very short reprieve from the selling in early September, it was straight back down again for the markets throughout the remainder of September and the first half of October. Third-quarter real GDP showed a decline for the first time in 32 quarters, or eight years. It looked again as if many things were going in the wrong direction, but then the market staged an interesting statement, similar to many we've seen in the past.

On October 12 the Nasdaq market was down 1% during the day and it looked like another typical selling day for the index. But the market reversed during the day and actually ended up 0.6%. This was a sign of support as the prior three days had experienced heavy selling and the index had closed right at or near its low for each of those days. The selling had been increasing and was quite heavy up to that point as the downtrend had dropped the Nasdaq nearly 31% in only three months. The Dow had given up 22.5% during the same time frame. On October 18, which would have been the fifth day of the new rally attempt, the Nasdaq followed through with a strong 2.2% gain on heavy volume. The broader S&P 500 also was up strongly, by 2.3% that same day also on heavy volume. These detailed signals have supported every upturn and bull market for over 100 years. They don't all last or mean that it's a 100% certainty that a major upturn will continue, but it at least gives the signal that the major trend is turning and more investors are now accumulating stocks as opposed to selling them. The very next day in *Investor's Daily* (still called by that name until Sep. 16, 1991) Cisco Systems was featured as a stock with solid fundamentals, an exciting new product, and one that had just surged out of a "shakeout + 3 points" basing pattern. This pattern was something that Jesse Livermore used to look for in his day, just proving once again that stock patterns keep repeating themselves throughout history. The day before (October 18) Cisco had soared 9.3% to $26.50 (adjusted for splits) in volume that was 421,000 shares, which was more than twice its average at the time. Most people had not heard of Cisco back then, but there certainly was some smart money being directed its way. The very next trading day, October 19, Cisco again soared, this time up $2.25, or over 8%, to a new three-month high on 837,000 shares, nearly twice the volume from the day before. This is a clear example of a new leader emerging and coming up off a bottoming market that confirmed its new upward direction. O'Neil viewed this stock as something similar to Pic'N Save — a new young company with a new product and concept and a similar chart pattern. Of course, we all know that Cisco would continue to be one of the best stocks of the 1990s. It would triple by November of 1991, and it ended up soaring over 70,000% until its top in 2000, when it would fall with the rest of the market during that severe downtrend.

While business kept slowing down as the fourth-quarter real GDP numbers came in negative again, the market was looking ahead as it always does. Coming up off the bottom and confirming its new uptrend in mid-October the Dow would chug its way higher and gain nearly 300 points from that October low until the end of 1990. The Nasdaq would add 50 points over the same time. Recall that when things look their worst the market may have exhausted its recent selling and turned the corner. That's why it's crucial to always stay in tune with the market's current action. That's what the best traders have always done; they don't get discouraged because they know that new opportunities can occur at any time. Roppel during this time was still making mistakes in option trades and listening to others. He would however be introduced to *Investor's Daily* in 1990, in what would become the first step in his learning process to turn around his performance. But he still focused mainly on low-priced cheap stocks and hadn't quite mastered market analysis or exactly how the paper (*IBD*™) really worked. So another unprofitable year would pass for him as he spent much of the time cold calling for commission dollars with his new firm. Despite the turnaround in the markets during October, the Nasdaq ended up losing 18% for the year following the heavy selling from July to October. The Dow fared better as it only lost 4% for the year.

After a brief pullback during the first two weeks of 1991 due to the uncertainty surrounding the impeding U.S. involvement with Iraq, the market turned around and began surging higher over the next few months as the U.S. campaign involving Iraq was a quick success. A few positives were also occurring in the economy at that time. The recession would end in March, and second-quarter real GDP would regain a decent showing ending the string of the previous four quarters of down and basically flat performance. So, with a short and successful military operation behind it and renewed growth in the economy, the stock market looked ahead and liked what it saw.

Some early leading stocks in 1991 included Costco, which came up off a cup-with-handle pattern in January and would rise 140% in just one year. International Game Technology (IGT) would turn out to be a huge winner as it soared 1,600% from its breakout in early 1991 to its peak in late 1993. Gaming stocks were a leader during this time, and IGT was its standout performer. Other leading groups that provided leading stocks included generic drugs, telecom, HMOs, biotechs, and semiconductors. The period also was experiencing lower interest rates as the Fed was making more cuts. The federal funds rate had already declined from 9.5% in January 1989 to 8.25% by the end of 1990. By the end of 1991 the federal funds rate would stand at 4%, the lowest in 27 years. These lower-interest-rate environments encourage companies to make capital investments. While the economy was picking up, the deficit was shrinking and capital research and development investments were picking up. Inflation was being contained, but there was rising unemployment mostly in the white-collar ranks.

One of the best groups of this run was the biotech stocks. Amgen was their leader, and O'Neil was adding to his position and reaping huge gains. Amgen was an established company with solid fundamentals. There were many other biotech stocks that were rising in price, but many only had a promising future drug and many had no earnings to speak of, as biotech is heavily dependent on research and development. Roppel sat on the sidelines and watched Amgen zoom higher and higher; he never bought into the stock, though he constantly watched its rise. His father had also invested in biotechs, so Jim jumped right in also. But we'll see another mistake being made here — he watched the leader (Amgen), both in terms of financial strength and stock price action, run right past him. Instead he focused on the cheapest stock of the group in hopes of hitting a grand slam. He read an article in *Money Magazine* about four "hot" biotech stocks, and that's when he chose the cheapest one and put himself and all his clients in the stock, which was Centocore. He did study the company well, and in September the FDA recommended for approval the company's new drug. The stock took off and climbed from $33 per share to $56 in just two weeks. He thought he had now mastered the stock market, as he finally held a winning position.

As the Dow crossed the 3,000 level again in early March the markets moved steadily higher throughout the summer and fall months. A sharp drop in November sent the Dow down 121 points in one day, but the market soon recovered. A very strong sprint during the last two weeks of 1991, mostly caused by the celebration of the breakup of the USSR, allowed the indexes to register solid gains for the year. The S&P 500 gained 26%, the Dow was up 20%, and the Nasdaq led all markets by rising an incredible 57% for the year. Smaller innovative stocks were clearly leading this new uptrend in the market as some new exciting companies were posting some very solid results.

The markets continued their end-of-year momentum from 1991 when 1992 began, especially on the leading Nasdaq. That index shot up another 12% just during the first six weeks of the new year. The Dow continued to lag behind with gains only half that size. After strong gains like the Nasdaq had been putting on, a consolidation of those gains seemed in order. Recall that many other times when the market marches upward in such a strong manner for an extended period of time that in many instances a correction becomes a part of the normal stock market cycle. Here in 1992 there were many good things happening that would create a positive environment for stocks. Interest rates were still coming down, inflation was falling and staying well contained, and corporate profits and real GDP were strong and rising. There were also many new companies that were really beginning to shine and bring new innovative and exciting products to the marketplace.

What did occur in early 1992 was that Centocore would begin to show classic topping signs in its stock price action in January. Roppel didn't know how to interpret this, as he was strictly sticking to the fundamentals and the story of the company. But Centocore was beginning to top at around $60 per share as heavy-volume down days began to overtake up days in the stock's daily action. This meant that many big investors and the smart money were beginning to take their profits out of the stock. Then the stock broke its key 50-day moving-average line. Roppel at the time didn't even know what that meant. He decided to hold on, and then on February 18, the FDA announced that it would not approve the drug it had recommended for approval months before. Roppel was fully margined in the stock and had been up approximately $20,000, which at that time was a fortune for him. After the FDA announcement, the stock crashed and Roppel was devastated. He actually had to write his firm a check to cover his losses on margin, and one client wouldn't even pay for his original purchase, which cost Roppel another $14,000. He ended up paying that back over an 18-month period. To make matters worse, his second biggest position at the time was in U.S. Bioscience, which soon afterward was also denied approval by the FDA for its chemotherapy drug called Ethiol. Again, Roppel and his customers were crushed. Roppel felt so bad about his losses that he became physically ill and had a hard time even getting out of bed at times.

There was also another blow to Roppel's account in 1992. He studied the fundamentals of a company called Royce Labs and liked what he saw, so he bought into the stock in the spring of 1992. He even spoke to the company's CFO about its future prospects. Of course, the news seemed too good to be true. Royce Labs soon collapsed, and Roppel took a 70% loss on the stock, again failing to exhibit the number one Golden Rule in the stock market — cut your losses short. As for learning from these major mistakes, Roppel had initially framed an article that was published in *USA Today* back when the FDA was contemplating the approval of the Centocore drug. He had originally kept that as a souvenir of his ingenious trade. He, to this day, still keeps that framed article next to his desk to remind him of his past mistakes. The year was a nearly total wipeout for him, and he actually contemplated leaving the business altogether.

By mid-1992 long-term bond yields were falling, and with short-term money market rates lower, more money was being directed into stock mutual funds. Also, 401k and other retirement programs were becoming more popular, and many participants had their contributions directed toward funds that invested in stocks. This powerful inflow of money, especially during a growing economy, is strong fuel for further stock market buying power. Near the springtime in 1992 a divergence appeared in the market. The Dow would continue moving upward, while the Nasdaq would begin a correction phase following its prior strong run-up. The Nasdaq fell from March until the end of June. It was a fairly normal correction with the index down 14%, especially considering how high it had run up over the prior 15 months, which was over 80%. But one sector that was especially hit hard during this correction was the biotech stocks just mentioned. Here we see another mistake by Roppel—not being in tune with the general trend of the market and not investing appropriately with that trend. The Dow would actually move higher all the way until early June, when it finally fell back as well. From July through September the markets traded in a somewhat choppy and sideways pattern seeming to more consolidate prior gains than exhibit more serious selling pressure. Then in October the markets blasted off again and would close the year with strong momentum behind them. The Nasdaq shot up over 22% in just the last three months of 1992, and the Dow climbed 9% over the same time. For the year the Dow finished with a 4% gain, while the Nasdaq scored another solid gain, up 15%.

The uptrending market continued gaining ground as 1993 began. Bill Clinton took over the White House, and the economy was still growing. Interest rates were low, and the mood seemed positive overall. After a rising market in January the markets pulled back in February. In March, Microsoft would break out of a basing pattern, and it would become a big winner in the 1990s as it would rise 1,800% from that point until its peak in 1999. Its innovative technologies would become widely accepted, and many of its software programs would allow companies to become more efficient in their operations. New technologies, similar to what Microsoft was introducing, would be key factors in raising the productivity levels of the 1990s. Higher productivity and greater efficiencies allowed more companies to trim overhead and overall costs and focus on their core missions to increase their bottom lines.

From March through April the markets traded in a whipsaw fashion with several weeks up and then several weeks down. From April through the summer and early fall the trend became more defined in a steady upward pattern. Many of the stocks that were rising were coming from medical, technology and gaming groups. The Nasdaq again outperformed and rose a solid 22% in less than six months from the end of April until mid-October. The Dow rose as well but at about half the rate as the Nasdaq during that time. By the first week of October the Nasdaq was rising on heavy volume at a faster pace. After a prolonged uptrend, these spurts can usually be attributed to climax runs in the market averages just as they show up consistently in individual stock patterns. From that top the Nasdaq would begin to fall. Rally attempts back up were met with further selling in late October and mid-November.

During this distribution in the market William O'Neil + Co., Incorporated, drafted a memo to its institutional clients. The memo was dated November 19. It stated that the company was adding more stocks to its sell and avoid lists. It mentioned that over the past four weeks the markets were coming under heavy selling after showing the topping signals that were described previously. Cabletron, Qualcomm, Tellabs, Best Buy, International Game Technology and Nextel were some of the stocks that the memo mentioned had reached tops and at that time were breaking down. These stocks were in addition to some others that were mentioned in an earlier memo, which included some big-cap names such as Nike, Novell, Phillip Morris and Waste Management. The memo also stated that it was clear the Nasdaq market had experienced a climax run in mid-October and that the S&P 500 index also experienced heavy distribution on November 2, 3, and 4. Other important details that were outlined in the memo were that laggard stocks had been picking up recently, which has always been an early sign of a weakening market. Two of the groups that had been leading the strong advance, which were gaming and technology, were breaking down. Other weakness was also showing up in banking, utility and insurance stocks. Also, gold was up, and there was a lot of excitement around. We've seen how in the past that when everyone is running around and excited about the stock market most miss out on the vital details that the market starts to exhibit as it begins to change its direction. It's the experienced and emotionally controlled market operators that pick up on these cues and then act appropriately. O'Neil was right there seeing this, and he was even telling many of the professional money managers what was happening through his market memo. One thing the memo did stress was that economic conditions overall were still positive and that this topping action may be more conducive to a normal correction type of market cycle than a full-blown severe market sell-off resulting in a major bear market. Nevertheless, the signals were clear, and they were the same signals that the market had displayed in many prior topping market cycles. So O'Neil acted on these signals and preserved a good part of prior profits made and avoided costly losses.

One who was still learning at this time was Roppel. He had not yet developed the market analysis skills needed to accurately adjust to key market signals by following price and volume action within leading stocks and the market as a whole. He actually was not as active in the market in 1993 as he was in prior years, mostly due to his devastating losses from the prior year. He would though experiment with some stock-screening software products that were out on the market. He also tried some artificial-intelligence programs that would give buy and sell signals. He had thought that maybe they were the key to success in stocks. But he would soon learn that they weren't the answer as he did experience a few more losses in his account, but he continued learning from experience and vowed to never give up.

The Nasdaq ended up whipping up and down again during the last few months of 1993. It was however unable to regain its high that occurred in mid-October as it struggled with choppy trading action. It ended the year up nearly 16% mostly due to its strong run from April through mid-October. The Dow exhibited some better strength during the last few months of the year as big-cap stocks held up better, and the index ended up 14% for the year.

The markets started off 1994 by shrugging off much of the topping action that existed near the end of 1993. The Dow actually crossed over the 4,000 mark by the end of January. Even the Nasdaq drove higher to cross the 800 mark, also by the end of January. Those peaks would be just about the highs for the markets that year as the Federal Reserve then ended its long policy period of no increases in interest rates. The Fed would become concerned about inflation, even though it still remained well contained, and it would then begin an aggressive campaign of interest rate hikes beginning in February 1994. The beginning of these rate hikes would send the markets down in early February. More than a few prior leaders were then exhibiting some classic topping action, much the same as we've seen in prior market tops, as it looked as if O'Neil's late-1993 assessment was coming to fruition. A few of those former leaders were:

Intervoice, Inc. This stock was a big winner during the 1992–93 market. It rose from a split-adjusted price of $5 per share in June 1992 to near $22 per share by October 1993. It then formed a head-and-shoulders topping pattern right before O'Neil was drafting his market memo discussed earlier. By January 1994 the peak of the stock was a distant memory, and the right shoulder of the topping pattern was formed at $17. It would then collapse from there on heavy-volume down days to under $8 by June 1994.

International Game Technology. As mentioned earlier this was a huge winner in the early 1990s. It peaked in October 1993 at near a split-adjusted $41 per share, which actually turned out to be the head of a classic head-and-shoulders topping pattern. As it fell off its peak, IGT would violate key support lines that it had never traded under on its way up in price. Attempts to get back over those areas failed in early 1994. It then formed the right shoulder of its classic pattern in February and March of 1994. From there it was all downhill on heavy-volume weeks. By late 1994, IGT was trading at near $15.

These topping signals in prior leading stocks were a clear warning sign to O'Neil that the general market lacked the strong support that it had during its upward trend and that selling was now overtaking the market. These chart patterns keep repeating themselves over time when markets top and begin to turn in direction. They have been pointed out in previous chapters already, and we'll see many more as we continue to analyze future cycle patterns. The Fed however wasn't done after its first rate increase. It aggressively raised the federal funds rate another four times just before May. Three quarter-point rate hikes were followed by a half-point increase in the spring. March was a bad month for the markets, as the Nasdaq fell over 10% in just the last two weeks of that month. The Dow also fell by approximately 10% as well on increased volume. With the Fed's aggressive rate hikes — and more to come — the bond market melted. As a result, the bond market experienced its worst days since the 1960s. Also, Orange County, California experienced huge losses on its derivatives portfolio, which wasn't helping the situation. While GDP was slipping a bit along with corporate profits, layoffs were on the rise. The markets would however recover somewhat from off their April lows, but it would end up being another whipsaw trading pattern for the next several months.

The Fed continued its rate hikes at an even faster pace as another half-point increase came in the summer. By the end of June the Nasdaq had already fallen over 10% for the year and the Dow was struggling as well. O'Neil, who had warned of something like this, was safely protecting himself. His experience by this time was invaluable, and he knew what to do when the market got into trouble. He had seen this coming many, many months ago and would save himself from major hits to his portfolio. At about this time however the market started to head back upward. We've seen this happen before. When just about everyone is scared to death, the market stages a change in direction. From a bottom in late June, the markets began to march steadily higher. Even a few stocks that were setting up in bases would surge forward to begin major moves. Peoplesoft would soar over 20-fold from this point in August 1994 to its peak a little over 3½ years later. Ascend Communications was another technology company that would blast off from an August 1994 base. It would rise 1,380% in just 15 months.

This newfound relief rally propelled the Nasdaq up 12% from its low in late June to mid-September. It was quite a sprint up after all the selling that had taken place earlier in the year. In fact, the short but sharp correction again was what O'Neil had mentioned might happen in his market memo from November 1993, due to the fact that the underlying conditions in the economy were still fairly strong. New technology issues led the way, while the Dow lagged behind, but not by much as the rally broadened out. One thing the economy had going for it back then was that computers and software programs were really having an impact on creating efficiencies within many corporations. The Internet was really just getting started, and excitement about more innovative technologies was beginning to build. Many new innovative companies were being created and introducing a host of products that were being adapted and implemented into many investment budgets from across numerous industries. While the market seemed to find its footing within an aggressive interest-rate-increase environment, the Fed would again raise the federal funds rate — this time by a whopping three-quarters of a point in the fall of 1994. This announcement sent the markets downward sharply in November. But again the recent resilience of the markets perked up, and they finished the year on an upward trend during the last month of the year. It definitely seemed that the trend had changed as mergers were also picking up, which as we've seen is a sign of confidence in the market. The other item the market was looking out and seeing as a positive was that corporate profits were strong again after a very brief respite. It was quite a comeback for the markets despite the tightening from the Fed that was occurring. The Dow would actually eke out a 2% gain for the year, while the Nasdaq would post a loss of 3%, ending its three-year positive run.

Jim Roppel in 1994 would experience his seventh year in a row of losses in his personal account as the year closed. It shows just how challenging the market can be. But he wasn't about to give up, and as you'll soon discover, that was a wise decision. And as it has already been mentioned, some of his losing years were outright devastating. He was nearly completely wiped out, from a financial perspective, three times, not to mention the psychological impacts those defeats must have had. For many who experience losses, it makes them wonder if it is possible at all to make decent money in the stock market. But Roppel, as we've seen with many others, refused to give up. The year 1994 was actually a turning point for him in many respects. He kept up his study, pulled himself up from bad periods, and continued on. He was really now starting to adopt the CAN SLIM™ method that O'Neil teaches. Roppel would continue attending *IBD*-sponsored seminars, even repeating ones he had attended before, just in order to get the correct principles, strategies and disciplines down so that he would start breaking old bad habits and start implementing successful time-proven methods. In fact, if you attend any of *IBD*'s sessions (which is highly recommended), you will find many participants who have been there before, many even multiple times.

One key for Roppel in 1994 was that he went back and reread O'Neil's classic "How to Make Money in Stocks." Roppel had read this book years before, but that was about it — he had read it, but he hadn't studied it and adopted its time-proven principles. It takes extra study to get all the aspects of the complex stock market down. Recall that Nicolas Darvas would reread Gerald Loeb's classic "The Battle for Investment Survival" every two weeks just to stay focused. Darvas, and his many years of mistakes before he turned it around for himself, are very similar to Roppel's experiences. Both of them prove that perseverance can overcome short-term defeats. Roppel even began to include many of O'Neil's CAN SLIM principles in the newsletters he was writing at the time. As time went on, Roppel's newsletter would consist almost exclusively of most of the rules from the CAN SLIM investment method. Roppel also read Loeb's book "The Battle for Investment Survival" for the first time in 1994 (he would, like Darvas, read it many more times as well). But the one major strategy that Roppel implemented in 1994, the lack of which had been detrimental to his turnaround, was that he finally adopted the Golden Rule — he began to cut all his losses short. He also started a subscription to *Daily Graphs*, which are chart books produced on a weekly basis by Daily Graphs, a company owned by O'Neil (also available today in an online version). He then began a discipline and ritual with *Daily Graphs* that he still follows to this day — he spends Sunday afternoons going through each page looking at every chart. For those not familiar with the *Daily Graphs* chart books, they contain thousands of charts. But after having read them religiously now for over 10 years, Roppel can get through them in just a few hours. A disciplined approach through many repetitious years of study now has his eye trained to focus in on only those chart patterns that qualify for further review. Recall Jack Dreyfus — the same patterns just kept recurring over and over again. For Roppel, he now knows exactly what he is looking for, and he doesn't waste time with other nonproductive tasks. The other important routine he added in 1994 was a year-end postanalysis of his trades. All the best traders do this, as it is one of the best learning tools in forcing them to see their mistakes so they stop repeating them in future market periods.

While he still lost money in the early 1990s because he didn't have the correct market analysis, chart-reading skills to recognize proper basing patterns, and selling rules down yet, Roppel did contain his losses. This was in stark contrast to the 50% to 70% losses he had experienced in other periods, as he would just hold on hoping for a comeback with a fundamentally strong stock. He also didn't understand how critical volume was in timing correct buy and sell points. One example was Micron Technology. He bought this stock twice in early 1994, both on very low volume breakouts and also when the general market was not in a clear uptrend and exhibiting strength. He kept his losses small at 7% each time the stock failed to move higher. But he made the mistake of not purchasing again later when it really broke out in heavy volume. Micron would soar 290% in just seven months from that confirmed breakout. After that mistake, he then made another classic amateur mistake — selling winning positions too soon. He bought Macromedia, Inc., in late October, after the market had turned upward after its midyear correction, and quickly sold out for a three-point profit. It later went on to surge nearly 700% without flashing any major sell signals. One other thing Roppel lacked at this time was historical knowledge of prior big leaders and market action. This, as we have already seen, was a major reason why the best in the business over the years have succeeded. Roppel would learn this lesson and employ it as major skill for his future success.

The markets in 1995 began where they had left off in the prior year — continuing an uptrend and moving higher. A final interest rate increase of another half a point in late January caused a slight drop in the indexes, but the market as always was looking ahead. After seven interest rate hikes in a row that doubled the short-term federal funds rate to 6% in just one year, the market sensed the tightening was over and began to look ahead to better times. As with any uptrending market there are always new leaders that step up. Leading stocks that were coming up off basing patterns came from technology groups such as software, Internets, and computer peripherals. Banking stocks also did well, along with stocks from the retail groups.

It's important to note again that prior corrections, such as the one that just took place in 1994, always help build the proper basing patterns for future leading stocks. Just as the market goes through its cyclical rotation, individual stocks have always built their patterns in much of a similar fashion. Recall that Jack Dreyfus mentioned in his early years of the 1930s, '40s and '50s that he kept seeing the same patterns in stock charts repeating themselves. O'Neil's historical study of past big winners in the market since the early 1950s also identifies the same type of base-building patterns just prior to when stocks begin their biggest moves. He always uses precedents from prior big winners in order to try and find the next big winners of the next market upturn that will always occur. And all patterns must have that downward slope to them at some point in order for them to come back up again and then continue to soar higher.

While the first two quarters of 1995 experienced positive but slow growth in real GDP, the future looked even brighter. By spring 1995, the Fed was done raising interest rates as inflation stayed very well contained. Corporate profits were growing, and the unemployment picture was improving as well. Long-term yields were also coming back down after spiking upward the prior year. There were many positives concerning the economic landscape, and there were more innovative companies that were coming public. Most of the best would hail from the technology industry. The markets took off in February 1995 and began a fairly steep upward trend that had the Dow crossing the 4,000 mark again by late February and then never looking back. Also adding momentum was the fact that there were many deregulatory legislations passed during the first half of the 1990s.

The Nasdaq sprinted forward and really took off until it finally hit the 1,000 mark in mid-July. It had experienced a 36% run already in just over half a year. After hitting the psychologically important milestone, the Nasdaq fell back over 50 points in just two sessions. It turned out to be just a pause and some profit taking as the market then resumed its upward move. The Dow was also surging higher, and with only normal pullbacks, a definitive positive trend was well established. The pullbacks on the indexes did not exhibit the heavy selling that we've seen so many times now when markets really begin to top and roll over. In the summer of 1995 we also get one of the more exciting new companies to come public. Netscape's IPO drew much attention, and the success of the stock was just a signal of things to come. The Internet was now generating quite a bit of attention, and investors were in a buying mood to get in on the next great innovation.

Roppel had made a change a few months earlier when he left the firm of David A. Noyes and landed a position with Northern Trust. One of Roppel's newest customers at Northern failed to pay for his purchase of Netscape when it gapped higher on an opening session by 35 points. Roppel had to pay the firm back for that, which amounted to approximately $75,000. It was just another setback for him in his early years. But the old saying that "mother knows best" was an inspiration for him. Roppel's mother never gave up on her son and his future ability. She actually had just received a small inheritance at that time, and she gave it to him to continue on with his passion and dreams of making it in the market. And he still refused to give up, and one thing he did do at Northern was stop trading in options. That was a wise decision for him as there were plenty of opportunities in stocks, as new issues would set records in 1995 and then again in 1996. Many IPOs that now came public doubled in their first day of trading, as demand was heavy. Also in the summer of 1995 the Federal Reserve reversed its policy of raising interest rates, and it actually cut rates in July. The markets responded favorably to this and resumed their climb. After a mild pullback in the early fall, the markets traded in a sideways manner until the end of October.

With the economy humming along and interest rates declining, the demand for stocks just kept increasing. The middle class was now more involved through 401k plans and also through mutual funds directly. The mutual fund industry was growing rapidly. The Dow, after pausing for a few months, took off in November and then crossed the 5,000 mark, only nine months after it had crossed 4,000. The Dow would end up finishing strong at a positive 33% for its fifth straight up year. The S&P 500 would end the year up by 37.5%. The Nasdaq didn't quite finish as strong as the Dow, as it continued its flat and choppy pattern that it began in the fall. But it ended up outperforming for the year and registering a very strong 40% gain. The year 1995 was also when Roppel began to improve a bit on his chart reading, market analysis, and observation and study skills. He still didn't make much headway as he still relied too much on basic Wall Street favorites like PE and valuation concerns. He also missed many big leaders that blew right past him due to inexperience. He felt he was making progress and getting better though, especially since he was sticking to a strict loss-cutting strategy, but there was still more for him to learn.

The markets started off 1996 by pulling back. In fact, the Dow dropped close to the 5,000 mark but remained above it and then moved strongly higher until mid-February. The Nasdaq would close below the 1,000 mark by mid-January, but it also soon turned back upward and drove higher as well. Mutual funds were really gaining in popularity, as the markets kept moving higher. Stronger demand for stocks, especially by big mutual funds that were being funneled with new money from a strong economy, kept the upward trend intact. Many of the leading groups during this time came from the technology sector. Personal computers and workstations, software, computer peripherals and LANs, and Internet stocks were out in front and posting big gains. Banks, retail and energy stocks were also doing well. O'Neil, of course, during a confirmed uptrend, was fully invested, and he held many leading stocks during this time.

Many economic issues continued to be favorable, including low inflation, growing real GDP, growing corporate profits, stable interest rates and an improving employment outlook. There were also no major military issues or recessions or slowdown periods on the immediate horizon. Notice how many of these factors were in stark contrast to other periods that caused major concerns for investors and resulted in very choppy market environments. The 1970s were dominated with many political, social and economic problems. The markets responded to those times with whipsawing trade and many uncertainties. Here in the middle 1990s many new innovations were under way due to favorable economic conditions and low tax rates (mostly due to the Reagan tax cuts that were introduced many years before) that encouraged entrepreneurial innovation and risk taking.

Here is where we begin to see the progression of Roppel's studies really take hold. As mentioned, he was now studying market action and stocks with price, volume and chart patterns on an in-depth level. He was continuing his attendance at *IBD* seminars and was determined as ever to turn around his performance. His first big trade was Iomega Corp. when he purchased 3,000 shares (split adjusted on chart; see Figure 10-3) as the Nasdaq was in a strong uptrend and Iomega had just risen out of a flat basing pattern on big volume. Quickly thereafter a sharp pullback forced him out of 20% of his position. Notice how he was quick to take action on the downside, though this time it was premature. The pullback came on lower volume, and the stock held

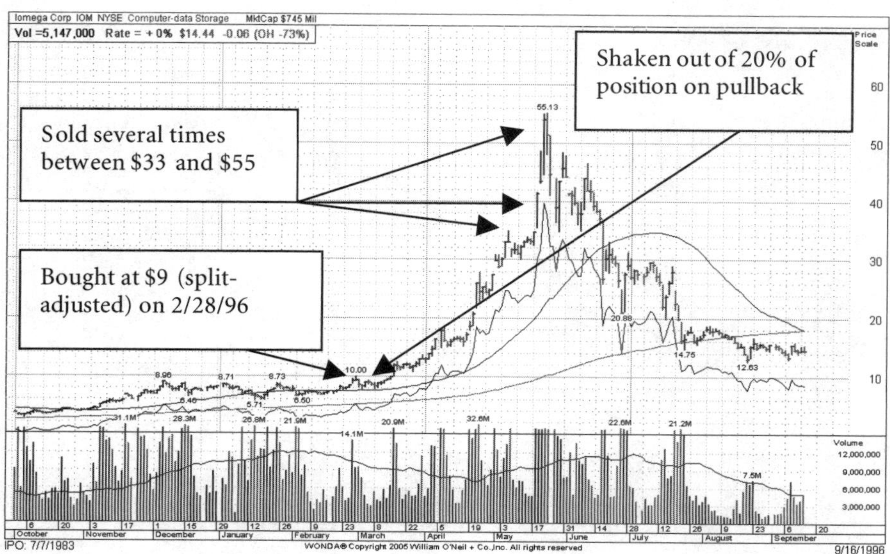

Figure 10-3 Iomega Corp. 1996 Daily Chart.
Source: © *William O'Neil + Co., Inc. All rights reserved. Reprinted with permission.*

above its 50-day moving average. But he stayed patient with his remaining shares and then the stock really took off on huge volume and then soared over the next three months. It then went into a classic climax run, and Roppel sold out like a master right near the top.

His selling off blocks of his position as the stock was rising was more conducive to an experienced Loeb or O'Neil transaction. Roppel ended up making just under $100,000 on this transaction, and it really lifted his newfound confidence in his long and hard study that he had been undertaking for many years. There were also other positions that Roppel was taking and doing well in at that time. He bought 1,500 shares of Action Performance at $9.75 (split adjusted on chart; see Figure 10-4) on March 13 as it had just lifted to almost a new high on very heavy volume. Riding the strong market, Action Performance zoomed higher throughout the spring and early summer. Roppel held fast as there was no reason to sell a well-performing stock. On June 20, 1996, Action gapped up at the open on a good earnings report but then started selling off on its highest volume in weeks. Roppel took that as a sign of weakness and that the big money was starting to take their profits. That's exactly what he decided to do, and he sold the entire position out. He netted a 100% gain on that stock.

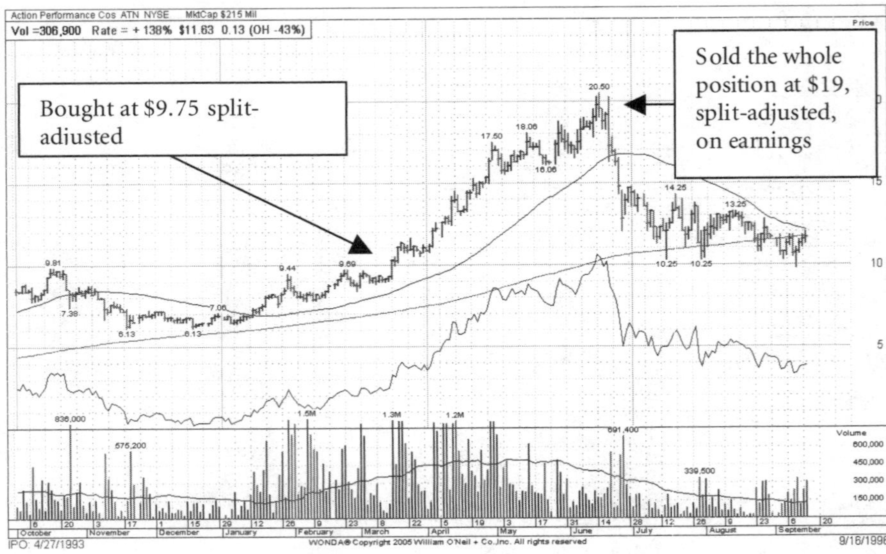

Figure 10-4 Action Performance 1996 Daily Chart.

Source: © *William O'Neil + Co., Inc. All rights reserved. Reprinted with permission.*

During this same time Roppel had purchased Dollar Tree Stores, Inc., as well. He bought on Feb. 29, 1996, at $24.375 per share as it had also come up off a flat basing pattern on heavy volume with the markets in their strong uptrend. This stock soared higher on excellent volume and then would quiet down on lower volume on down days on its way up. When volume picked up to its highest levels in months and the stock started falling on this heavy volume, Roppel sold out. It was another winner for him, and he was noticing how these strong stocks by mid-June were flashing classic topping signals. He didn't know what was ahead — he just followed the stocks and their actions and then he implemented proper sell rules. Notice how his behavior was in exact contrast to how he would operate years earlier. He was now buying fundamentally strong stocks coming out of proper basing patterns when the market was strong. He then held them as they worked out correctly, while always keeping his eye out for changes. When selling signals were present, he acted. This is how a stock operator matures from someone who earlier had no skills, disciplines, or trading rules. It shows how his hard work was beginning to pay off for him as he kept studying the best traders and the history of the market and kept up and refined his chart-reading study.

As the markets consolidated their early 1996 gains in early spring, the Nasdaq would then continue its strong upward rise during April and May. The Dow however lagged behind as the Nasdaq and its leaders sprinted higher. By early June the Nasdaq had already risen over 18% for the year. The Dow was up approximately 15%. The frenzy over mutual funds was continuing to grow. The dollar was strong, which helped as well. But by the summer the markets began to look a bit tired again after many strong months of gains. This is exactly what the strong leading stocks were exhibiting as we just saw in the three transactions from Roppel. A sharp pullback occurred in June and July, especially on the Nasdaq. That index would then correct nearly 20% from its peak in early June to mid-July. It was a scary and rapid fall. The Dow's decline was more modest at 10%, but still worthy of a decent pullback. Both indexes, though, seemed to find support just above their recent milestone marks of 5,000 on the Dow and 1,000 on the Nasdaq. Those psychological levels holding up bolstered confidence for many. But notice how Roppel avoided this hard 20% correction on the Nasdaq. This again was in stark contrast to how he would have acted just a few short years ago. Remember that most leading stocks will drop far further than the averages during corrections and especially during bear markets. One can just look at the chart of Iomega above to see how hard that stock fell during the summer correction. Roppel's trades were now like a marksman hitting his mark. He retained excellent profits, and those trades boosted his confidence, which is critical for future success, though in a well-managed and measured way. From those levels in the markets just mentioned the markets turned right around and continued a strong upward trend.

A few new leaders helped bring this market up. Dell Computer, with its new innovative and low-cost PC business model of direct-to-the-consumer delivery, soared out of a basing pattern in July 1996 and climbed over 500% in just 15 months. As the fall months wore on, the markets just continued climbing higher and the Dow crossed the 6,000 mark in October. By this time excitement was beginning to run high as new business magazines were coming out, CNBC was gaining in popularity, and new mutual funds were coming to market in droves. Money was pouring in to these funds, as the year would bring in $235 billion just to stock funds. This was by far a record number. As the money came in, the managers of those funds put it to work in the market. In 1996 fund managers had 6.2% of their funds in cash, versus 13% in 1990. This heavy demand for stocks from big money is what moves markets. For the individual traders of those days, following right in sync with that big money is where they would have wanted to be.

The markets by November 1996 were in a strong upward trend, and many leading stocks were producing big gains for their holders. Increased productivity, strong corporate profits and a strong growing economy all factored in as the economy seemed to be running on all cylinders. This fast-rising market was of course the talk of many, and it was catching many people's attention. One of those who would comment was Alan Greenspan, when on Thursday December 5 he uttered his famous words of "irrational exuberance" during a speech to describe his views of the rapidly rising stock market. His well-known comments had a very short-term effect on the market as the markets fell approximately 2% the next morning, while other exchanges globally actually fell even more. But by the following Monday, the Nasdaq registered its second biggest point gain in its history up to that point. The year 1996 turned out to be another solid one for the markets as the S&P 500 rose 23% and the Dow was up 26% for its sixth straight positive year in a row, which was a record string at that time. The Nasdaq matched the S&P 500 with a solid 23% gain. Some of the best groups for the year included semiconductors, which soared 80%; computer hardware, which was up 41%; and software, which gained 36%.

Roppel Follows the Market's Action

The upward momentum of the recent market action continued as 1997 began. January was another solid month as the markets continued higher. Consolidation was dominant in February as the Dow traded sideways, though it did cross the 7,000 mark, but the Nasdaq began to slip downward. In March the Federal Reserve raised interest rates by a quarter of a point, which helped send the markets downward. Sharp drops in the markets occurred until mid-April. After some profit taking and a scare from the Fed, the markets would again turn right around and resume their upward trends. Roppel was right there, and he noticed a new leader taking shape. He bought into Jabil Circuit, which was a technology leader from the electronics–contract manufacturing group. Roppel bought this stock perfectly when it broke out of a base on May 2, 1997, and made a new high at $25 per share, which can be seen in Figure 10-5 on p. 204. The market had also just turned back upward, and Roppel was right in sync with the market and a strong stock. He held on to this stock as it kept gaining in price. In mid-June 1997, the company reported outstanding earnings and the CEO was featured on CNBC touting the bright future that lay just ahead for the company. The stock really exploded upward after that. Roppel still hung on, and the stock reacted perfectly by rising on heavy volume and pulling back or pausing on weak volume, indicating that the big investors were content to hold the stock. Roppel would go on to hold this stock until it finally showed selling signals, which included heavy down days on very strong volume. It also would slice through its 50-day moving average, which it had never done all the way up on its rise. As we'll see later, the market was set for a major correction in the fall and Jabil Circuit would head lower with that market correction. Roppel was out of his position when its action flashed sell cues, and he acted correctly and retained another 100%+ gain. We are really starting to see now how Roppel was beginning to turn things around and how his profitable transactions would begin to mirror the same strategies of the best stock traders who have already been featured.

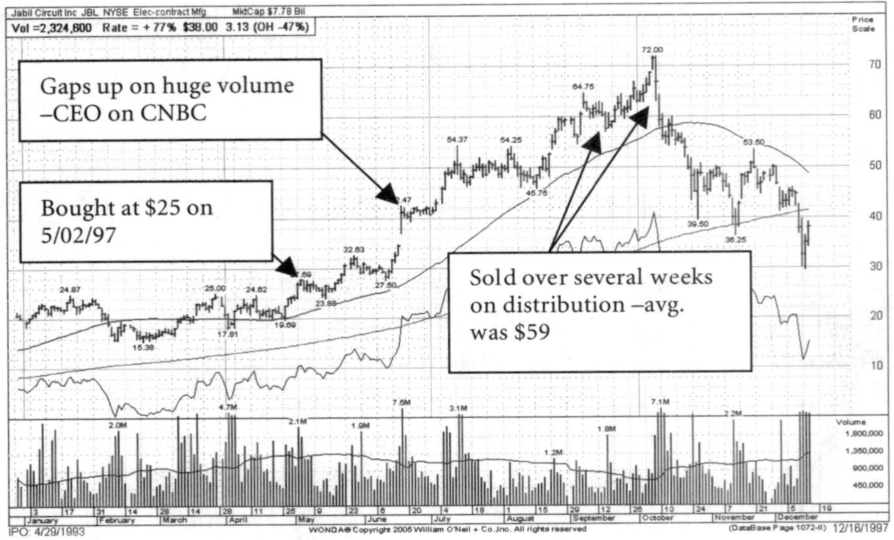

Figure 10-5 Jabil Circuit, Inc., 1997 Daily Chart.
Source: © *William O'Neil + Co., Inc. All rights reserved. Reprinted with permission.*

For the next four months, from mid-April until early August, the markets sprinted higher. The Nasdaq gained over 35% in that span, while the Dow was not far behind, as it passed the 8,000 level in July and climbed 30% in just four months. During this time the Fed also refrained from further increases in rates, which pleased investors. In fact, it would begin cutting rates and not raise them again until June of 1999. During the strong upward run, technology-, media- and telecom-related stocks would post the best gains. These were good times as capital investment was booming and prices were falling for central processing units (CPUs) and memory components for computers. Consumers were reaping the benefit of new technology products at lower prices. Corporate profits were still growing at a healthy clip, and real GDP numbers were solid. Productivity was the new engine driving growth and keeping inflation well contained. New advancements in technology were beginning to pay off in many economic statistics that supported a positive and increasing growth phase.

A few of the other new leaders that were breaking out of sound basing patterns during the time included Home Depot again, as it would break out of a cup-with-handle base in May 1997 and shoot up another 431% over the next 32 months. Yahoo was another new technology leader that broke out of a cup-with-handle base in July, and it would rocket up 7,443% over the next 30 months. When the market moves up strongly like it was doing in the first part of 1997, there are many opportunities to latch onto big leading stocks that are being accumulated by big money funds. And that was exactly what was happening, just as we've seen in past upward-trending markets. One mistake that Roppel made in 1997 was when he took a position in Siebel Systems, Inc., in June. Roppel knew the company well, and it had impressive fundamentals and was in a major leading group — software enterprise. Its customer-relationship management software program was being adopted by many large organizations, and Seibel was reaping the benefits of strong revenues and earnings. As it broke out of a cup-with-handle pattern he bought in at $27 to $30 per share (adjusted for a three-for-one stock split). He went in with a huge position and was leveraged on full margin. Having taken his biggest position yet he was too nervous when the stock quickly pulled back in what turned out to be a normal minor fluctuation. He then quickly unloaded his full position and ended up losing about one point on the transaction. Seibel went on to be a huge winner. Roppel would learn from this, as we'll see later, but that is one of the traits of the best traders — they always remember their mistakes so in the future they try not to repeat them.

As we get back to the markets' action, recall that when the markets rise very fast over an extended period of time it usually means that a top may be just around the corner. In 1997 the Nasdaq was leading all indexes as it raced up to hit over 1,700 in early October. The Dow had slowed down somewhat and traded in a choppy fashion during August and September. After normal pullbacks in mid-October, the markets were hit with some international issues that sent them down hard. During the summer of 1997 overbuilding in Asia caused excess capacity, and the Thai Baht declined 12% against the dollar. Other devaluations soon followed, and as the "Asian flu" spread, it was feared that U.S. companies doing business in Asia would get hurt. This expansion of globalization to the Pacific Rim would then begin to stumble as the fast growth track that it had been on began slowing down. A near panic ensued as the U.S. markets then reacted to this crisis. On Monday, October 27, the Dow would fall 554 points, or over 7%. It would be the largest point loss in the Dow's history, surpassing the crash in 1987. But the markets soon recovered, as the crisis did not have as much of an impact as most had feared, and the U.S. economy was still very strong and for the most part unaffected. As many also looked to the U.S. for growth, they would find stability and a strong economic environment, and foreign funds would continue to flow to the U.S. markets.

As the markets recovered quickly from the late October sell-off the Dow actually recovered to the point where it had been before the sell-off within just over a month. By early December, the Dow was just a few points shy of its early October level. The Nasdaq didn't recover as quickly but still managed to move higher by year-end. Other new leaders also came to the fore, including Cisco again as it broke out in September; it would soar another 900% to its peak in March of 2000. Network Appliance was a huge winner as it broke out of a cup-with-handle base in October and gained 3,700% in 30 months. In December, CMGI Info Systems would blast up off a cup-with-handle pattern and surge 8,958% in just 24 months. It was another solid year for the markets and the U.S. economy. GDP grew 4.5% that year, and the markets kept moving higher as the Dow gained a solid 23%, for its unprecedented seventh straight positive year. The Nasdaq finished up 22% for the year.

A sharp drop during the first two weeks of 1998 was quickly reversed, and the markets resumed their incredible runs. A sharp drop in crude prices in early 1998 reduced any inflation jitters. In fact, it looked as if economic conditions couldn't get any better. Interest rates were stable, long-term yields were falling, corporate profits were still strong, unemployment was continuing to improve, and the discount rate was now holding under 5%. The stock market kept reflecting good times ahead, and new innovative companies seemed to come to market on a daily basis. Improved productivity reigned, and the U.S. was the economic powerhouse. The Internet was really fueling excitement, much as the automobile and radio did decades before. From February through April the Dow shot almost straight up, gaining over 20% in just a few months and breaking through the 9,000 level. The Nasdaq would rise even more, by over 30% from just mid-January to late April. Nokia Corp. was a new leader breaking out of a classic cup-with-handle base in March. It would ring up an 800% gain in 30 months from that point. Roppel didn't get in on this one at that point, but Nokia offered up other strategic buy points during its climb, and we'll see later how Roppel took advantage of one of those opportunities when the market was resuming an upward trend. EMC was an even earlier leader, as it broke out in January and would soar 478% in just 15 months.

After a normal pullback and consolidation of its prior gains during May and through the midpoint of June, the markets turned right back around again and surged higher into the middle of July. The Nasdaq even broke through the 2,000 level. This spurt in July looked similar to the climax run that has accompanied many topping stocks and markets in the past. In fact, O'Neil would view this current time (from July 1995 to July 1998) in the market as similar to the 1962–66 market uptrend, which had the Dow rising 85% in four years. As the market and many stocks began showing those classic topping signals here in the summer of 1998, O'Neil acted again and began to sell his holdings that violated his time-tested sell rules. By mid to late July the markets really began to show classic selling or distribution signs. Roppel, though active during this time, didn't have many positions open. He was looking for proper basing patterns in his chart reading and wasn't finding very many good candidates, as many stocks had already broken out and were well extended from proper buy points. He knew the much higher risks involved in buying stocks that were in extended upward runs, and his experience by this time was telling him to heed caution.

By the third week of July, distribution days started showing up in the major averages. Heavy selling was beginning to take place, and many leading stocks were cracking. A few examples, which started to weaken before the major index averages, were:

Cliffs Drilling, Co. This stock was a big gainer from April 1996 through November 1997, as it rose more than 10-fold from a split-adjusted $8 to near $80 per share. It fell back in early 1998 to near $60, which is not unusual considering how far up it had gone in less than two years. But by May 1998, key selling signals were flashing that resembled more than just normal fluctuations. Heavy volume became prevalent on many down days. The stock would then break with the market, and by August it was trading at near $15 per share.

Saville Systems PLC (ADR). This leading stock had soared nearly 500% from April 1996 to April 1998. By June it had formed a classic head-and-shoulders topping pattern at near $50 per share. Then it really fell apart as heavy-volume down days ruled the day. By late August 1998, it was trading near $15 as well.

CIBER, Inc. This was another leading stock that doubled in price from September 1997 at near $20 per share to near $40 by June 1998. It too would form a classic head-and-shoulders topping pattern and experienced heavy-volume down days that would begin to dominate its trading sessions. Volume really picked up as the stock headed down, classic signs that big traders were cashing in profits and heading for the exit. Once again, this prior leader would fall to the $15 price range by September.

O'Neil Avoids Another Major Market Break

While the leaders discussed before were starting to flash selling signals by June, William O'Neil + Company was putting Gillette on its sell list for its institutional clients. Gillette at the time was one of the most widely held and highly regarded blue chip companies. His firm received some criticism for putting such a stalwart stock as Gillette on the sell list at near $60 per share. But O'Neil's experience was telling him it was time to sell as the market looked like it was topping and Gillette's run had been about over — it later sank. Experience and objectivity go a long way in the market, and it proves again that not listening to the crowd and others' opinions but instead to the market itself and the action within a stock from its price and volume action is what leads to profitable transactions. The last week of July is when the selling started to really begin, which can be seen from Figures 10-1 and 10-2 on pp. 181 and 182. The Dow would lose over 500 points in just one week. Big-cap stocks (Proctor & Gamble, etc.) were especially getting hit hard. The market actually experienced five distribution days within 10 trading sessions. All five of those selling days came before the market really broke down. The S&P 500 experienced six distribution days within a span of 13 trading sessions. By early August the market had experienced even more selling. The Dow fell 299 points on August 4, which was its third largest one-day point decline in history up to that point. What happened was the Russian default was causing quite a bit of panic. During the summer of 1998 the Russian economy was suffering due to the Far East problems that were occurring. The Russian government then called a moratorium on its debt, which in turn instigated a default. Foreign investment basically then came to a standstill. Here was another international issue that was affecting the U.S. markets due to the expansion of globalization.

By mid-August the markets at least temporarily stopped declining, but it was a brief settling. In late August the market really fell apart. O'Neil by this time was well out of his holdings, which is again a main reason why the best traders can put together triple-digit yearly returns — they act when conditions give them signals to act. Here O'Neil was again reaping huge gains during a strong upward trend in the market and then selling, locking in prior profits, and avoiding major market breaks, when the same signals that accompanied prior topping market cycles gave off warning signs. On August 31 the Dow would lose another 6% (502 points) in that session alone. This heavy break in the market had a major impact on a large hedge fund at that time. Long-Term Capital Management (LTCM), which was supposedly being run by academic market "experts," was basically destroyed by the bear market that hit at a pretty rapid pace. The Dow would lose over 20% in just over a month. The Nasdaq lost approximately 27% over the same span. LTCM got into trouble because it was heavily overleveraged. By mid-1998 many of its leveraged bets were going against it. Its system was based on efficient market theories, and what really happened should not have happened, according to their models. But here again we see that the market is always right and that LTCM's model and its academic assumptions about the future were totally wrong. You simply cannot predict future prices and human behavior, especially through a computerized modeling system. The Russian default crisis brought a panic to the U.S. stock markets, but early signals were there to the most astute observers who were watching the markets' action. By the third week of September, LTCM had to be bailed out by a consortium of 50 banks and investment banks. This announcement just sent the markets down even further, and by early October the Nasdaq had fallen 33% from its peak just from late July. The Dow had lost 1,900 points during the same short period. No one knows how bad things can get, which is why it pays to act on the selling signals the market will always display.

To calm investors fears the Federal Reserve even had to pump money into the economy by reducing interest rates in three quarter-point increments. This was actually a positive for the market. As we've seen many times already, when many give up after a severe drop, the market may turn right around and begin a whole new uptrend. Again, no one knows how long downtrends will last, but when you stay tuned into the market's action no matter what, you'll see when these turning points occur. Bernard Baruch did it; Richard Wyckoff did it; Jesse Livermore did it; and Loeb, Dreyfus and O'Neil all did it as well. They looked for those turning points, as they all knew they would eventually come. That was a major key to their huge successes. In October 1998, after hard and fast breaks on the market, there were many underlying positives. Most of the break in the market was attributed to another outside influence — the Russian default. Back in the U.S., the economy was still solid and many of the positive and favorable conditions that were present during the middle 1990s still prevailed. Productivity, which was a huge catalyst for the strength of the economy, just kept getting stronger. The prior investments made in capital equipment and new technologies were a key that was driving profits for many and a reason for stable inflation.

On October 6 the Dow, S&P 500 and the Nasdaq fell hard during the day, all on heavy volume, but then they came back and ended in the upper part of the day's trading range. The very next day, all the major indexes surged higher, and they all closed right at the top of their highs for the day on heavy volume. These two days' action hinted that a new rally might be in the making. Of the next three trading sessions on the S&P 500, two were higher. On the fifth day of the attempted rally, all the major indexes soared on huge volume. On October 16, *Investors' Business Daily* stated that the short but hard bear market had ended as the markets had confirmed their new uptrend with solid follow-through price and volume action. As the market began its change in direction some new leading stocks would begin setting up and breaking out of well-formed bases. The hard bear market helped correct many stocks and their price charts. It is corrections and bear markets that help shape proper basing patterns, and this has occurred over and over again throughout history. One of the stocks that set up was Nokia, which was mentioned earlier when it originally broke out in March 1998 (see Figure 10-6). But the bear market correction actually formed the stock's classic double-bottom base.

Roppel actually cheated a bit and bought his position in Nokia in the handle of the double-bottom pattern. It turned out to work for him though, and in Figure 10-6 you can see how he then pyramided his position at $47.50. Nokia was a strong leader in the telecommunications group, and its fundamentals were top-notch. WorldCom was another leader from this leading group, and it too set up in a near perfect basing pattern during the same

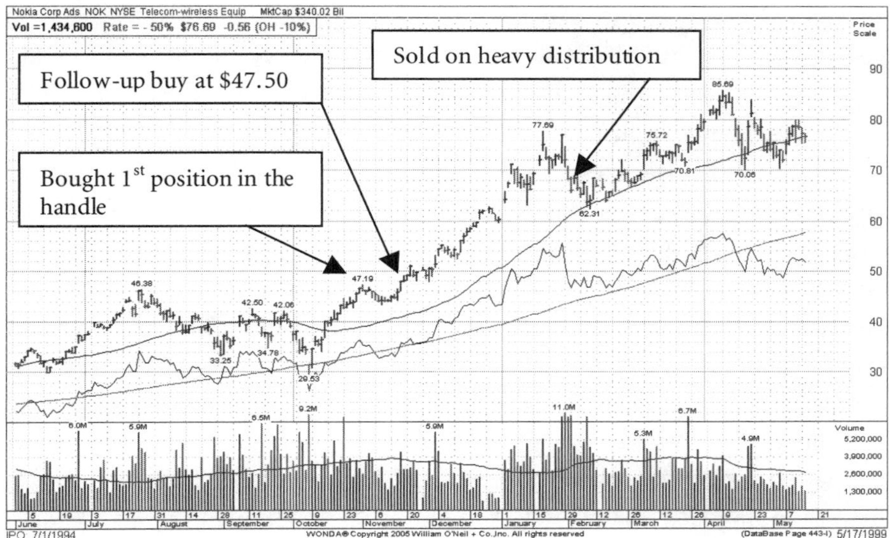

Figure 10-6 Nokia Corp. 1998–99 Daily Chart.
Source: © *William O'Neil + Co., Inc. All rights reserved. Reprinted with permission.*

time. Roppel bought into that stock as well, and he of course sold out long before problems surfaced with that company. Roppel ended up making decent profits on his WorldCom and Nokia stock transactions. Though it seems as if Roppel had become the success he had always strived for, like all the other great traders he still made mistakes. The difference at this time was that Roppel corrected them quickly. One mistake he made at this point in 1998 was when he bought JD Edwards on September 22. One thing to note is that the market had moved up during September, but it had not flashed the classic follow-through and confirmation signals it finally did portray in early October, as detailed earlier. JD Edwards reacted just as the market did back then. Roppel bought on a breakout on September 22, but the stock didn't follow up on its breakout. It just drifted sideways for over a week, and then it gapped down hard $8, which fell below Roppel's buy point and the stock's 50-day moving average. Roppel made a mistake and hung on, even though the stock was not exhibiting any strength after its one-day plunge. The next day the stock broke down again as it fell another $8. Finally, Roppel sold out, but he learned his lesson and was humbled by the transaction.

As the market kept its newfound rally in an uptrend other new leaders joined in. Yahoo broke out in the fall of 1998 and soared 500% to its peak in

1999. Sun Microsystems surged 700% from a breakout in October 1998 to its peak in March 2000. O'Neil was a buyer of this technology leader, and it would turn out to be a huge winner for him. Charles Schwab took off in October 1998 and climbed 439% in just six months, since it became the leader in the strong discount brokerage business as the Internet was transforming another industry and providing low-cost efficiencies. O'Neil also bought into this leader, and he held on for most of that increase. He scored a 313% gain on Charles Schwab. Notice again how O'Neil moves with the market and always stays attentive to it. He made great profits early in the year, and then sold out before the market broke. Then he came right back in again when the market confirmed a new uptrend. O'Neil then looked for new leadership that consisted of very strong fundamentally sound companies that then set up and broke out of classic basing patterns, be it the cup-with-handle, flat-base, double-bottom, high-tight-flag, ascending-base, or three-weeks-tight patterns. These stock patterns have occurred over and over again throughout stock market history and cycles. His experience and discipline taught him to be patient and wait for those right times, as they always occur at some future point. He also was right there buying into companies that were introducing new products and services in the exciting technology arena. Notice he always stays in touch with what is being introduced into the economy that is in strong demand. He doesn't limit himself to one or two industries — he becomes knowledgeable about many new industries and does his homework on the new innovative companies that are introducing exciting products that enhance our lives. Recall that Loeb as well would always seek out knowledge about many different industries so he would be able to invest successfully across many different sectors of an always expanding economic landscape.

O'Neil Uses History to Land a Huge Profit

Other stocks that were breaking out in late 1998 included VeriSign, which would rise 2,543% in only 15 months from its breakout in November 1998. Qualcomm, another technology leader, soared 2,567% in only 12 months from a December proper buy point. This was another winner that O'Neil latched on to. ARM Holdings blasted up 1,385% in 13 months from December 1998, and Optical Coating Labs soared 1,957% in the same 13 months from its breakout also in December. These leaders show just how far strong stocks can rise during strong market environments. Probably the best example in the late 1990s of a master stock market operator making big money is O'Neil's purchase, hold, and sale of his America Online (AOL) shares. In the last week of October 1998, with the market uptrend confirmed, he bought into AOL at $60 per share just as it blasted off from a cup-with-handle base. The PE ratio of AOL at the time of his purchase was 158. The stock jumped 25% in just three weeks. For O'Neil, and through his studies and experience, that means you may have a big winner and you hold on to it. The stock then moved up again and was up 50% in just five weeks. What he did next is a classic lesson on how to use history and past big winners to find the next big winners. In 1965, he had bought Fairchild Camera exactly right but was shaken out of the position on its first correction. He then missed out on the huge move it made shortly thereafter. But he remembered that mistake, here at this time in 1998, thirty-three years later. He even pulled out an old chart of Fairchild when AOL pulled back hard just as Fairchild did after it ran up 50% in about five weeks. What AOL did after that was exactly what Fairchild did in July 1965. It formed an ascending base pattern and quickly found support. Because of the precedence set by Fairchild many years before, O'Neil knew what to do. He held on to AOL until it finally gave him the sell signals to act correctly. He ended up making a 456% gain on that stock, as AOL made a 557% move in just six months. Here was an example of experience and history aiding a legendary trader in producing a huge gain. It pays to learn from your mistakes, do your homework, remember key market facts and prior cycles, and study the best performers from the past.

The markets ended up recovering quite well during the later part of the year in 1998, and the Dow would actually end the year just slightly under the peak it had attained during July, just before the bad break in the market. The Dow finished up 16% for the year. The Nasdaq, home to many of the leaders mentioned earlier, actually soared in early December right past its peak before the break. It then really picked up all the way into the end of the year. It finished way out in front of the Dow, by soaring 40% for the year. Many may say, "If you would have just sat tight through the mini bear market, you would have finished on the positive side." But again, no one knows how far and severe a bear market will get, as we'll see when we get to Chapter 11. But even more impressive than how the markets rebounded in 1998 is how the best traders of all time moved with the market. O'Neil's personal account in 1998 was up

401%. That beat the best market average of that year by 10 times! He did that by staying in sync with the market, sidestepping a major break, and then reentering when the conditions were right to score huge gains. Ten of O'Neil's in-house money managers at his firm were up an average of 221% in 1998. That's outperforming the market by a long shot, and that is why O'Neil is considered one of the greatest stock traders of all time.

The year 1999 continued the recent strength of the markets, and the major indexes moved higher during the first week of the new year. While the Dow would fall back during the remainder of January and then trade sideways throughout February, the Nasdaq kept rising during January but then pulled back as well throughout February and then traded in a choppy fashion until mid-March. As the Y2K scare, which actually contributed to some of the massive capital investments throughout the 1990s, was still present, more investments were still driving growth, and this also contributed to some impressive stock gains. Leading sectors in early 1999 seemed to all consist of technology issues, such as computer software (Internet), computers (memory), electronic (miscellaneous electronics), computers (mini and micro), computers (mainframe), electronics (semiconductor manufacturing), and computers (local networks). Other leading groups were medicals and biotechs, telecom equipment, and fiber-optic components. The economic landscape was still very strong. Unemployment was low, inflation was still well contained, corporate profits were still strong, and real GDP was healthy. The productivity surge was still driving efficiencies and profits for many firms. In fact, productivity growth was over twice the rate it had been averaging during the 1973 to 1995 periods, which was 1.4%. From 1995 to 2000, the growth rate for productivity was 2.9%. Stock buybacks were also popular, and they would fuel more demand for stocks. The IPO craze continued and would soon get to a point where things were getting clearly out of control.

Roppel Trades with a Strong Market Trend

By the beginning of March the Nasdaq once again found its footing and began moving upward. The Dow, in March, broke the 10,000 level for the first time in history. It was viewed as a major psychological milestone and was clearly a stamp of the strength the market had exhibited throughout the 1990s. Once the average hit that level, it quickly retreated below it but then blasted up past it again in early April. The Nasdaq was also rising fast, and Jim Roppel was right there studying and looking for new solid buying opportunities. He would discover a few, and he used his prior successful experiences and observation to land some new winners. One of those was NetBank, Inc. The fundamentals were strong, the market was moving higher, and NetBank had formed a near perfect cup-with-handle basing pattern. Roppel bought in on March 26 at $30, as the stock surged past its pivot point on massive volume. He later added shares on a pyramid buy at just over $35. In only 12 days, the stock would hit $83. Roppel only held this one a short time as it raced up quickly and he thought it had staged a quick climax top. He therefore sold out and retained a nice solid quick profit.

Near the same time, Roppel saw Knight Capital Group also setting up in a proper basing pattern. On March 29, he bought into this new leader as it also broke out perfectly from its basing pattern on huge volume. Roppel got in at $31.25. This stock also ran up very quickly. After only 12 days, it more than doubled to $66.75. Roppel again took another short-term profit here as he thought this stock was exhibiting a climax top. Knight Capital Group later fell back but found support at its 50-day moving-average line and then bounced up off that support area and soared upward to hit $81 by mid-May 1999. Roppel though hadn't seen many stocks race up as fast as NetBank and Knight Capital Group, and he thought they were reaching climax tops, which is why he sold and retained excellent short-term gains. He didn't hold the stocks for any predetermined time frame — he only stayed with them until the stocks presented the selling cues to him. So it didn't matter how long he would held a stock; he held it until it was time to sell it. In this fast-paced market environment in the late 1990s, taking shorter profits on classic sell signals was somewhat similar to what had happened in the late 1920s. Recall then that Baruch and Loeb would many times buy stocks on strength one day and then sell them the very next day for decent gains. Then they would come right back into the market the next day and purchase other shares as the market kept racing higher. Staying with the market's action has rewarded great traders with the best returns over history. Here in 1999, Roppel was moving with the market and reaping big gains. In fact, he had taken his own personal account from only $14,000 in 1997 up to $311,000 after taxes by the third quarter in 1999.

As the markets were racing higher, the Dow surpassed the 11,000 level in early May, gaining 1,500 points in under two months. Trading volume was picking up and above already high levels. Mergers were rampant, and many deals were growing in size, while 401k programs were already increasing the wealth effect of many participants. Day trading was becoming popular, which seemed similar to the days in the late 1920s when many would leave work to go and watch the tape. History just keeps repeating itself. Many socials and work breaks in the late 1990s centered around people discussing stocks, and it seemed as if everybody had become experts in the market. Recall also in the late 1920s when shoeshine boys and beggars began giving stock tips to some of the best market operators in history. CNBC was vastly popular, and many new investment books were hitting the shelves. Many success stories of millionaire stock traders would surface, and many would make their way to published pages, but the big key question is how many would retain their profits and sell properly, as did Baruch, Livermore and Loeb when another market offered up great opportunities but then corrected in a major way? We'll see shortly how two successfully acted in a similar fashion as the legends just mentioned.

By June the markets were once again rising. What was happening was that technology stocks were acting much like some other groups in prior market eras. In the late 1990s, IPOs of new companies, many with "dot-com" in their name, seemed to be coming out on a daily basis. It also seemed that if they had "dot-com" attached to their name, then that was about all they needed in order to raise large amounts of capital. Many were just stories, and many had no earnings and no revenues to speak of. Was this the first time in history that this had happened, and was it really different this time? The 1990s actually resembled much of what happened in the 1920s. Back then it was the introduction of the radio and the advancement of the automobile that were transforming people's lives. In the late 1990s it was just something else — the Internet and the proliferation of the personal computer. As the frenzy grew with technology and the Internet in the late 1990s due to increased demand and rising capacity, there would be an overbuilding that would eventually lead to a corrective phase in order to get back to a more normal growth phase. Recall many chapters ago that the railroad industry also experienced an overbuilding that led to a correction. In the 1920s there were, at one point, 166 different automobile companies. That's another example of overexpansion. Even the airline industry had its day of overexpansion. During the 1919–39 period there were over 300 airline companies. Many ended up going bankrupt. Recall also that it was only in the late 1950s, as the market was racing higher, that electronics and electrodes were the hot new industry. Many new companies were coming out with the words "trons" and "electros" in their names. Even mature established companies were trying to diversify into that industry. It was no different in the late 1990s as hundreds of companies were trying to take advantage of the Internet craze. Some new IPOs, when the frenzy would be at its peak, would rise 500% or more within days of their issue date.

A pullback in early August did hit some Internet stocks, but it was short-lived. While the Dow was bouncing back and forth throughout the summer, the Nasdaq would step up and take center stage. By the time mid-October came around the Y2K scare was abating and the market would begin a major move upward that would become a classic climax run. Analysts were caught up in the excitement, and many recommendations were not objective but turned out to be just hype as target stock prices were rising faster than the market and many seemed to have no end in sight. The list of stocks hitting new 52-week highs was expanding almost on a daily basis. A few leaders that broke out, all from cup-with-handle bases in August, and then rode the late 1999 market to incredible gains included Siebel Systems, up 420% in seven months; E-Tek Dynamics, up 507% in just six months; and BroadVision, up 949% in seven months. O'Neil was there riding this incredible market, and he still held shares in Qualcomm. He would end up taking a large profit in that stock and sell it right into its climax run when it seemed everybody was talking about Qualcomm and analysts kept raising price targets to absurd levels. O'Neil's experience, discipline, and most importantly, emotional control, allowed him to ride this winner and retain a huge profit, as it soared to its peak in late 1999.

Roppel Takes His Biggest Position

So many technology stocks were racing up in late 1999 it's hard to list them all. VeriSign, C-Cor.net, Yahoo!, Oracle, Network Appliance, MicroStrategy and Broadcom were some of the big gainers. Emulex Corp. was a stock that formed the rare high-tight-flag pattern in October 1999. Recall that other big winners from prior market eras formed this exact same pattern. E.L. Bruce, which produced a major profit for Darvas in the late 1950s, and Syntex, which O'Neil landed many years before, are a few examples. Emulex would zoom 404% in six months as it broke out of its high tight flag. Roppel was right there as this market environment was what he had been waiting for for quite some time. He purchased many leading technology stocks such as Redback, Juniper Networks, Elantec and Foundry Networks. As for Broadcom, Roppel was very familiar with the company, as he had traded it in its earlier days. But it was now highly profitable, and it set up in a perfect base. When the fundamentals are solid, the base is near perfect, and the market is in a very strong uptrend, that is what great stock operators wait for. Roppel began purchasing in late October at $64 per share when he bought 2,500 shares. He made a follow-up pyramid buy shortly after at $68 for another 2,500 shares. He then made a final buy at $75 (also 2,500 shares), as the stock kept moving up on heavy volume. Roppel went all out on this stock, and he leveraged his buys on full margin. His experience was showing him one of the best setups he had ever seen. We'll see in Chapter 11 how he sold it almost perfectly and retained a $1 million profit!

The market just kept soaring all the way into the close of the year. The Nasdaq passed 3,000 in November and then 4,000 in December. It was an outstanding year for the markets as the Dow gained 25%, which looked pale in comparison to the unprecedented 85.5% gain on the Nasdaq, good for its fifth straight year of gains of 21% or better. Market opportunities don't come along like that very often, but the best traders take advantage of them when they do arrive. O'Neil would have another outstanding and outperforming year. He was up 322% in 1999, and for the 1990s he again averaged over 40% annually for the entire decade. His in-house money managers gained 363% in 1999. In fact, O'Neil's in-house managers would score a 1,500% return from 1998 through the beginning of 2000. How about Jim Roppel's performance? He really turned it on in 1999 as he was up 483% just from April through November. He was then up another 68% in just the last two months of the year. In fact, in October he would resign from Northern Trust and land a position with a major wire house firm as a seasoned and very successful stockbroker.

11

Avoiding Bear Tracks Keeps Prior Profits in Expert Accounts (2000–2004)

Jim Roppel Knows That the Health of the Market Is Paramount

As the new century began and the Y2K issues turned out to be nothing much to be concerned about, the markets turned right around after selling off during the first few days of the new millennium, and it looked as if the only way was "up." But by mid-January the Dow peaked and was being hit by some heavy sell-offs. This action caused a divergence in the markets as the Nasdaq, after pulling back during the last two weeks of January, just kept powering upward. This was a major divergence that had not really occurred

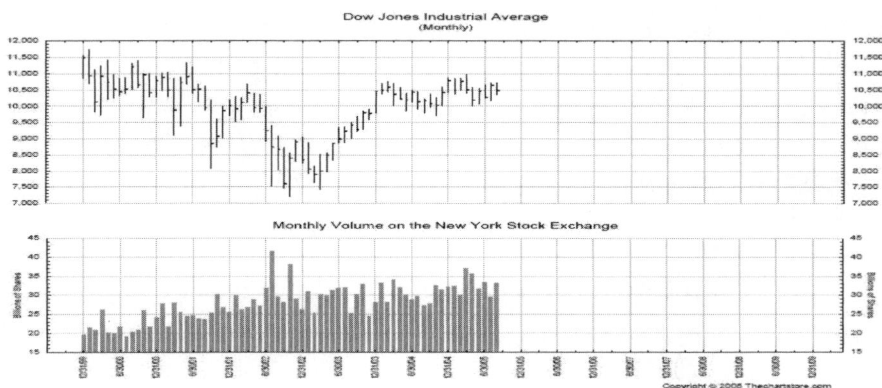

Figure 11-1 The Dow Jones Industrial Average 2000–2004.
Source: *www.thechartstore.com.*

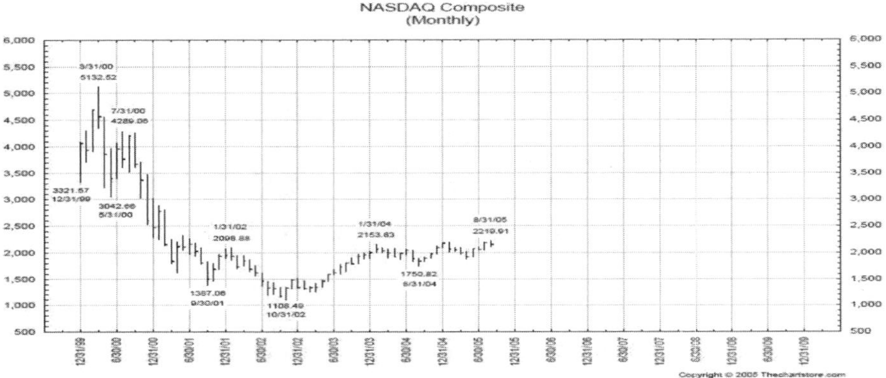

Figure 11-2 Nasdaq Composite Average 2000–2004.
Source: *www.thechartstore.com.*

before to this extent. The Dow was falling and crumbled 2,000 points in just under two months from mid-January to early March. During the same time, though, the Nasdaq just rocketed up and broke through the 5,000 level by early March. This was a climax run on the index like no one had really seen before. In fact, nearly everyone it seemed was piling into technology and Internet stocks in early 2000. Many things seemed to be getting out of hand as all caution was tossed aside. We even witnessed the biggest takeover of all time during early January, as AOL merged with Time Warner. Sell-offs in other industries seemed to free up capital to go after high-technology shares of all sorts. The new-issue craze was at an all-time high. But this had happened before, and the latest times occurred not that far back— the early 1960s and then in early 1983. But since human psychology rules the stock market and a heightened frenzy was in full force, many ignored the lessons from the past. There are only a minority of standout investors who can control their emotions and really make the sound trading strategies that need to be employed to succeed in environments like these. Most investors end up giving back big paper gains.

An Expert Keeps His Emotions Intact

In early January 2000 Enzo Biochem, a biotech stock, illustrated perfectly how a frenzy was in full force and also how an expert trader used controlled experience and strict rules to lock in a huge gain. Jim Roppel, while still working for a major wire house, had an in-house broker talking this stock up as the company was rumored to have a cure for AIDS. Roppel was experienced in biotech stocks, and he saw the stock form a near perfect basing pattern in late 1999. He took his initial position on Dec. 12, 1999, at $36 per share as it broke out of a classic cup-with-handle base on heavy volume. It zoomed nearly straight up to over $48 within weeks and then pulled back to consolidate its solid gain, as it was downgraded by an analyst. Then it really blasted off in mid-January 2000 on huge volume, and Roppel doubled up his position at $49 per share. After that, the stock really took off and shot up nearly 90 points during the next six days. The broker in Roppel's office got so excited he thought the stock was on its way up to $1,000 per share. But Roppel, now experienced with some major wins under his belt, thought this was the most classic climax run he had ever seen. When one studies chart patterns and historical models of past winners, which is what Roppel had now been doing for many years, one tends to focus on reality and facts instead of outside influences. The stock would continue to gap up session after session on massive volume. On Jan. 24, 2000, Enzo gapped up again, but then it reversed, which it had never done on its incredible, but short run-up. Roppel began selling his shares as he thought the reversal off the top was the loud warning signal that the frenzied buying had exhausted itself. He ended up selling out the entire position, and he reaped a huge short-term profit. The broker in his office couldn't believe Roppel would sell a stock that was headed to $1,000 per share, or so he thought. The chart in Figure 11-3 on p. 222 shows the story of what happened next to the stock, and Roppel doesn't think that broker ever sold his shares. This transaction for Roppel was very similar to the huge gain William J. O'Neil also made in Qualcomm, when that stock also formed a huge classic climax run and it seemed nearly everyone was projecting that stock to keep rising and rising. O'Neil's experience, strict rules and trained controlled emotions moved him out of that winner right near the peak. The Roppel transaction in Enzo Biochem was classic trained stock-trading skill at work. Roppel didn't listen to all the chatter around him, and he kept his emotions intact during probably one of the most emotionally hyped market cycles in history.

While the Dow kept falling during February, all the attention was on the Nasdaq. But there were some small details that were playing out and would start to send key signals to the more astute traders, just like many times before in prior cycles. Here in early 2000, the Dow had already peaked and

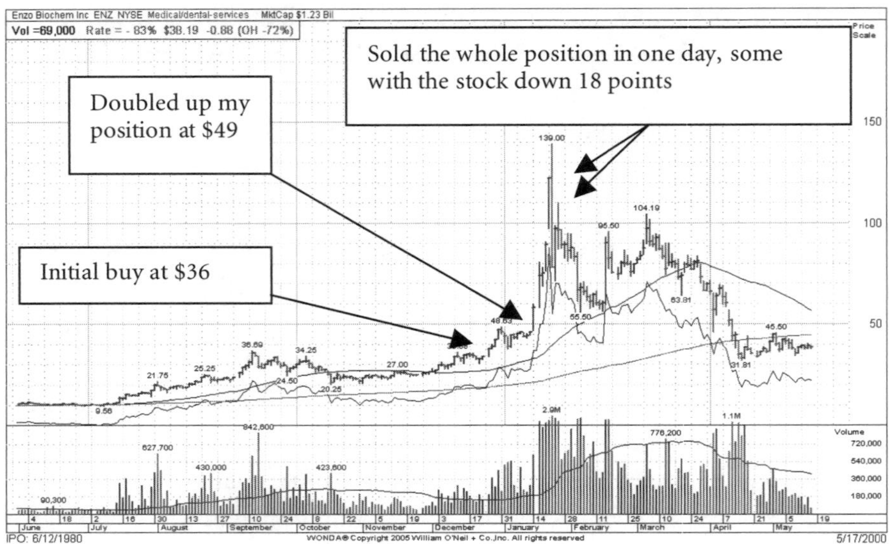

Figure 11-3 Enzo Biochem 1999–2000 Daily Chart.
Source: © *William O'Neil + Co., Inc. All rights reserved. Reprinted with permission.*

was in a correction mode, as it had lost over 10% in just under four weeks by mid-February. Insiders at companies were really beginning to take advantage of the incredibly high prices for their stocks. Other small details included the beginning of a slowdown in economic activity. After the Fed had pumped the economy with billions of dollars in late 1999 thinking there may be a liquidity crunch due to Y2K fears, they then started aggressively raising interest rates. From its beginning in June 1999, the Fed would continue raising rates, in total six times, until May 2000. It was now concerned about the wealth effect that the rising stock market could cause, which could in turn fuel high consumer spending, which could then ignite a spiraling of inflation. We've already seen in more than a few instances that higher interest rates can seemingly choke off the growth of a surging economy. By early 2000, inventories were rising, orders were declining, and corporate debt was at sky-high levels. The economy had already experienced overbuilding and overextended increases in the hot new technology areas. We've already seen a few of the past eras where that had occurred before, and those instances preceded sharp market breaks. It is vitally important to remember that history constantly repeats itself in the stock market through its cyclical behavior. The exact same events, of course, won't repeat, but the psychological behaviors of investors will.

Roppel Scores Big and a Few Experts See the Top

As the first quarter of 2000 was winding down, the frenzy really hit its peak in the market. On March 10 the Nasdaq broke the 5,000 level for the first time. By March 1, the Nasdaq had climbed 108% over the preceding 12 months, but the Dow was up only 9% and the S&P 500 up almost 12% during the same time span. It was clearly a technology-based frenzy, as technology-sector mutual funds were soaring. In March 2000, mutual fund cash positions were at a low of 4%, indicating that most of the funds available were already invested. As the Nasdaq blew past 5,000 it would hit a high of 5,132 on March 10. But a few leading stocks by that time had already exhibited climax runs and tops after their huge run-ups. Roppel was heavy in the market; in fact, he was margined to the hilt, as the market kept racing upward. His holdings in all his technology shares were showing him huge profits. Broadcom continued to be his biggest winner yet. It had pulled back sharply on two different occasions (once during January and once during February), but it held up over its 50-day moving average. Now, he held 7,500 shares in this stock and was on full margin, so he watched it closely. And when a 7,500-share position corrects 20 or 30 points, you can image how nervous one would get. But Roppel kept his calm and just stuck to his now time-tested rules. Also, his other positions were still racing up in price and cushioned the temporary pullbacks that Broadcom caused in his overall portfolio. After Broadcom bounced up off its 50-day line in early February, it really took off from there. Roppel held fast to a winning stock — a key strategy to massive gains. The following details the action on the Nasdaq for certain key sessions in early to mid-March 2000. It should be noted that on March 6, the Nasdaq had risen 86% in just the preceding five months.

March 7. The Nasdaq started higher but then reversed and lost 57 points, or 1.2%, on very heavy volume of 2.1 billion shares. This was the index's first heavy loss since Jan. 3, 2000. The S&P 500 fell 2.6% that day, and the Dow sank 3.7%, as NYSE volume increased.

March 8. The Nasdaq ended up 1% higher, but volume came in 7% lighter than the day before.

March 10. The Nasdaq sprinted up 85 points to hit a high of 5,132 in the morning. It would end up only 1.76 points higher at 5,048. This was a major reversal off the top, another sign of a tired market.

March 14. The Nasdaq sank 4.1%, or 200 points, and volume climbed to 1.98 billion shares, or 17% higher than the day before. Biotech stocks got crushed (down over 13% as a group), as President Clinton and Prime Minister Blair make an announcement that they want free access to raw data in order to map the human genome.

March 15. IBD™ stated that it would be wise to take some profits and ease off margin as heavy selling was overtaking any buying power and distribution was building. The Nasdaq sank 2.6%, or 124 points, though volume eased up a bit. The Dow and S&P 500 however rebounded and scored gains of 3.3% and 2.4%, respectively.

Because of the heavy selling that began showing up on the Nasdaq, O'Neil sold his holdings and moved to a cash position. He had seen this type of topping action many times before, so he knew what to do. He also retained some very solid profits, and he made sure he wasn't about to give them back. Jim Roppel hadn't really been through a climaxing market quite like this before, but he wasn't about to give back his huge gains either. He almost started to believe that climaxing stocks had become the norm in the market, since almost all his holdings were racing up in climax runs at the same time. He'd seen climax runs before, and we've seen him make some excellent profits on a few, but he never witnessed so many at one time. But March 14 finally changed his views. On that day Broadcom broke hard and fell 29 points. In fact, his account that day was up by $300,000 in the morning, but it closed down $400,000 by the close. That was it for him, as he now knew he was right at the peak of the market. Many of his other holdings also gapped up that day but then reversed as well. That price and volume action alone was a clear wake-up call to him. He then knew that this time was not different and that history was about to repeat itself again. The very next day he sold it all, nearly everything, and went from a 200% long position (fully margined) to a 100% cash position in just one day. He had made over $1 million on Broadcom alone, or nearly 200% just on that stock, as he sold his positions at over $200 per share, as can be seen in Figure 11-4. He kept 1,000 shares as a memento of his million-dollar transaction, but he later sold that as well over the $200 level to cash out completely. His total personal account value when he finally sold out was now worth over $2 million. That's a far cry from the $14,000 base he had left when, in 1997, he finally began to turn things around for himself. By March 17, 2000 (St. Patrick's Day), Roppel was golfing in Arizona, just before the really heavy selling was about to hit the Nasdaq. Roppel had finally made the big money he had been working so hard to attain for so many years. And we've seen how he struggled in the past. He had no idea what the market was about to do, but to him it didn't matter — he had cashed out and was now a millionaire and a very successful broker, as he had also earned great returns for many of his wealthy clients. He, of course, had cashed them all out as well in March 2000 to protect their profits. When describing that time during his career, Roppel says he once joked to his friends that he might end up working at Dunkin' Donuts if a major bear market hit, since he was fully invested and margined completely. His great timing and staying in sync and attuned to his rules — not his emotions — made sure that if Dunkin' Donuts was to be in his future, he most likely would be the owner and not the employee. As he also stated, when he decided to get out and stay out of a bad market, as he did stay out of the market for most of 2000 and realized a 50% return for the year, *"Knowing the future is not important, knowing the trend is."*

While O'Neil and Roppel were now sitting mostly in cash and out of the market, the Nasdaq was actually able to produce a mild rally from March 16

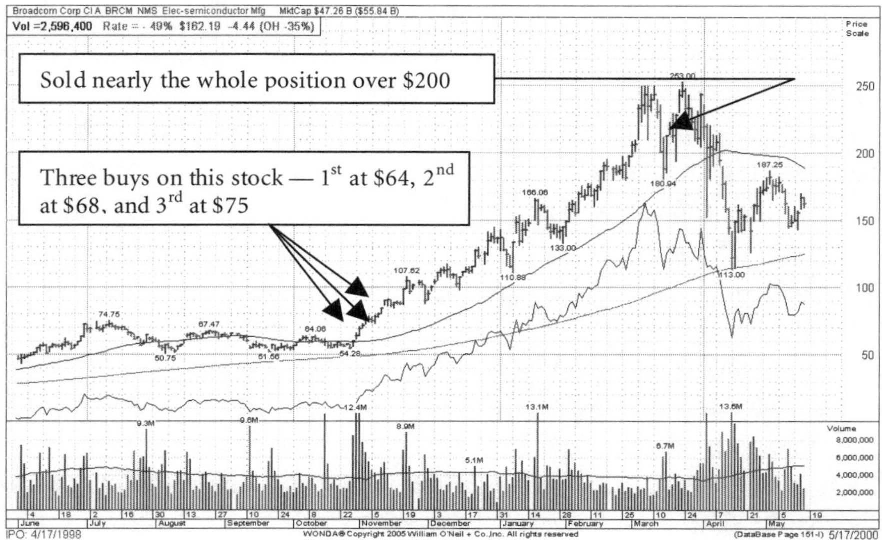

Figure 11-4 Broadcom 1999–2000 Daily Chart.
Source: © *William O'Neil + Co., Inc. All rights reserved. Reprinted with permission.*

through March 24. But it was accompanied by lower volume levels, and many leading stocks had already begun to crumble. So many stocks hit climax tops in early 2000 that it's hard to list them all. But some of the more notable ones included Analog Devices, QLogic, Human Genome Sciences, TriQuint Semiconductor, Biogen, VeriSign, MicroStrategy, JDS Uniphase, Comverse Technology and Seibel Systems.When many leading stocks like that top and break down and then cannot make new highs on rebounds, the peak has usually just passed in the market. Again, this type of price and volume action has occurred many times in the past. That's why O'Neil never seriously gets hurt by major market corrections. He always knows that this is how the market has worked in the past through so many years and different cycles, and so he is quick to recognize those warning signs and take action to protect himself.

After moving up through the 5,000 level again by late March, the Nasdaq reversed again and headed lower. On March 28, 29 and 30, the Nasdaq experienced three large sell-offs on heavy volume as the index sank over 10%. While the Dow had sprinted higher during March, the Nasdaq was really getting into trouble. When April began, the Nasdaq really began to fall apart as more big investors were heading for the exits. Selling was clearly overtaking buying, and it was time to be in a defensive position. We already saw Roppel cash out his whole portfolio, and that was already weeks before by the time April rolled around. The week ending April 14 was a disaster on the Nasdaq, as that index lost 25% in just one week — its worst weekly performance ever up to that point, as can be seen in Figure 11-2 on p. 220. Many dot-com new issues were totally wiped out. By April 17 the Nasdaq was already 37% off from its peak reached just a little over a month before. The Dow even fell heavily during April, as it shed over 1,000 points in just three days from April 12 to 14. Volume on the downside was heavy, and any buying power was weak even though many analysts kept telling people to buy on the dips, as technology stocks had always come back up in price before — so they stated. One leader that did hold up well during this time was Cisco Systems, which may have fooled many. Cisco hung in there during this first break in the market, but it eventually came tumbling down with the rest of them as the market continued to weaken throughout 2000.

From April through August the Dow whipsawed up and down in a sharp trading range. The Nasdaq actually put together a short rally during the end of May that lasted throughout the first half of July as analyst projections continued to be positive, but the index still couldn't get over the 4,300 level. Besides, many leading stocks had come down hard and their basing patterns looked damaged. That is why Roppel stayed mostly out of the market — he didn't see many solid buying opportunities. Many leaders had sunk under their key support, or 50-day and 200-day moving-average lines. Also, first-quarter real GDP showed a major slowing and was actually the weakest reading since early 1995.

While the second quarter showed a marked improvement in economic performance, the third quarter showed a decline for the first time in 10 years, since the last recession in the early 1990s. This slowdown just worsened things for the market, and interest rates were still rising into the summer of 2000. William O'Neil + Co., Incorporated, kept updating its NSMI list of stocks to avoid throughout this rough market period. While TV market talking heads kept telling everyone to come in and buy on the dips, O'Neil's list stuck to the facts, not opinions. The following table lists just a few of the stocks he recommended as sells or to avoid.

Stock	Date Listed	Price at Time	Price on 10/30/01
Conexant Systems	3/03/00	$84.75	$6.57
Yahoo!	3/03/00	$175.25	$8.02
Exodus Comm.	3/30/00	$69.25	$0.14
Cisco Systems	8/01/00	$63.50	$11.04
PMC-Sierra	8/01/00	$186.25	$9.37
Enron	11/29/00	$72.91	No comment

After a decent rebound in August, the markets hit another top in early September. From there the Nasdaq displayed five distribution days within 10 trading sessions. Those five heavy-selling days occurred on heavy volume, and each time the index closed at its low for the day. *IBD* was again pointing this out to its readership base and suggesting to investors to take profits, raise cash, and get off margin. Even Cisco, in mid-September, began to really crumble as well. It sliced its 200-day moving-average line during the week of September 15 on heavy volume. It then fell hard over the next five weeks. From its peak in March 2000 at $82, when many thought it wouldn't fall, it ended up plunging 90% when it hit $8.12 in October 2002. Rebounds up in price were on weak volume not exhibiting much strength. Even the mightiest of them all eventually succumb to heavy selling. It happened to RCA in late 1929 and the early 1930s; it happened to Xerox, Coca-Cola, Gillette, and many other blue chip names over the years and decades of the past. Key selling signals from the market and individual stocks must be studied and watched in order to know when it's time to get out. Cisco was a stock, along with others such as AOL, Lucent Technologies, and WorldCom, that was owned by so many mutual funds, that when big selling hit, many funds ran for the exit at nearly the same times. That heavy selling can bring down prices in a fairly quick and painful manner, for even what seemed like the best stocks of all. That's why some very skilled traders who know how to short stocks correctly can usually make decent profits by shorting the former leaders when a brutal bear market is in full swing and those former leaders begin to display major weakness.

Starting in September 2000 the market really fell apart. The Nasdaq plunged 29% from 4,259 on September 1 to 3,026 by October 18. Leading stocks were getting crushed as the selling really intensified. Many analysts kept telling investors to continue buying on the dips even at that point. Most of O'Neil's in-house money managers had been in cash positions for months. Roppel was still in cash as he instituted a few of the vital traits from the very best traders — patience and discipline, as he stayed on the sidelines. Many of *IBD*'s serious readers had long since cashed out, and they were protecting their capital as well. The IPO market was really drying up now, as over 400 IPOs came out in 2000 and raised a record $100 billion. But most of those came out during the first nine months of the year. While the Dow rebounded back a bit in late October and early November, it still couldn't make any progress. The Nasdaq was much worse, as small rally attempts didn't take and just led to more intense selling. While the Dow finished the year down only 6% and the S&P 500 lost 10%, the Nasdaq was damaged by 39%. It was a brutal year for technology stocks as many really broke hard — much more than the average, which is usually the case. As for Roppel, he stayed mostly out while the market was sinking for most of the year, posted a 50% return in 2000, and joined the millionaire ranks.

The slowdown in business activity continued as 2001 began. On Jan. 3, 2001, the Federal Reserve announced an interest rate cut of half a point to 6%. The markets jumped on the announcement, and it was finally some positive news. January actually was a good month for the Nasdaq, as it gained over 600 points. The Dow lagged behind. The Fed, by the end of January, cut rates again by another half a point. But earnings were falling and growth was nonexistent. A decline took over, and it once again seemed as if the market accurately forecasted what was about to come, just as it had done many times before. After a January rally, the markets turned right back around again and headed lower. Again, the Nasdaq led the way falling all the way to 1,619 by April 4, or down 28% for the year already and down 44% just from its peak only about two months earlier. The Dow even fell below 10,000 and was sitting at 9,106 on March 22. Following a free fall, and again when many would now come to view things in the worst way and give up, the Nasdaq perked up and looked as if it would turn around to the upside. On the fourth day of its rally attempt, the Nasdaq shot up 6.1% on big volume, greater than the previous day by 48%. *IBD* called this and alerted readers to look for fundamentally strong companies that had been building sound bases during the falling market.

Roppel Finds a Few Gems in a Difficult Market

Roppel had kept up his study, and he discovered a few potential candidates. He had been staying mostly in cash still while following one of the best traits of the very best traders over history — patience. But because he was still working for a major brokerage firm, he lost several clients out of frustration because they didn't like the fact that he wouldn't put their money to work. It turned out Roppel was making the right decision and protecting his own and his clients' capital. One of the stocks he discovered during the spring of 2001 was Metro One Comm. It broke out of a nice base on April 18 on massive volume, and Roppel was right there, but he waited until the market confirmed its uptrend before he committed. He held this winner as it continued to show strength even when the market's current rally fizzled out by the end of May. Once it finally showed its selling signals to him and began to weaken during a tough market environment, Roppel was out quickly and retained a decent profit.

Another winner Roppel was watching was Krispy Kreme Doughnuts. The fundamentals were solid and there was quite a bit of attention being directed to the company and the stock, but the base setup was even better.

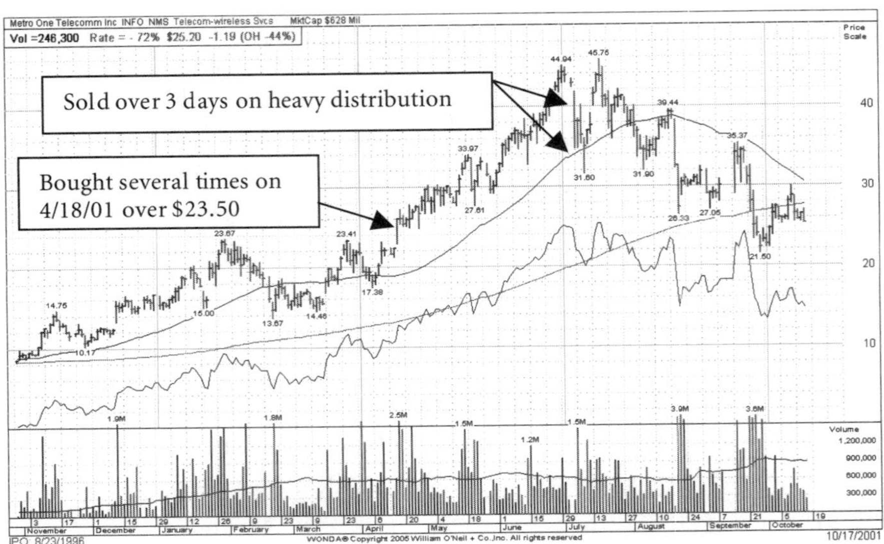

Figure 11-5 Metro One Comm. 2000–2001 Daily Chart.
Source: © *William O'Neil + Co., Inc. All rights reserved. Reprinted with permission.*

He also knew that the stock had a large short position outstanding. Roppel thought that if the stock broke through its base the shorts would have to cover their positions, just adding more buying power to the stock. That is exactly what happened as Krispy Kreme blasted up on huge volume, also on May 7, and Roppel took his initial positions. As it kept getting stronger he pyramided up just like he did on Enzo Biochem and some others he scored big gains with. While the market began to really weaken in the summer of 2001, Krispy Kreme would follow, proving once again that most stocks eventually follow the general trend of the market. As it pulled back Roppel hung tight, but when it finally broke its 50-day moving-average line, he sold it all. It was a modest profit but one he was content with considering the rough market environment.

While the market sprang up in April, the rally wouldn't last long. By late May the Nasdaq was flashing topping signals again. Many stocks began breaking down as well, and many new recent breakouts were failing all over the place. In late May, *IBD* again correctly analyzed the market's action and pointed out that five distribution days had occurred during the last 17 trading sessions. Of the five heavy selling days, the last four of those all closed at their lows for each of those days. Also, the sessions in which the index was up all occurred on lower volume. Again, this detailed action was signaling that the buying power that had brought the market up in April had dried up. Instead, selling came right back into the market as the overall longer-term trend was still down. Roppel was also mostly staying away from the market, and he held very high cash positions, as the market was getting weaker and offered no good new solid buying opportunities. Economic conditions continued to deteriorate, and third-quarter GDP again came in negative. Corporate profits continued to fall back as well, and unemployment was rising. The market slid downward throughout the remainder of the summer in 2001. By early September the Dow was again under 10,000, and the Nasdaq had fallen back to under 1,800. It was clearly a downtrending market environment. Then on September 11, terror struck on that horrible and tragic Tuesday morning. The exchange did not open that day and stayed closed for the rest of that week. I recall an *IBD* reader posing a question to O'Neil on the investors.com Web site that they were worried and didn't know if they should sell or hold their stock positions when the market reopened the following Monday. O'Neil's response was somewhat to the point that if that investor had been following the market and how *IBD* was assessing it, they should have had nothing to worry about as far as their stocks were concerned, as they probably should not have held any open positions in such a bad market environment. Here was experience again following the market's action and implementing sound strategies, and O'Neil was even giving advice through his national publication, well before the 9/11 tragedy, that being invested in a difficult market is extremely risky. It again seemed as if the market sensed something was coming, though no one could have expected what actually happened.

When the markets did reopen the following Monday, it was as expected—a sell-off. The Fed even lowered interest rates to hopefully ease an ensuing panic. While the country bonded together, the markets sold off the entire week and the Dow fell to a low of 8,062 by Friday, September 21. The Nasdaq hit a low of 1,387, also on that Friday, as it fell 18% in just that one week. The following week, though, offered up some hope in many ways. Monday, September 24, was a strong day for the markets, and with lowered interest rates coming down fast and new incentives for many goods (zero percent interest on autos, etc.) the market looked ahead and continued to move upward. On the fifth day of its rally attempt the markets surged ahead on higher volume, and *IBD* again noted this as a possible confirmation of a new trend to the upside. Remember, when things look their worst, the market may change directions and sense better opportunities ahead. But this environment still held many uncertainties. It looked like an impending war was just around the corner, the market was still in a major downtrend from a longer-term perspective, and business and economic conditions were still weak. From the fall until year-end the markets actually put together a nice strong rally. The Nasdaq rose a solid 48% in just over two months, while the Dow rose 26% off its bottom. Many defense-related issues led the way as air strikes began and were very successful in Afghanistan. Also, in November, O'Neil would advise his institutional clients to buy into home-building stocks. The rapid interest rate reductions would become a boon to the home-building industry. One stock he recommended was NVR on Nov. 1, 2001, at $180 per share. As of this writing, NVR has broken through the $900 level, which is an all-time high as it has continued to climb higher since late 2001.

The markets ended 2001 with at least some hope, and the current trend was up. But it was still a brutal and difficult year from all the early, midyear, and fall selling that took place. The Dow fell 7% for the year, the S&P 500 fell 14%, and the Nasdaq again led the downside with a 21% decline. O'Neil and his in-house money managers stayed mostly in cash and averaged a positive return in the low single digits. They would come back into the market in a small way when it looked as if a confirmed uptrend had occurred, but they would then quickly retreat if things didn't work out so well. Jim Roppel ended up with a 10% gain for the year, again outperforming all the major indexes. It was a frustrating year for him even though he still managed to stay on the positive side. He experienced several losses during the year, but he kept them small and contained. He stayed in cash about 80% of the time during the entire year, and because of that, he lost several more clients due to their impatience with him adhering to that successful strategy.

When 2002 began, it looked as if the recent rising market at the end of 2001 was going to continue. But it was short-lived. After just one week, the markets turned back around and headed lower again. A criminal investigation into Enron would begin an inquiry into many corporate abuses that had taken place during the excess of the anything-goes 1990s. Here again, this wasn't the first time corporate wrongdoing was going to be discovered, but this time it seemed the magnitude would be greater and affect more people. Since many were involved indirectly in the market through mutual funds and retirement plans, the magnitude of the loss looked to be greater than in the past. These types of greedy behaviors tend to get out of hand when it seems the good times will last forever. Investigations would end up uncovering fraud at some highly visible institutions such as Tyco, Adelphia, and of course, WorldCom (which would file for bankruptcy by summer 2002) and Enron. As investigations into fraudulent activities continued, it looked as if several firms just cooked their books in order to meet Wall Street's expectations. As profits soared throughout the 1990s, comparatives to prior periods kept getting more challenging. A few just decided to fudge the numbers to keep their stock prices and their egos up. Prosecutions were in order, and many would be tried and convicted over the course of the next few years. Investor confidence seemed damaged again, as it had been in prior eras when these things occurred. These investigations also led to the passage of a new strict accountability law called Sarbanes-Oxley, which is supposed to safeguard against conflicts of interest in auditing procedures and requires stricter corporate disclosure, among other things. One thing to note, since this a book about how great stock traders made money in the market, is that both O'Neil and Roppel were unaffected by the fraud and bankruptcy issues that affected several companies and many individuals during this time period. We already saw O'Neil remove Enron from his new-ideas list way back in late November 2000 at near $72 per share because its price and volume action were flashing sell signals left and right. Also, the market was in terrible shape back then. Roppel, as we saw earlier, actually made a nice profit on WorldCom several years back and sold out when it flashed selling signals to those who paid attention to the details. He wasn't invested in the others, as their chart bases didn't warrant any good buy signals based on time-tested strategies and their base patterns were a mess.

By February 2002 the markets were back in a downtrend. By this time nearly $5 trillion in wealth had been lost in market value since the spring of 2000. Numbers that large have a psychological and real effect on how consumers and businesses act. Businesses reigned in spending, as they had spent heavily during the mid to late 1990s upgrading systems, adopting new technologies, and readying themselves for Y2K. By 2002 capital spending was down and falling. While real GDP would end up growing again in 2002 and take the economy out of a minirecession, the markets just kept falling. More than a few times the market would bounce back up and begin short rallies, but then the trend would turn right back around again to the downside. This declining steep stair-step pattern has occurred before in falling markets. In fact, the 2002 Nasdaq, and even for that matter, the entire 2000–2002 market period, was looking very similar to the Dow and its pattern from late 1929 through the early 1930s. Recall that during the brutal selling in the early 1930s, Gerald Loeb actually made money each year during 1930 through 1932 from the long side by getting in quickly when the market turned up for a bit and then realizing and taking quick profits when the selling took over again. As the market kept sliding in the early years of the first decade of the 2000s, the dollar broke down in May 2002 and would begin its own long decline. Many negatives were hitting the market, and the mood was one of extreme gloom from an equities standpoint. It sometimes seemed the end would never come, just as Bernard Baruch had commented on how many felt in prior market cycles many decades before during his time. After another rally attempt in May failed, it was nearly straight down through July as the selling just intensified.

Another rally occurred during August, but that one as well was short-lived. Rally attempts like these after over two years of selling can get very frustrating, even for the best traders. Roppel came back into the market during these short upward spurts, but he found it very difficult to gain any ground. There was basically a total lack of strong leading stocks sustaining any real advances. He, therefore, would exit quickly as he stuck to his tight loss-cutting rules. He didn't experience any major losses; he was just picked apart by a dangerous market that couldn't sustain any advances. He was really similar to Darvas in that his style was to stay nearly completely on the long side of the market. Roppel had taken such efforts to make sure he had that side of the market down, that he spent nearly all his efforts trying to perfect correct buying and selling rules. Therefore, he didn't feel comfortable going on the short side and risk losing money in something that was quite risky in and of itself, and especially since he didn't have much experience shorting stocks. What he did eventually learn that year was that if several breakouts keep failing, it is better to just walk away and stay out. Recall, from my first book, that the all-time greats all agreed with that assessment — sometimes the best thing to do in the stock market is to do nothing at all.

After several failed breakouts, which seemed to keep recurring more often, Roppel finally just stayed out completely.

Another sharp decline in the markets occurred throughout September and the first part of October. Then the Nasdaq finally found a bottom on October 10. At that point the Nasdaq had fallen 78% from its peak in March 2000 over the next 31 months. It was the second-worst market decline in history, second only to the Dow's 89% decline in the 34 months from October 1929 to July 1932. During the bear market of the early years of the first decade of the 2000s the Dow would fall 38% and the S&P 500, 51%. The S&P 500 alone fell 33% just from Jan. 1, 2002, to the October 10 bottom. Many investors were hit hard by this major bear market, just like others had in past market cycles. Many that were affected by the recent bear market hadn't seen anything quite like this before, and many were unaware that the market was capable of such a severe decline, especially since most were so ecstatic during the run-up that they failed to do any historical homework to see that the market's pattern is cyclical and does repeat itself over time. Even old stalwart AT&T couldn't hold up during a major bear market. Its stock price, which was near $99 in January 1999, had sunk to $17 by July 2002, proving just how brutal the market can get. Remember Loeb didn't call it a "battle" for nothing.

O'Neil Studies a Gem and Buys It Right Off the Bottom

While most had given up long before the market would find a bottom in October 2002, O'Neil kept up his meticulous study. In fact, it is outright impressive what he had been doing during the long decline. One stock he was watching all throughout the decline was eBay, and he noticed how it had actually held up fairly well throughout 2002. It had formed a 16-week double-bottom base, which was quite constructive considering the bad market period. For those fortunate and diligent enough to have attended one of O'Neil's advanced sessions, he provided a copy of his personal chart analysis of this stock from 1999 through 2002. Though the chart is already filled with data on the fundamental and general informative side, O'Neil made no less than 68 different handwritten notes to himself concerning proper buy points and chart action, references to history, notes about the fundamentals, and so forth. This is a master market operator doing the required homework. And though this was probably impressive to most, as he was doing this during the worst market in generations, it was just routine homework for him, and he probably had a feeling this might be a big winner. Why? Because he knows an upturn will always occur and that it would most likely occur when the news is at its worst. He'd been through tough markets before and knew a new opportunity would come along sooner or later. One of the key notes on the eBay chart was that he compared the chart action of eBay at that time to the 1962 chart of Delta Airlines and to the 1990 chart of Cisco Systems. Both of those stocks have been mentioned in this book during those respective time frames as they became huge price winners coming up off of similar chart patterns that he was now studying. He bought into this new emerging leader (eBay) near $60 per share (prices on chart are split adjusted from a two-for-one split) right off the bottom of the 2002 market, very similar to what he did with Chrysler almost exactly 40 years earlier when he bought that leader off the October 1962 market bottom. Chrysler was a huge winner for him, and eBay would turn out be another huge winner for him as well.

As the markets moved higher off their lows the Nasdaq gained over 500 points in less than two months. The Dow gained nearly 1,850 points over the

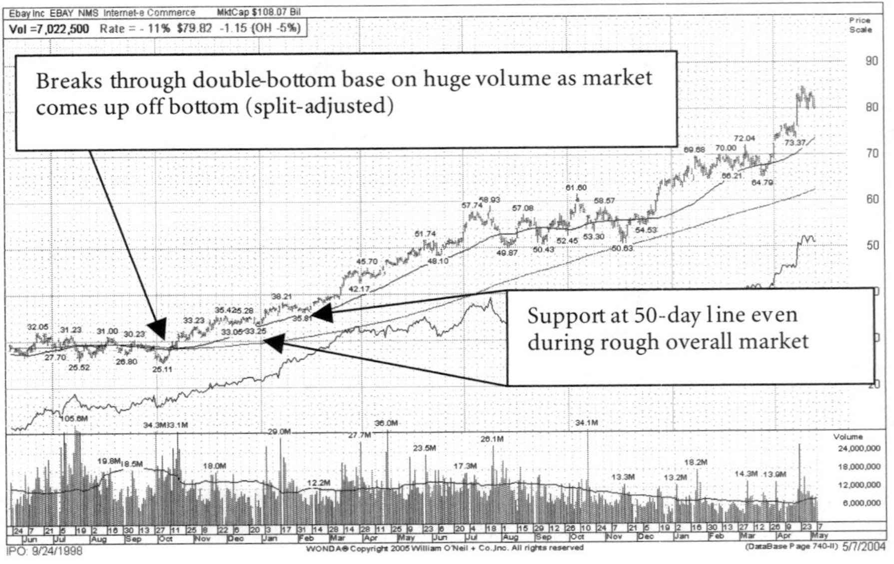

Figure 11-6 eBay 2002–2004 Daily Chart.
Source: © *William O'Neil + Co., Inc. All rights reserved. Reprinted with permission.*

same time span. A consolidation occurred throughout December as the markets pulled back. The Dow ended up losing 17% in 2002 and the Nasdaq was down 31%, as early-year selling really took its toll. While most of O'Neil's in-house money managers still stayed in cash most of the year, they did have approximately 10% of their funds in stocks. They also reentered several times when the market seemed to have established a confirmed upward trend, but they again would quickly retreat when those short rallies failed, so they wouldn't get hurt too much during a major downtrend. Roppel ended up taking a 15% loss for the year as he landed no major winners and took several small losses with a portion of his capital. Despite the loss for the year, he still outperformed the major indexes again.

The year 2003 started off with the markets climbing higher during the first two weeks of the year. It seemed the upturn off the October 2002 bottom was firmly established. But from mid-January to mid-February the markets turned right back around and headed lower in a sharp slide. It then looked as if the rally was going to be another short-lived upturn. Many breakouts that occurred off the October 2002 bottom were failing, and lower-quality stocks seemed to be coming up faster than the better-qualified and more fundamentally sound stocks. The Nasdaq lost over 200 points in just a month, and the Dow lost 1,200. One stock that held up well was eBay, as it barely lost any ground, a strong sign of strength during a very scary and rocky market period. The strength of eBay, as an early leader, would allow O'Neil to hold on to it as it didn't violate any of his sell rules. It actually created opportunities for taking new positions in the stock as it formed a flat base and also found support at its 50-day line and then bounced up off that line. That price action, especially during a break in the market, is a very strong sign of a leading stock's strength. After a few strong up sessions following the sharp break until mid-February, the markets continued falling into early March. Each index had undercut the low from mid-February, but each held up above and did not undercut its low from October 2002.

One key signal that was occurring during the period of mid-February to early March, even though the market was losing ground, was that accumulation was actually taking place on the Nasdaq. There were 13 sessions (over 21 trading sessions) in which the index moved higher on higher volume. Sessions when the market fell back during that time usually occurred on lower volume. That net accumulation buying was a detailed signal to the more experienced market operators. It was a slight but major market signal. Many were so discouraged with the stock market by March 2003 that they had given up on the market long ago. Even Jim Roppel, by the spring of 2003, was wondering if things would ever turn around. He had stayed disciplined and in effect had stayed out of the market, but he was really beginning to get concerned. It had been a brutal three years since the Nasdaq peaked, and the losses many suffered were outright devastating. By this time many securities analysts were being fined and penalized, and some were banned outright from the industry altogether, due to securities law violations during the prior few years. But we've seen many times before already that when most give up that is when the market may be finally ready to make a change to the upside. On March 17 the Nasdaq, on its fourth day of a new rally attempt, jumped 3.9% on heavy volume. That action, along with confirmations on all the major indexes, confirmed the new trend of the market for O'Neil. He then issued a market memo to his institutional clients that a new uptrend in the market was in the making. As U.S. troops were bombing Iraq, the market would begin to take off in a new direction. After losing nearly 18% from just December 2002 to early March 2003, the Nasdaq led the new direction to the upside. Many leading stocks jumped out front, which is always a good sign when a market attempts to turn around its trend. Genentech, Shuffle Master, NetEase.com, Yahoo!, Amazon.com and Sohu.com were just a few new leaders breaking out of well-formed base patterns that sported top-notch fundamentals and new products, services and ideas. While corporate profits in 2003 fell 28% from their 2000 peak levels and nearly 36% from their 1997 peak, things were looking up as the economy was beginning to pick up steam. GDP growth was picking up, interest rates were near historic lows, recent major tax cuts were igniting new growth opportunities, and there were new leading stocks showing exceptional profit growth. But there were still many uncertainties such as unemployment and international issues surrounding the Iraq War. But in mid-March the market, as it always does, was looking ahead and seeing brighter times.

Roppel's Patience and Observation Skills Lead to Big Gains

Roppel saw the new confirmation take place on March 17 even though he almost couldn't believe it. He had almost become totally accustomed to the bad market period. But many investors miss the best opportunities when a market finally confirms its upward trend simply because they don't believe it, because the market has been so bad for so long. Most then miss these golden opportunities because they simply aren't paying attention. Roppel was paying attention, and he quickly moved into the market and into some of the great opportunities that were presenting themselves. On March 25, he bought into eResearchTechnology. He actually missed the correct buy point on this stock as it actually broke out in early February — way ahead of the market. But Roppel wasn't comfortable buying stocks without the market first confirming its trend. You can see the strength of the stock during its run throughout 2003 in Figure 11-7. The stock rose with the rising market and constantly used its 50-day moving-average line as a support base. Roppel more than tripled his money on this transaction.

As the market pulled back slightly during the last week of March and then consolidated its gains during the first part of April, Roppel was taking other positions in some new leaders as well. He bought OmniVision Technologies and would end doubling his money on that big winner. By mid-April the market really began to pick up speed as the Nasdaq surged 2.2% on April 17 on very strong volume. After a long brutal bear market, more

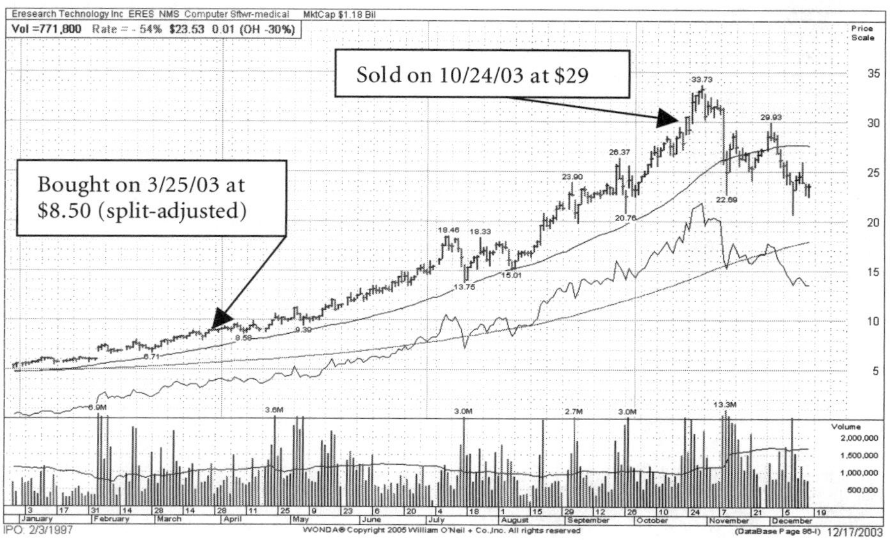

Figure 11-7 eResearchTechnology 2003 Daily Chart.
Source: © *William O'Neil + Co., Inc. All rights reserved. Reprinted with permission.*

funds were finding their way into the market. The momentum of the rally was really starting to build, and it looked as if the rally would last instead of falling back and failing again as it had done so many times during the past three years. The key to the strength of this uptrend was the amount of new leading stocks that were blasting up off sound basing patterns, just like strong leaders have done in all the other uptrends from prior eras. As the market was strengthening, Roppel was doing his homework, and he was finding more opportunities shaping up as well. One particular leader he was watching was Gen-Probe, Inc. This leader from the medical-biomed group had exceptional fundamentals and formed a near-perfect base, as can be seen in Figure 11-8. It broke out on huge volume six days before its earnings report on April 22. When the earnings came out, and they were exceptional, Gen-Probe really took off. Roppel then really piled into this one, and he pyramided this stock seven times over the next nine weeks after its initial move upward. The action in this stock really proved to Roppel that the rally was here to stay, and its strength was only just beginning.

In the period from late March to April 2003 the leading groups were taking shape. Telecom (fiber optics), Internet (Internet service providers), semiconductors, Internet (e-commerce), and Telecom (wireless equipment)

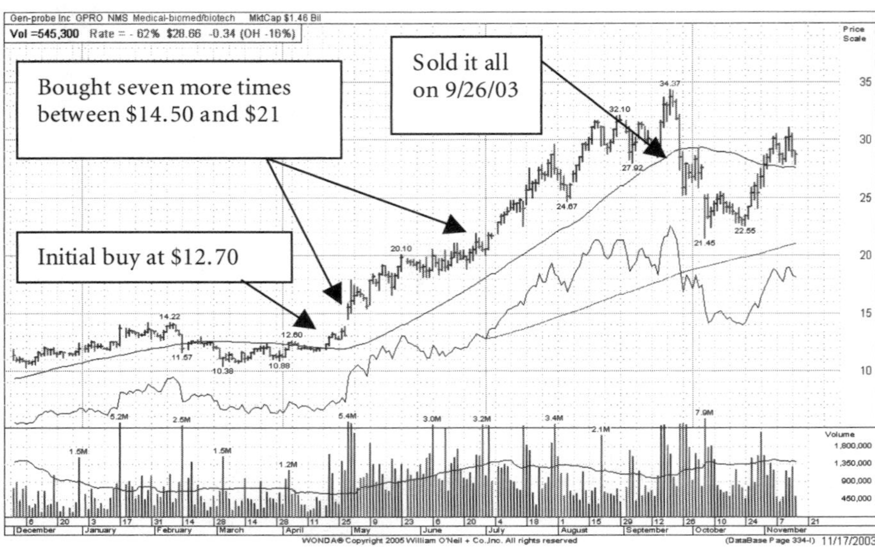

Figure 11-8 Gen-Probe, Inc., 2003 Daily Chart.
Source: © *William O'Neil + Co., Inc. All rights reserved. Reprinted with permission.*

groups were just a few that were moving up in rank and providing some interesting opportunities. O'Neil of course was right there making the most of the new market uptrend. This, for him, was textbook strength, as he had been through periods like this many times before. Omnivision and eResearchTechnology were also big winners in the O'Neil circles. Amazon.com and NetEase.com were new leaders in the Internet groups that were growing revenues and earnings at very high rates and were breaking out of classic basing patterns. Coach, Harman International Industries, Mobile TeleSystems and Ceradyne were other solid leaders that formed classic time-tested historical basing patterns and offered up the experienced and watchful stock operator great profit opportunities. All the stocks mentioned made triple-digit gains during 2003, and each one offered up excellent pyramiding opportunities as they would either consolidate prior gains to their 50-day moving-average line or create a three-weeks-tight pattern on their way up. Then they each would display the classic sell signals as well that have been mentioned throughout this book in prior periods. Some would make climax runs after their already incredible increases in price, while others would then break through their 50-day moving-average lines, which they did not violate on their runs upward, on large volume. That sell signal is a favorite of Roppel, as you'll see when you study the charts of his trades.

Roppel Finds More Opportunities

One stock that caught Roppel's attention during the spring of 2003 was SanDisk Corp. SanDisk was a dominant leader in memory sticks that were used in digital cameras. Its earnings power was top-notch, and it gapped up on massive volume on April 17 on a solid earnings report. Roppel had run a screen of percentage increases on huge volume, and SanDisk was at the top of the list — he thought this one could be a huge winner. He really piled into this one (taking a 5,000-share position) and then pyramided up on May 2 after it had just digested its huge gain weeks ago, which was positive action. Notice how Roppel really took a position in this stock when it made its move (see Figure 11-9 on p. 242). He didn't hesitate; it was almost an impulsive move, but it was an experienced impulsive action, one he was very comfortable in making. He knew from prior strong markets that making quick decisions, when the time was right, was a big key to huge gains. It needs to be noted though, that if the position doesn't turn out the way one intended, it is even more important to make those quick decisions on the exit side. Notice how SanDisk ran all the way up during the year, never violating its 50-day moving average, and then when it finally broke its 50-day line, Roppel sold the remainder of his shares. He scored a huge gain on this stock as his initial positions had quadrupled for him.

Near this same time Roppel was also watching JetBlue Airways. Airlines were in terrible shape back then, and some were declaring bankruptcy. Many brokers in Roppel's office said he was crazy for considering a purchase of an airline company. But JetBlue was taking market share, and its fundamentals were sound. It had also set up in a near-perfect base. Roppel studied the chart extensively, and he bought into this unique opportunity. He would end up doubling his money in this stock by sticking to many of the key strategies that lead to big money in the stock market. He did his own research and didn't listen to all the others around him who thought he was crazy for making that purchase. He also moved with the strong market and made sure the fundamentals and the chart base of the stock were top-notch. Then the volume action within the stock really convinced him he had a

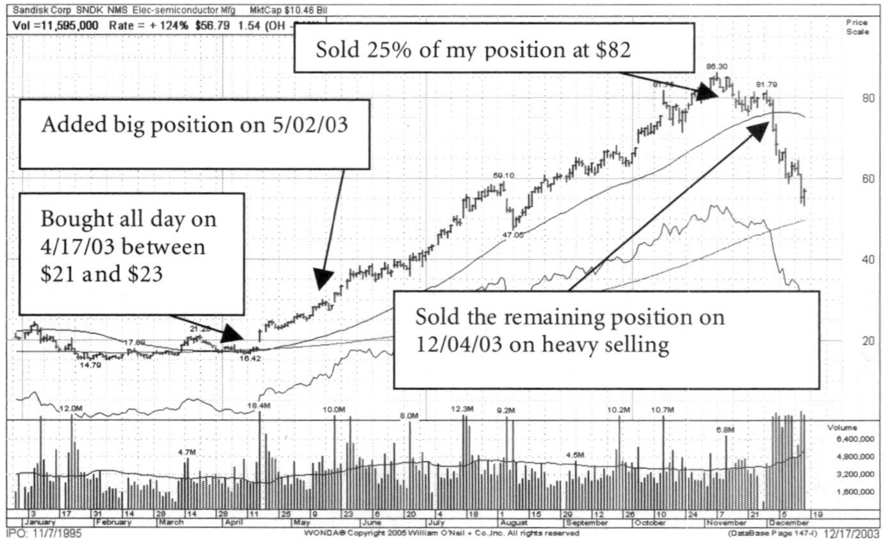

Figure 11-9 SanDisk, Corp. 2003 Daily Chart.
Source: © *William O'Neil + Co., Inc. All rights reserved. Reprinted with permission.*

major winner. He then held his winner as it clearly was just getting stronger as the market kept moving up. He then stayed attentive to its action and then sold — unemotionally — when the time was right. It may look like he stayed too long at the top (see Figure 11-10), but remember that no one is going to sell right at the absolute peak, though at times it looks as though Roppel hits that mark fairly well in many cases.

Through May the markets just kept rising, and Roppel and O'Neil held their profitable shares and took additional positions if their stocks' actions warranted it. Roppel was already on full margin by then, and he really took some heavy positions in his best stocks. Other leaders he held that he would make solid gains on were United Online, j2 Global Communications, Netflix, eBay, and American Pharmaceutical Partners. This here is another key strategy of the very best traders — when the market is ripe, they really pile in and take advantage of the key opportunities. They don't sacrifice their risk strategy, as they keep their loss control tight, but they do take bigger positions, and many utilize margin to the fullest extent, when the market is in a clear strong uptrend and leading stocks are powering higher. On May 27 the Nasdaq zoomed up another 3.1% on huge volume as the rally was really kicking in. By June 2003 the Federal Reserve once again lowered interest

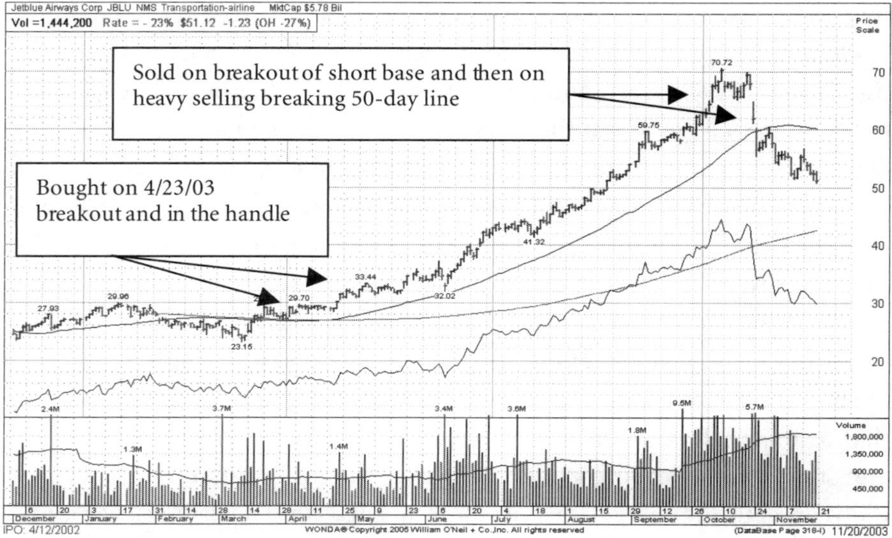

Figure 11-10 JetBlue 2003 Daily Chart.

Source: © *William O'Neil + Co., Inc. All rights reserved. Reprinted with permission.*

rates, as its continued easy monetary policy had now brought rates down to a new 45-year low of 1%. The housing market was really responding to these low rates, and housing- and building-related stocks were standout achievers during this uptrend.

Roppel Outperforms Again

As the rally kept strengthening, the market's leadership began to broaden, which is always a classic strength signal for a powerful market. As the market was moving higher we again see the great foresight of the market's action. Third-quarter GDP rose solidly and was the best reading since late in 1999. The market in the spring of 2003, when it began its uptrend in earnest, was obviously looking out and sensing solid growth in the near future. We've now seen this occur time and time again throughout history. With rock-bottom interest rates, contained inflation, a somewhat improving but still wobbly employment outlook, and growth and corporate profits increasing at a good pace, the market was responding in kind with solid opportunities in excellent groups that were sporting many fundamentally strong stocks. After a strong August, the markets fell into a trading pattern of increasing for a few weeks, then pulling back constructively, and then resuming the uptrend for a few more weeks. This pattern persisted throughout September, October, and most of November 2003. In early December the Nasdaq finally crossed the 2,000 mark again. The Dow also crossed the 10,000 level again by mid-December, and it sprinted to the finish line until the end of the year. It was a solid year for the markets in 2003 as the S&P 500 rose 26%, the Dow was up 25%, and the Nasdaq outperformed all the major indexes with an impressive 50% advance. O'Neil took full advantage of the new uptrend, and he scored solid gains for the year. Roppel had another incredible year as he ended up 109% in 2003, outdistancing himself from the best market index by over two times! But what he once again proved was that to materially outperform the market, one must move with its action and stay with the leading stocks. He stayed patient during the early part of the year until the market gave its clear signals. He did his homework and landed some major gains that resulted in major profits for him. He utilized margin and a pyramiding strategy, let his winners run, and stuck to time-tested sell rules to lock in profits when he had them. He watched the stocks and took appropriate action when it was time to sell.

Another outperforming statistic during this time was the independent real-time, month-to-month study that was conducted by the American Association of Individual Investors (AAII). The AAII tracked major stock strategies from many different best-known methods. The strategy that produced the best results was the CAN SLIM method that O'Neil created from his historical studies of the best-performing stocks over the past half decade. Monthly from 1998 through 2003 the CAN SLIM method produced a total compounded rate of return of 705%. The S&P 500 returned just 14.6% over the same time frame as the severe bear market kept returns low. How did CAN SLIM produce such a great return that included three years of severe declines? Its strict selection criteria would only lead one to leading stocks during a bear market, which really limits the choices. But there were a few strong sectors such as small regional banks and housing stocks, as mentioned earlier. The low-interest-rate environment was a benefit to many of those companies, and their stock prices reflected that, as they registered solid gains during a dangerous market environment.

As 2003 wound down, Roppel took a new position in Research in Motion (RIMM), another technology leader. He made good progress on this stock in 2004, but a few details are worth noting concerning some of his trades during 2003. Notice in the charts for eResearchTechnologies, Gen-Probe, and SanDisk (Figures 11-7 to 11-9 on pp. 239, 240 and 242) that he sold out his entire positions in late 2003. Even though the market was still rising, these leaders, many of which were some of the first to really break out strong, were experiencing some serious selling. Roppel of course noticed this, and that is why he took his profits when those stocks broke some key areas which they had never violated on their way up. As the market continued to rise during most of January 2004, a few issues were causing some concern. Commodity prices were hitting record highs, mostly due to increased demand and strong growth in emerging markets, mainly those of China and India. Commodity prices had been increasing for much of the early part of the first decade of the 2000s, but they were now beginning to cause quite a concern. Huge deficits were being talked about, the Iraq War wasn't going as smoothly as many had hoped, and the dollar was falling hard. But the real issues were soaring oil prices and increasing interest rates. As with any market cycle there are always a few strong sectors. Housing was still red-hot due to historically low interest rates, and energy stocks were taking off as the rising price of oil was a big benefit to many oil-related companies.

The market began to wobble in late January, especially the Nasdaq. From there selling began to take over, and the trend of the market changed direction. Sharp drops occurred on the Dow in early March, and the Dow lost nearly 700 points in about a month. Those types of selling bouts were basically nonexistent during 2003. The Nasdaq then began to whipsaw during the spring of 2004. One change made during this time was that Roppel quit his position as a stockbroker with the major wire house he had worked for. At 39-years-old he would officially retire as a multimillionaire. His new life would be to trade for his own and his family's account. By mid-March with the market now heading down he again mostly stayed in a cash position except for a small position in Genentech. Selling his transactions in late 2003 was another wise decision, as those stocks came down along with the market in early 2004. As the markets bobbed back and forth during the spring and summer months of 2004, Roppel was in cash on the sidelines exercising patience again and waiting for a better market environment. One opportunity he did let pass him by was in the energy groups. Because of the continued rise in oil prices, energy stocks were the standout leaders in mid to late 2004 and into 2005 as well. Many fundamentally strong energy leaders would triple in price during 2004 alone. This had happened before with energy stocks in the late 1970s and early 1980s when O'Neil took advantage of that opportunity. There have been many market cycles when a single economic event provides the most astute investors with great profitable opportunities. Housing stocks also continued to do very well in 2004 even though interest rates were on the rise. But rates continued to stay low because they were coming up from historic low levels, which just kept fueling the demand for homes, as GDP growth stayed positive, registering decent increases.

The markets really took a dive during July and throughout mid-August 2004. But on August 18 the Nasdaq had a follow-through session, though the volume was suspect due to it being less than average at the time. But some stocks were setting up in proper base patterns, and Roppel saw this action on the Nasdaq and kept his watch to some interesting opportunities. One mistake he did make during this time was when he took a position in Shanda Interactive, a Chinese Internet company. Roppel bought it on its breakout on

August 10 even though the market had not confirmed its new direction just yet. Because of the weakness still in the market, he took a small position. On its first pullback he was shaken out as he didn't want to take a big risk in a weak market. Even though he missed the big move in this stock, he kept his loss-control strategy extremely tight in a suspect market environment. That is a key reason why he has retained the millions he has made in the market.

While Roppel quickly shook off the small loss in Shanda, the market as mentioned earlier showed some strength shortly thereafter. Roppel felt more confident since the market confirmed an uptrend, and he latched onto Apple Computer as it broke out perfectly on August 26 on huge volume. Roppel only took a small position, mostly due to his lack of confidence in an older computer company, which was his opinion of Apple. Even though he was well aware of its hot new iPod product, he underestimated its impact on the company. But the action in the stock soon convinced him it was for real, and he made excellent add-on buys as Apple kept blasting upward. This is a great example of an experienced market operator not letting his own thoughts overcome the action that was taking place in the stock. He instead listened to the market's action, changed his own views, and then rode this leader up and retained a solid profit when he sold out in January 2005, due to weakness in the market. Another leader he noticed during August 2004 was Chicago Mercantile Exchange (see Figure 11-11 on p. 248). He took a much larger initial position in that stock, and he held on to it on its way up until it broke its 50-day moving-average line in early 2005 when the market was really hit with some selling. He still ended up making a 48% gain on this stock. Chicago Mercantile Exchange would rebound in 2005, and Roppel bought back into it then as it continued to be a leading stock sporting solid fundamentals.

As the market kept making its way upward throughout August and into September 2004, there were several solid accumulation days occurring during the later part of September. This gave Roppel more confidence that the market was trending up with some strength behind it. He then piled into a very strong issue that was generating quite a bit of attention. Roppel bought into Google on September 28 at $125.00 per share. As it would keep rising he really loaded up on this stock. The fundamentals and the business plan were exceptional, and he saw the heavy institutional interest that was accumulating the stock. Even though the stock had not much of a history on its chart, due to it being a new issue in August 2004, Roppel still saw the impressive strength, and he began to take some very sizable positions himself. In fact, when he was fully invested in this position, he had 32% of his account balance in this one stock. This is a strategy that the very best traders can get away with. Through their experience and strict loss-cutting policies they really hit home runs when they see just about everything falling into place. All the best would take big positions as a percentage of their capital if things were working out, they knew the company inside and out, and they kept their attention to the price and volume action of the stock. It is vitally important to totally separate emotions from facts when one decides to take such huge positions in certain stocks. Livermore, Baruch, Loeb, Darvas and O'Neil would all do this when they thought the risk/reward ratio was as near perfect as it could get. Darvas took a 50% capital position in Texas Instruments when he landed that leader. Remember though that this strategy, which Livermore referred to as "the big money comes from the big swings," was only undertaken by these experts after they had gained the experience and had already established themselves as millionaire investors.

Roppel kept riding the market higher during the fall months of 2004 as the market was rising quickly. The Dow ended up shooting higher by over

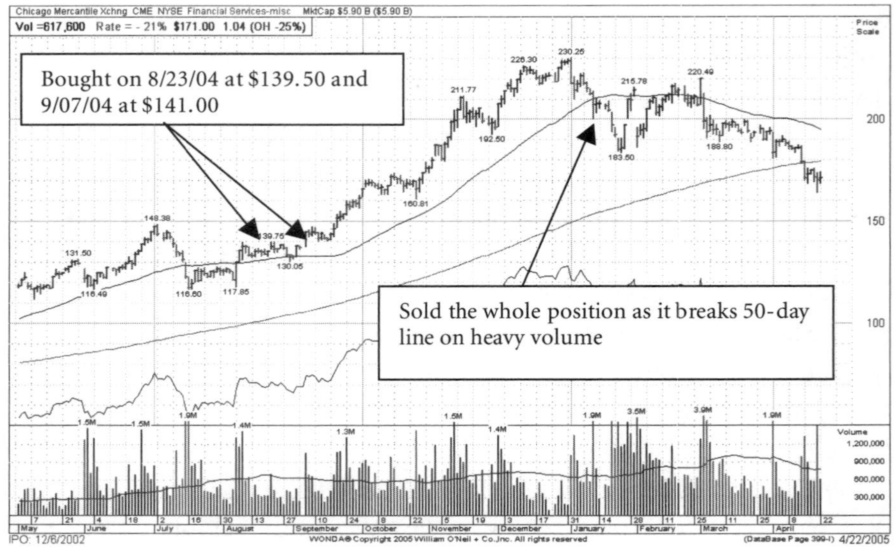

Figure 11-11 Chicago Mercantile 2004 Daily Chart.
Source: © *William O'Neil + Co., Inc. All rights reserved. Reprinted with permission.*

1,000 points just from late October through to the end of the year. The Nasdaq also had a great run during the fall and into the winter months of 2004 as well. Roppel's stocks were moving right along with the market as his positions in Apple, Chicago Merchantile and Google were producing nice returns. By early December, though, the run may have seemed to be continuing, but there was a warning sign that Roppel became aware of. On December 7 the Nasdaq experienced a big distribution day. After it recovered, the Nasdaq then began to sell off and experienced heavy volume on those additional down days. Apple was one of his holdings that pulled back in December to start forming a new base. Roppel stayed with his key holdings as the averages moved back up and ended the year near their highs. The first few days of 2005 experienced some heavy selling, and Roppel sold out of every position he had to retain his profits. He therefore was back to a full cash position by the end of the first week in 2005. As for 2004, the Dow gained 3% for the year and the Nasdaq led again with an 8.6% gain. Roppel again beat the major indexes as he registered a solid 18% gain in 2004. He still made plenty of mistakes that year, but again he adhered to the number one rule in the market — cut your losses short. It was a challenging year as the market broke deep during the first part of the year and then rebounded strongly during the second half. Those types of markets require keen observation, quickness and the ability to move properly with the changes of the market.

The first half of the new decade of 2000 was a very challenging one for investors in the stock market, to say the least. We witnessed the worst decline in 70 years, and many leading stocks again proved that when the market melts, the former leaders can come down fast. But we also saw two experts sidestep the worst decline in a generation. Their attentive skills and sound, proven strategies allowed them to conduct their operations like the professionals and experts they've become. Both outperformed the markets by a long shot and avoided the painful losses that many experienced who refused to implement sound selling rules. It seemed nearly everybody was an expert at buying stocks when the market was racing up, but few have possessed the necessary skills, disciplines and trading rules to outmaneuver a very challenging market environment. O'Neil proved again that he is one of the best, if not *the* best, legendary stock operator of all time. Roppel, while maybe not a legend as yet, proved that his hard work and study would finally pay off.

12

Learning from the Lessons of History and the Greatest Traders

"You can always learn from history, because human nature doesn't change and there's really not as much that's new in the market as most people believe. Cup-with-handle patterns have appeared and reappeared in every cycle throughout market history. In every stock market and economic cycle through the entire twentieth century, the big funds and professional pools went after the best growth stocks at the time, ran them up, and eventually pushed PEs to levels no one could justify. It's just history repeating itself over and over again, human nature continually on parade."

— William J. O'Neil (2004)

It pays to listen to one of the most successful stock market operators in history and the one who has probably studied more than any other person, and in meticulous detail, the history and action of the stock market and the leading stocks that made the best gains throughout history. So not only are you receiving advice, wisdom and experience from possibly the best student ever of the market, you are also learning from one of the best real-world participants who has achieved enviable returns over many decades. How many individuals do you know of who have achieved over 40% annual returns on average for over 25 years? Those types of almost unheard-of returns come from study, experience, discipline and following time-tested trading rules. And when I say study, I mean he conducted the most in-depth analysis ever on the stock market for decades, built the first stock market historical database, and then utilized that data to create the models for success he has used for over 40 years. As a young man, William J. O'Neil also purchased a library of nearly 2,000 books on the market — and that was more than 40 years ago. So he's read almost everything that has been written about the market. His conclusion after reading these many books, and more since then, is that most of them were useless. The best of the best according to him, other than his own writings, which rank among the best ever written on the stock market, are as follows:

"Reminiscences of a Stock Operator"	Edwin Lefevre
"How I Made $2,000,000 in the Stock Market"	Nicolas Darvas
"The Battle for Investment Survival"	Gerald Loeb
"How to Trade in Stocks"	Jesse Livermore
"My Own Story"	Bernard Baruch

You'll notice that all the authors listed are discussed in this book (recall that Lefevre's book was the fictionalized biography of Jesse Livermore) and that these books were all written by and about people who made a lot of money in the market, not by academics who wrote about investment theories but had no track record of long success in the market. Also, my first book summarizes the profiles of many of those listed and references most of these books, so a reader can have access to the best stock market operators and their books in one convenient guide.

So instead of trying to figure out if academic theories concerning random walks, efficient market theory, capital asset pricing models, and so forth really work, one should understand that simple supply-and-demand psychology decisions from millions of participants is what moves the markets. Gerald Loeb stated in his book "The Battle for Investment Survival" back in 1935, "The most important single factor in shaping securities markets is public psychology. This is really another reason why I am not particularly impressed with academic calculations purporting to show what this or that stock should be worth." Price and volume action within the market and within leading stocks based on profitability, expected profitable growth (which usually comes from new and innovative companies that are creating new services and products), historical cycle movements, and how investors react to those attributes along with certain other economic trends is what causes the movement of the stock market. As this book has pointed out repeatedly, if you understand how history has worked in past stock market cycles, it can surely assist you in future market cycles. This book has analyzed the market decade by decade and has pointed out references that were made to prior cycles in the market and how the greatest and most successful stock market operators used history as a precedent. Here are just a few of the real-life examples that many used to reap profits in their current times:

Bernard Baruch. The 1924 market upturn off the bottom looked very much like the 1897 market upturn to him. He remembered that profitable time and used that knowledge and experience to reap new returns. He also saw the parallel in the 1904 market to that same market in 1897. Therefore, he used his first initial success in 1897 to profit two more times in market cycles that repeated a similar pattern. He also saw a similar situation of a market top in late 1960 (at age 91) to prior ones he was involved in when other major market tops occurred, and he warned about it at that time.

Jesse Livermore. The strategies he implemented during the market top in 1903, from which he successfully profited, were the same ones he used with the market tops in 1907 and 1929. He did just what Baruch did; he used parallels to his first huge success in the market to reap huge returns in two following market cycles as well. His study of how markets top after long and strong advances was something he always remembered so that he could sell correctly and then short former leaders on the way down in future market cycles.

Gerald Loeb. He saw a parallel to the market top in 1937 with the market top of 1929, when he had sidestepped the Great Crash. That allowed him to sell and keep his profits in 1937. He also knew that the bottom to the market in 1932 looked very similar to the market bottom in 1942. He then saw similarities to the 1943 market top from prior market tops that had occurred in both 1937 and 1939. That knowledge helped him make the correct decisions during that market period.

Jack Dreyfus. He saw a market topping in 1957 after a very strong and sustained advance that looked very similar to the market situation he had studied back in 1937, then very early in his career, when he went against the advice of the experienced voice in his firm. Dreyfus was right on both accounts, and he retained big profits and avoided large potential losses.

William J. O'Neil. His first great success came from his study of the 1962 market top and how it looked like the market top that Livermore saw in 1907. So not only does O'Neil use his own experience, he also is familiar with market cycles that occurred well before his time and that other great stock traders were involved in as well. O'Neil's comments in early 1982 from his ad placement in the *Wall Street Journal* used prior market cycle precedents that looked similar to that time in 1982. Those that looked similar were from 1974, 1949 and 1932. He also avoided the worst single day in market history (in October 1987) because the market topped in August of that year (when he sold and went to a 100% cash position) and it reminded him of the market tops of 1907 and 1962, thereby forcing him to sell stocks and raise cash. O'Neil also uses similar cycle and chart patterns in stocks as well, as that is a major component of his CAN SLIM™ system. His big win in Pic'N Save initially reminded him of the same early action that occurred in Kmart and Jack Eckerd. His huge win in AOL reminded him of the time he missed Fairchild Camera's big move 33 years earlier. Both followed the exact same pattern. Those are just two examples of hundreds of successful stocks that O'Neil has bought over the years in which he related current price action to other great stocks in the past. In fact, historical models of the best stock market winners in history is the cornerstone to his successful CAN SLIM investment method and is the real key to how he expanded on and refined the strategies of his predecessors.

Jim Roppel. He constantly refers to charts in his study of price and volume action of the best historical winners in stock market history. He also always refers to historical charts of specific market environments. These references to history are a daily part of his study and observation disciplines that keep him in tune with the current market and have led to many of his successes.

For those who still don't think it's important to understand history in the market and that market cycles don't repeat themselves, just take a look at some of the following charts. These charts show similar patterns during different years in the market. These examples show how uptrends may look similar to prior uptrends and how downtrends also can follow similar paths of prior cycles that moved in a downward manner. These charts also only show calendar time periods. There have been other market cycles that overlapped simple calendar periods, as the market trades without time periods in mind. If these patterns looked similar during the same months of different periods, just imagine how many others were similar if we remove the same monthly time periods. Also, during many sideways patterns in the market, which occur just about as often as the uptrending and downtrending cycles, the patterns can look even more similar to other prior time periods as well.

It's hard to argue with history because the facts speak for themselves. It's also interesting to see that if the best traders over history have used historical information in the market to profit in the present, then the message becomes that much clearer. And as the quotes in the Introduction of this book stated, repeatable behavior just keeps recurring in the market. This message was repeated throughout this book as we analyzed the decades. It is especially true when the market hits tops and bottoms throughout its cyclical rotation. We saw numerous times that tops in the market indexes occur when heavy selling (down days on increased volume activity) begins to overtake buying power and the stocks that led the uptrend begin to wobble, then weaken, and eventually crater. It doesn't matter what time frame it was, or what time frame it will be in the future. And don't let overexuberance and phrases such as "this time it's different" confuse you. Phrases like that appeared in the 1920s, 1950s, 1960s and 1990s. All markets rotate through cycle patterns, so the more you realize how they have behaved in the past, the better your chances will be that you will become one of those "smart money" sellers at or near the top of the next market cycle. And market bottoms almost always occur when the major indexes follow through on confirmations (upside trading on increased volume activity) within a few days to near two weeks after they have hit bottom. Today, investors have the convenience of having *Investor's Business Daily®* instruct you on when these tops and bottoms are occurring in the market.

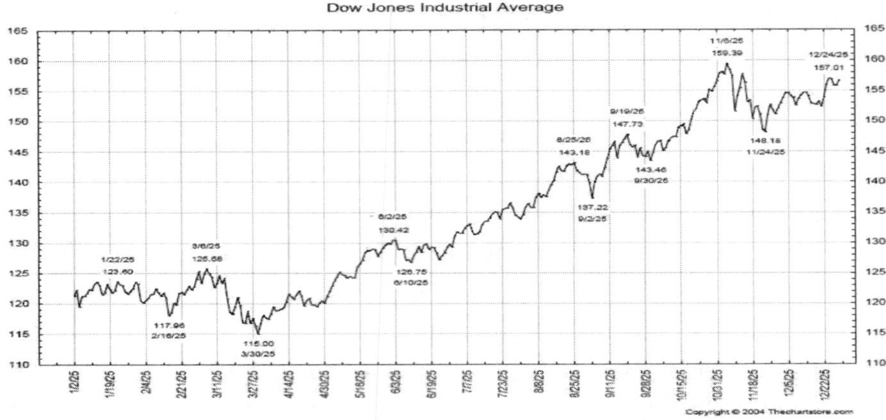

1925 Dow Industrial Average :+30%. Source: *www.thechartstore.com.*

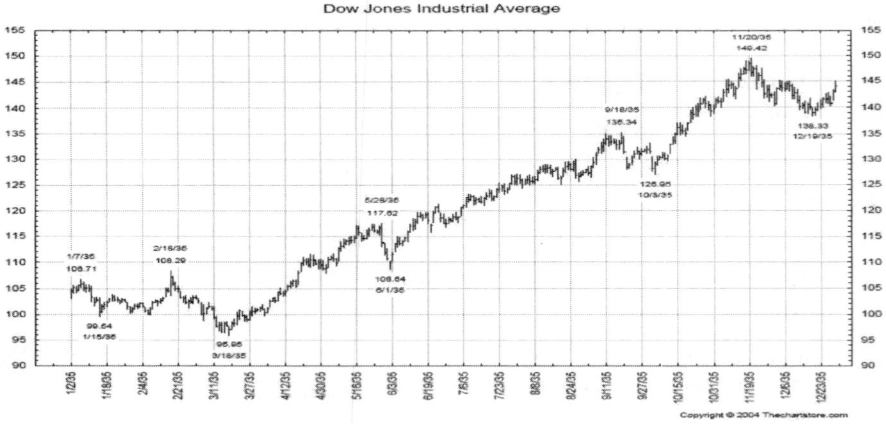

1935 Dow Industrial Average: +39%. Source: *www.thechartstore.com.*

How Roppel Turned It Around

My first book, "Lessons from the Greatest Stock Traders of All Time," profiled the common traits, skills, disciplines and trading rules that five of the best traders throughout the past century implemented. In this book I introduced a new trader, Jim Roppel, who also achieved great success as we've seen. How did he really turn it around and become the success he worked so hard to attain? He did just what the other great traders before him did to achieve their successes. When I asked Roppel what was the main reason for

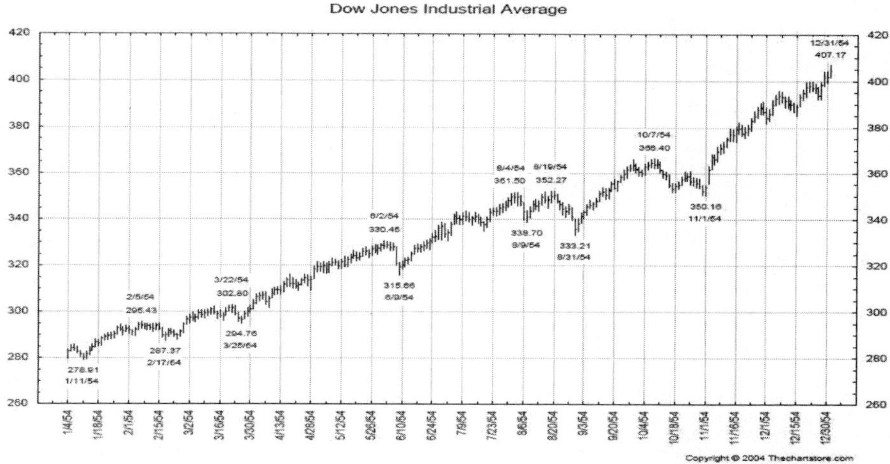

1954 Dow Industrial Average: +44%. Source: *www.thechartstore.com.*

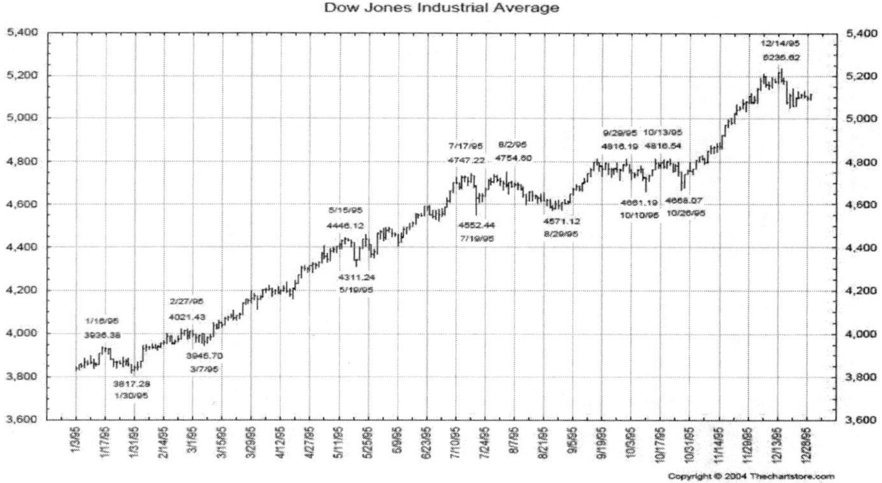

1995 Dow Industrial Average: +33%. Source: *www.thechartstore.com.*

his turnaround, he said without hesitation, "Without a doubt — cutting my losses." On his desk in his office is a sign above one of the seven flat-panel monitors he uses that states "3%, 5%, 7%." This sign hangs above the monitor that directly faces him. It means that if he takes a position in a stock and it falls 3% from his buy point, he will sell one-third of his position. If the stock then continues to fall 5% below his buy point, he sells another third. If

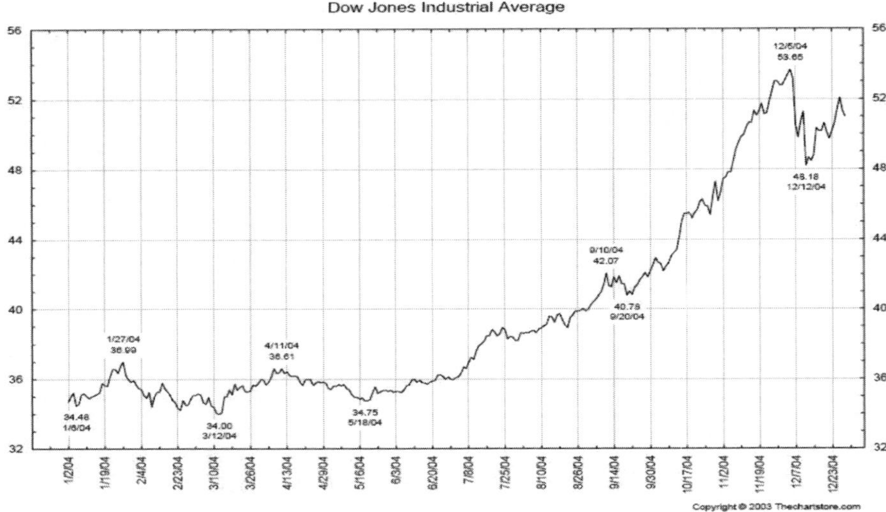

1904 Dow Industrial Average: +42%. Source: *www.thechartstore.com.*

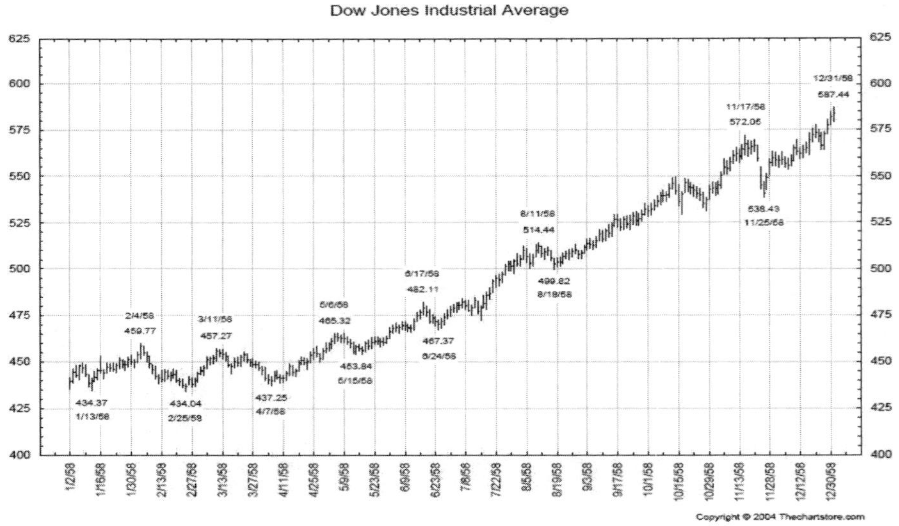

1958 Dow Industrial Average: +34%. Source: *www.thechartstore.com.*

the stock then continues down and falls 7% below his buy point, he will sell out the remainder of his position. He religiously sticks to this rule with *no* exceptions. The only time his losses exceed those limits is if the stock gaps down hard and breaks through those areas. In cases like those, which can

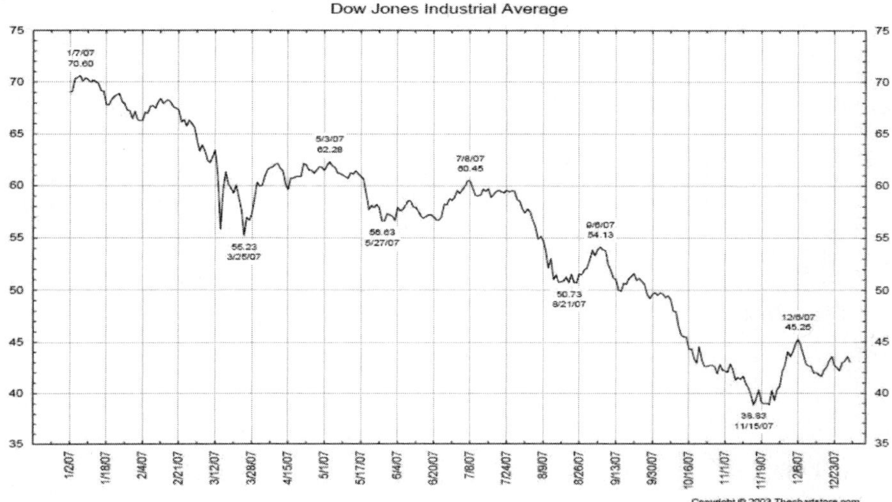

1907 Dow Industrial Average: –38%. Source: *www.thechartstore.com.*

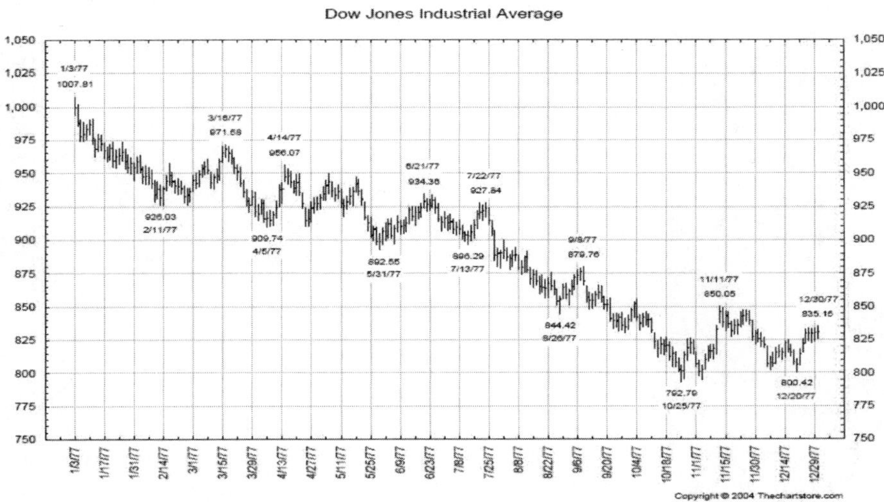

1977 Dow Industrial Average: –17%. Source: *www.thechartstore.com.*

happen at any time to any stock, he sells out completely at the market price. It should be noted that he does not use stop-loss orders. Instead he watches with intense focus his positions throughout each day and utilizes market orders on his buy and sell transactions. But how did he get to this rule? He studied, and he studied hard after he made the major, and sometimes devastating, mistakes

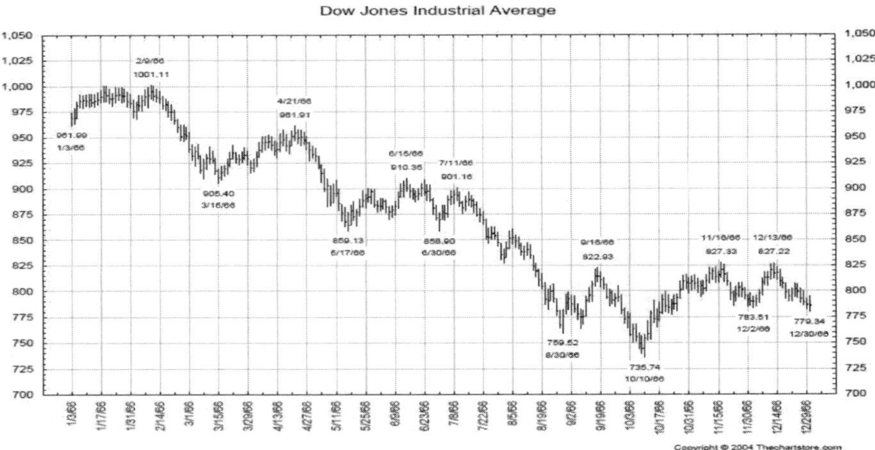

1966 Dow Industrial Average: –19%. Source: *www.thechartstore.com.*

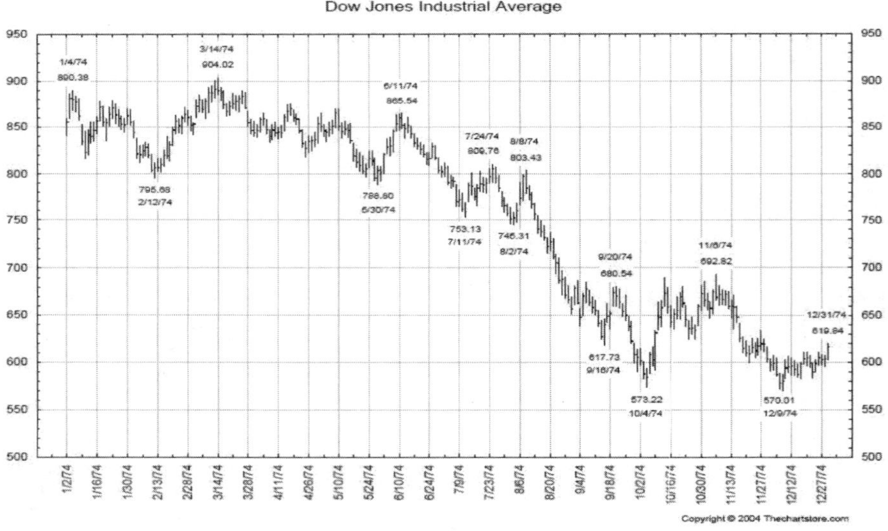

1974 Dow Industrial Average: –28%. Source: *www.thechartstore.com.*

early in his career. As mentioned, he went back and read O'Neil's book "How to Make Money in Stocks." I asked Roppel how many times he has read that classic. "Probably no less than 30 times" was his response. It takes time, repetition and dedication to get down all the strategies needed to succeed in the market. Recall that both Livermore and Loeb, two of the most successful at Wall Street, both agreed when they implied something of the following sort

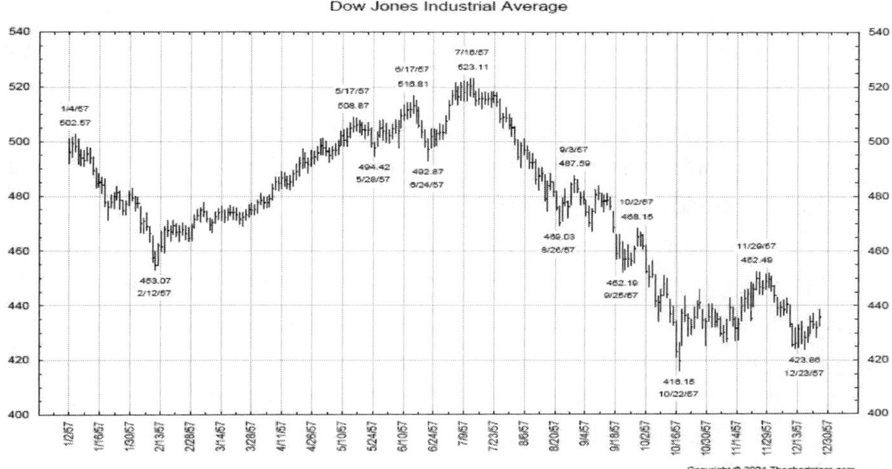

1957 Dow Industrial Average: –13%. Source: *www.thechartstore.com.*

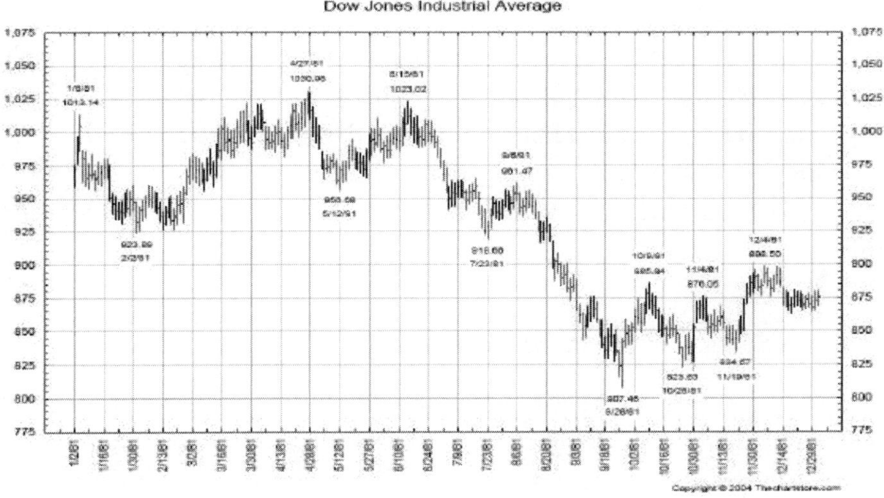

1981 Dow Industrial Average: –9%. Source: *www.thechartstore.com.*

"there is nothing harder to succeed at — in my opinion — on a consistent basis, than that of stock speculation."

Roppel's home office library is stacked with books on the market, but he has a dedicated shelf for the very best ones. Not surprisingly, they include many of the same titles that are listed under O'Neil's favorites as well. For Roppel, O'Neil stands out as his major mentor. He also learned extensively by reading the books by Gerald Loeb (one of his favorites) and Jesse Livermore. Roppel's passion for market knowledge is something to admire. In fact, you would be hard pressed to find someone with more passion for the stock market today than Jim Roppel. His passion has even taken him to places where the great ones once went. He went to Florida one time just so he could stand where Jesse Livermore stood, in the Breakers Hotel in West Palm Beach where Livermore would retreat from the market and vacation, so Roppel could "feel" what it was like to be where he once was. I even asked Roppel, now that he has made enough money to more than live comfortably, "Why continue on?" His response was that he would never quit because his passion for the market is too strong for him to ever give up the challenge.

Looking for "Basketballs under Water"

While Roppel kept learning and attending *IBD™* sessions (he doesn't recall exactly how many but says it's probably about a dozen), the other major factors that resulted in his turnaround were (1) better selection criteria for purchases, (2) refining his chart-reading skills, (3) constant study and hard work and (4) learning and implementing the proper selling rules.

Better Selection Criteria for Purchases

Roppel only invests in the very elite companies that have great fundamentals. He likes liquid stocks since he now takes much bigger positions and it is easier to get out if he needs to. He never buys cheap low-priced stocks. In fact, he will rarely buy a stock if it trades under $20 per share. Here he agrees with the experts before him — if you want quality, you have to pay for it, even in the stock market. If you want bargains, go to the flea market. He wants to own the very best stocks that are producing the very best profit growth, are providing great products and services, and are forecasted to grow at very high rates. He also really does his homework to get to know the company and its products. He wants to know the company's story inside and out.

Refining His Chart-Reading Skills

Here Roppel looks for all the classic stock chart patterns that have repeated themselves over the many market cycles from prior decades throughout history. He looks for exactly what O'Neil, who was responsible for naming some of those patterns, looks for. These patterns are cup-with-handles, double bottoms, flat bases, ascending base, the rare high tight flag, and three-weeks tight. Roppel gets his best ideas from the weekly *Daily Graphs®* chart books produced by one of O'Neil's companies. Roppel spends each Sunday afternoon looking at every single chart. Even during bad market periods, he keeps up the hard work — a characteristic that distinguishes the people who really succeed and excel from most everyone else. What Roppel is looking for during his screening process when the markets are bad is what he calls "basketballs under water." If you've ever been in a pool of water before and held a basketball under the water, you know how you need to apply force in order to hold it down and keep it under water. Once you let go, the basketball springs out of the water with great force behind it. He's looking for stocks with bases that are setting up and that may then break through their bases on huge volume when the market turns around to begin a whole new upturn. This is exactly what Dreyfus, Darvas, O'Neil and the others were looking for. For Roppel, if he sees 20 or 30 fundamentally strong stocks setting up, while the market environment is usually bad, he becomes pretty confident that the market may be getting ready to make a move. Remember, you always need strong leadership to drive a new market rally, and great stocks setting up are the "basketballs under water" that will eventually lead the next market cycle. Roppel also runs chart screens each night after the market closes. He reviews about 150 different charts each night — both daily and weekly charts. He'll run them looking for heavy volume increases and positive relative-strength divergences. He reads the electronic edition of *IBD* every night and then formulates his strategies for the next day.

Constant Study and Hard Work

In Roppel's office he has two large wall-sized charts of historical market activity. He constantly studies past market cycles and past big winning stocks. He's created his own resource through his own intense study and from the big winners that are listed in many of O'Neil's publications. He doesn't use fancy software programs but does have Level II quotes, and he's a subscriber to WONDA® (William O'Neil Direct Access) where he gets all his online charts and can run historical charts of past winners (used throughout this book). His only sources of information are *IBD*, WONDA, and *Daily Graphs*. He has a plasma TV in his office where he keeps CNBC on throughout the day under one condition — it stays on mute. He works hard to remove all biases, and he listens to no one else, as he sticks to the facts and his historical study. This is exactly what all the best traders have done as well. Though it may sound like he constantly works, he does leave the market for periods of time and vacations, as the other greats did too. It's that time away to refresh and reflect that puts you back into the proper perspective when you come back into the market under the right conditions. Roppel also learned quite a bit from his early losses as he implemented a postanalysis of his trades. He likes to learn from his losses, as that, he says, is the best teacher of all. He still does some postanalysis but mentions it was more of a benefit to him earlier on as he kept learning how to avoid the basic and major mistakes.

Learning and Implementing the Proper Selling Rules

Everybody knows the hardest thing to do in the market is to sell properly. Roppel doesn't waste time with fancy and complicated technical analysis tools. He strictly sticks with price and volume action. He may hold up to 15 stocks at one time if the market is strong, but most of those will make up small percentages of his total portfolio. He'll then sell off the worst performers to weed the total down to 10 or so. That concentration is another key strategy of the very best. For Roppel it's also important for him to "not swing at every pitch." Staying disciplined to that rule allows him to avoid one of the classic mistakes in the market — overtrading. Because of his patience on the buy side he will then work with the best five or six stocks in his portfolio as that is where most of his attention and money will be. Two other signs on his monitors in his office read, "Rules Not Emotions" and "Follow the Volume." Those are self-explanatory, and we already know that his first measure for selling would be to look at the action of the general market and to see if distribution is starting to overtake buying. If distribution is taking place in either the market or his stocks, he will act quickly if major sell signals arise for him. He keeps the selling side simple, and he uses the 50-day moving-average line as a key area and how a stock behaves at or near that line to help him determine what to do. We've already seen many of his trades on the charts included in this book that illustrated his exit positions — many times it was when a strong leader was finally breaking down and would pierce through that 50-day area. Roppel usually doesn't wait around after that — he takes action. His other favorite sell signal is the classic climax top. When this happens, he watches very closely because he knows the end is near. And while I haven't mentioned much about Roppel using shorting strategies, he has been improving and increasing this skill set as well. He will, when the time is right, allocate approximately 10% of his capital to short sales if he sees a major break coming in the market.

Roppel, in 2005, realized another milestone and lifetime goal when he opened Roppel Capital Management, his own private money management firm in his hometown just outside Chicago, which is open to qualified investors only. He is also one of the most humble people you'll meet. That humbleness comes from living through many rough market periods and never forgetting how difficult it was to get to where he currently is. An avid golfer as well, Roppel says the two most humbling things are golf and stock speculation — how true.

What the Very Best Do to Beat the Market

To summarize the successful common strategies that were mentioned throughout this book and that were implemented by the best traders over history, I will outline the key aspects that were utilized by the individual stock traders (Baruch, Livermore, Wyckoff, Loeb, Darvas, O'Neil and Roppel) that were responsible for most of the millions of dollars in profits that these great stock traders realized.

Understand the General Trend of the Market

This is the first key to success. You must be in tune with and trade with the trend and rhythm of the market. One must be observant of its action at all times and then follow its lead. Don't try to predict what it will do as no one ever has been able to do that with reliable accuracy for any sustained period of time. We saw many times how the market can turn around quickly. Many times throughout history the market would top and begin to turn down when just about everyone was running around and was as excited and jubilant as they could be. Then, many other times, the market would turn up and begin a new uptrend when most people had given up on the market and were scared to death and licking their wounds from prior losses that were not managed properly. It is very critical to study the market's action day-to-day as it is occurring to understand what kind of environment you are dealing with. Even Loeb, during the market's worst years ever in the early 1930s, managed to make money each year on the long side. This is to this day one of the more remarkable profitable feats in market history. He did this by understanding that the dominant major bear market cycle he was currently in offered short-term upside rallies that were then slapped back down. Therefore, he traded in quick fashion, kept his losses very well contained, and reacted to the market's actions.

Use History in Your Study and Observation of the Markets

The best traders knew that knowledge of history was very important to success in the stock market. I have already listed many of the times when great traders used history to profit in their current market environment. We also see Roppel going back to market and stock charts that are nearly 100 years old as he knows how important historical knowledge is to succeed in the market.

Do Your Own Study and Research and Don't Listen to Others and Their Opinions

All the best traders made money by making their own decisions. Listening to others and others' opinions all led to losses for the best market operators early on in their careers. That is what forced them to study and conduct their own research in order to get on and stay on the profitable side of the market.

Buy Fundamentally Strong Stocks That Are Leaders in Their Industry

Leading stocks are ones that are leading profit generators and that usually have a new product and/or service that has been introduced and has been widely accepted by the general public to increase the quality of many lives in some positive way. Strong revenue and profit growth accompanies these leaders. The leaders always change with each new market cycle, so flexibility is an important trait that must be implemented. Of utmost importance is knowing the fundamentals of the stock. This fact is *vitally important.* All these great traders made their big money in stocks that displayed great fundamentals. O'Neil believes that in addition to learning to read charts skillfully to improve your selection and timing, it's key to make sure your selections contain the following fundamentals (from his CAN SLIM investment method):

- Each of the last three years' earnings per share are up a minimum of 25%, plus at least the last two quarters' earnings are up sharply and in most cases five or six quarters in a row up and showing acceleration in their rate of increase — the bigger the increase, the better.
- A superior new product or service with sales up 25% or more, or accelerating in their latest quarterly reports.
- A superior return on equity (ROE) of 25% to 50% and a minimum level for ROE acceptance of 17%. A stock must have either strong pretax profit margins or a high return on equity, and the best stocks are entitled to a bigger PE ratio.
- You should be looking for the real leaders, the number one company in its field in terms of these fundamentals — not the lower-quality number three or number four company. You are looking for the top 1% or 2% of all stocks, and you should know and understand their products. This is easier to do with consumer companies. O'Neil's biggest winners have been unique retailers, drug companies and Internet leaders — all consumer-driven.
- Eighty percent of all new leaders in the past 20 years either had a recent new issue or IPO in the prior eight years. So it's entrepreneurial America that creates more real leaders.

Buy Those Leading Stocks in Only Uptrending Markets and When They Break Out of Proper Basing Patterns on Large Volume and Then Use a Pyramiding Strategy to Add to Those Winners

The key to making the really big money in the market was when these traders had the patience to wait for the market to confirm an uptrend and then they purchased strong stocks breaking out, mostly into new high ground on heavy volume. Then if, and only if, the stock kept moving up as they expected, they would make pyramid or add-on purchases in addition to their initial positions. Strategies varied on exactly how their pyramid buys would occur, but the key was that they added to their strongest stocks in order to compound their gains. The pyramiding strategy, on the buy side (or sell side if you're shorting), is a major buying strategy that led to millions for these traders.

Cut Your Losses Short on the Ventures Where You Have Been Proven Wrong

This again is the number one Golden Rule for success in the stock market. It was repeated over and over in my first book and was the main reason for Roppel turning his performance around, as mentioned before. Without this, you can rest assured your results will be mediocre at best. The very best know this, and they actually improve on it as they continue to go along. While it is probably the most difficult discipline to implement, it is the one that clearly separates the very best from everyone else. What does seem to stay the same from era to era is the amount of successful trades versus the unsuccessful trades. All the best still experienced win/loss ratios of near 50%. O'Neil may be one of the best ever at approximately a 66% rate for successful trades. Roppel's records show a success rate of approximately 55%. Because of that, implementing a strict loss-cutting policy is essential to success and big profits in the stock market.

Hold On to Your Winning Positions Until Classic Sell Signals Tell You to Unload Your Position

This is the other classic phrase that most hear about: "Let your winners run." Again, this is easy to say, but extremely difficult to do. But with practice and study, especially using charts of the best winners from the past, you have already seen two successful traders gain the benefit of this classic strategy. Day trading didn't make the money for these great operators and neither did "buy-and-hold." It was somewhere in between, and it was never the same throughout any cycle. These traders didn't call themselves short- or long-term traders or investors. They instead moved with the market and watched their holdings until sell signals warned them to do something. O'Neil will hold positions for years, if they act right. If they don't, he doesn't look at the calendar and say he can't do something because the stock hasn't been held for this or that length of time. If he's close to a tax consideration period, he might work with that on a big winner, but that is a secondary decision, far behind the importance of what the market, price and volume action of the stock is doing. The other thing these traders proved was that, believe it or not, timing is everything in the market. And with proper study and observation, one's timing can actually improve to the point where, with the proper time-tested strategies employed, profitable transactions can occur.

So it pays to study these great traders, their big winning transactions, their mistakes and losses, and the history of the market in order to try and better your performance in the future. The progression of time and the traders learning from their predecessors is proof that it is possible for some to really rise to the top and succeed at high levels in the stock market. After all of this, I would like to conclude by citing a quote from Gerald Loeb, which comes from the book by Ralph G. Martin titled "The Wizard of Wall Street — The Story of Gerald M. Loeb," when Loeb once described what constituted a successful person with regard to taking on the challenge of the stock market environment:

> The truly flexible man in the market is the man who can be foolish at times, bullish at times, bearish at times, borrow money at times, be short at times, the person who can learn to be an expert on gold stocks in one period and some other style of stock in some other period. These men are exceedingly super-super rare. But they exist. And these are the men to watch, the men to learn from, they are the men who really make money on Wall Street.

Bibliography/Resources

Baruch, Bernard. "My Own Story." Buccaneer Books, Inc. 1957. Copyright © 1957 by Bernard Baruch. All rights reserved.

Chapters 1–4: Relates to Bernard Baruch.

Darvas, Nicolas. "How I Made $2,000,000 in the Stock Market." Lyle Stuart books published by Kensington Publishing Corp. 1986. Copyright © 1994, 1971, 1960 Nicolas Darvas. All rights reserved.

Chapters 6, 7, 12: Relates to Nicolas Darvas.

Fridson, Martin S. "It Was a Very Good Year: Extraordinary Moments in Stock Market History." John Wiley & Sons, Inc. 1998. Copyright © 1998 by Martin S. Fridson. All rights reserved.

Chapter 8: Relates to economic statistics, other general events, and certain market activity that occurred during the time frames analyzed.

Geisst, Charles R. "100 Years of Wall Street." McGraw-Hill. 2000. Copyright © 2000 by McGraw-Hill. All rights reserved.

Chapters 4–10: Relates to economic statistics, other general events, and certain market activity that occurred during the time frames analyzed.

Geisst, Charles R. "Wall Street — A History." Oxford University Press. 1997, 2004. Copyright © 1997 by Charles R. Geisst. All rights reserved.

Chapters 4, 7–11: Relates to economic statistics, other general events, and certain market activity that occurred during the time frames analyzed.

Grant, James. "Bernard Baruch: Adventures of a Wall Street Legend." John Wiley & Sons, Inc. 1997. Copyright © 1997 by James Grant. All rights reserved.

Chapters 1–4: Relates to Bernard Baruch.

Lefevre, Edwin. "Reminiscences of a Stock Operator." John Wiley & Sons, Inc. 1994. Originally published in 1923 by George H. Doran and Company. Copyright © 1993, 1994 by Expert Trading, Ltd. Forward © 1994 by John Wiley & Sons, Inc.

Introduction, Chapters 2 and 3: Relates to Jesse Livermore.

Loeb, Gerald M. "The Battle for Investment Survival." Copyright © 1935, 1936, 1937, 1943, 1952, 1953, 1954, © 1955, 1956, 1957 by Gerald M. Loeb. Copyright © 1965, and renewed © 1993, by H. Harvey Scholten.

Chapters 3, 4, 12: Relates to Gerald Loeb.

Mahar, Maggie. "Bull! A History of the Boom and Bust, 1982–2004." HarperCollins Publishers, Inc. 2003, 2004. Copyright © 2003 by Maggie Mahar. All rights reserved.

Chapters 9–11: Relates to economic statistics, other general events, and certain market activity that occurred during the time frames analyzed.

Martin, Ralph G. "The Wizard of Wall Street — The Story of Gerald M. Loeb." William Morrow & Co. 1965. Copyright © 1965 by Ralph G. Martin. All rights reserved.

Chapters 3–7, 12: Relates to Gerald Loeb.

O'Neil, William J. "How to Make Money in Stocks." McGraw-Hill. 2002. Copyright © 2002 by William J. O'Neil. Copyright © 1995, 1991, 1988 by McGraw-Hill, Inc. All rights reserved.

Introduction, Chapters 6–10, 12: Relates to William J. O'Neil.

O'Neil, William J. "How to Make Money Selling Stocks Short." John Wiley & Sons, Inc. 2005. Copyright © 2005 by William O'Neil + Co., Incorporated. All rights reserved.

Chapters 7–10: Relates to William J. O'Neil.

O'Neil, William J. "The Successful Investor." McGraw-Hill. 2004. Copyright © 2004 by William J. O'Neil. All rights reserved.

Introduction, Chapters 9–12: Relates to William J. O'Neil.

Saito-Chung, David. "Investor's Business Daily and the Making of Millionaires." McGraw-Hill. 2005. Copyright © 2005 by William J. O'Neil. All rights reserved.

Chapters 9–11: Relates to William J. O'Neil.

Sarnoff, Paul. "Jesse Livermore: Speculator King." Traders Press. 1985. Copyright © 1967 by Paul Sarnoff. All rights reserved.

Chapters 3–5: Relates to Jesse Livermore.

Smith, Mark B. "Toward Rational Exuberance — The Evolution of the Modern Stock Market." Farrar, Straus, and Giroux. 2001. Copyright © 2001 by B. Mark Smith. All rights reserved.

Chapters 1–3, 5, 6, 8–10: Relates to economic statistics, other general events, and certain market activity that occurred during the time frames analyzed.

Sobel, Robert. "The Big Board — A History of the New York Stock Exchange." Beard Books. 2000. Originally published in 1965 by The Free Press. Copyright © by The Free Press. All rights reserved.

Chapters 1–7: Relates to economic statistics, other general events, and certain market activity that occurred during the time frames analyzed.

Wyckoff, Richard. "Wall Street Ventures & Adventures through Forty Years." Traders Press. 1986. Originally published in 1930 by Richard D. Wyckoff. All rights reserved.

Chapters 1–3: Relates to Richard Wyckoff.

Wyckoff, Richard D. "How I Trade and Invest in Stocks and Bonds." Copyright © 1983 Fraser Publishing Company. Originally published in 1924 by *The Magazine of Wall Street*. All rights reserved.

Chapter 1: Relates to Richard Wyckoff.

Investor's Business Daily®. Numerous articles, stories, and statistical information.

Charts

Provides Dow Jones Industrial and Nasdaq decade charts.

Provides individual company stock charts.

Profile

John Boik is a controller and former stockbroker. He is the author of "Lessons from the Greatest Stock Traders of All Time," which was chosen by *Barron's* as one of the Best Books of 2004. He has been the featured guest on business investment radio shows that have been broadcast throughout Canada and the United States. Please visit his website at www.johnboik.com.

INDEX

Note: Page numbers in **bold** indicate chart.

ABOUT THE AUTHOR

John Boik is a controller and former stockbroker. He is the author of "Lessons from the Greatest Stock Traders of All Time," which was chosen by *Barron's* as one of the Best Books of 2004. Boik has been the featured guest on business investment radio shows that have been broadcast throughout Canada and the United States.